Leadership Development for Healthcare

A Pathway, Process, and Workbook

Merida L. Johns, PhD, RHIA

ISBN: 978-1-58426-463-7

AHIMA Product No.: AB126016

AHIMA Staff:
Jessica Block, MA, Project Editor
Chelsea Brotherton, MA, Assistant Editor
Megan Grennan, Senior Production Development Editor
Elizabeth Ranno, Vice President of Product and Planning
Caitlin Wilson, Project Editor
Pamela Woolf, Director of Publications

Cover image: © simon2579; iStockphoto.com
Icon image: © Blablo101; iStockphoto.com

For more information about AHIMA Press publications, including updates, visit http://www.ahima.org/publications/updates.aspx

American Health Information Management Association
233 North Michigan Avenue, 21st Floor
Chicago, Illinois 60601-5809
ahima.org

Brief Table of Contents

Detailed Table of Contents

About the Author

Merida L. Johns, PhD, RHIA, has more than 40 years of health information management experience on national and international levels and is a noted author and presenter in the field. She currently heads up The Monarch Center for Women's Leadership Development and is professor and director of health informatics and information management at Resurrection University in Chicago.

Preface

Healthcare organizations are seeking health professionals who can lead operational effectiveness and efficiency in a complicated environment. Every element of society is shaped in some way by a far reaching network of interrelationships. Today a local and global market impacts the programs, strategy, direction, and operation of healthcare organizations in many ways. Minimizing costs; increasing quality, effectiveness and efficiency; and improving value are challenges facing the healthcare industry. In a complex environment, leaders and leadership are essential for organizational growth, profitability, and well-being. Leadership is a key strategic objective for today's organizations. Too often, though, leadership is viewed narrowly as a collection of traits, acquisition of skills, a process, or even an inherent ability existing at birth.

For over a century researchers have studied leadership and developed theories to describe it. Until the 1930s leadership was framed as the control and centralization of power to induce obedience. Up until the 1950s, leadership was seen as a set of specific individual personality traits that could guide group attitudes and activities. Vision, shared goals, mobilization of people, and influence were common leadership principles from the mid to late 20th century. Concepts of leadership related to authentic, servant, and adaptive leadership were introduced in the early 21st century.

In this book leadership is defined as a commitment to excellence and leveraging personal awareness in cultivating a shared vision that inspires and motivates others to act ethically, embrace change, and develop and use their talents in creating an environment where people and organizations flourish. Leadership is different from management. Management is concerned with maintaining the status quo, ensuring operational efficiency, and establishing order and consistency within organizations through planning, organizing, staffing, and controlling. Leadership, however, challenges the status quo and promotes opportunities for growth, innovation, and improvement and fundamentally seeks to produce change.

As its value increases, leadership is increasingly commoditized and monetized through books, courses, workshops, and presentations. The assumption underlying commoditization is a leader can be trained. Read a book, become a leader. Attend a workshop, become a leader. Go to a presentation, become a leader. These strategies focus on attaining skills that can be learned in discrete parts and mastered and achieved by following a sequence of steps such as learning negotiation skills, time management, meeting management, and communication skills. The assumption is a competent leader materializes from mastery of discrete skills. Using training strategies, however, does not produce a leader who has the requisite leader characteristics nor one who is prepared to carry out the purpose of leadership. Being a leader who practices leadership is far more than possessing a set of skills or following a formula of prescribed steps. It is a journey and developmental process and has no discrete destination.

The Developing Leaders for Leadership Model

The goal of this book is to advance the health professional's capabilities in meeting current healthcare organization challenges through both leader and leadership development and is not intended to provide a background on the evolution of thought on leadership or leadership theory. For those interested, the appendix provides an overview of the evolution of thought on leadership and describes many of the common leadership theories developed between the early 20th century and today.

To meet its goal the book takes a developmental—not a training—approach by providing a leadership development framework that helps guide one in acquiring the characteristics and behaviors associated with good leadership that is defined as incorporating both moral and technical competence (chapter 8). The framework's underlying premise is that opportunities for being a leader and practicing leadership are available to everyone and leader behavior and leadership practice can be cultivated by anyone. Leader development is accomplished by generating personal change through shifting, clarifying, and expanding individual awareness. Leadership development focuses on applying individual awareness and ethical practice to situations of social influence, interpersonal relationships, organizational context, and team dynamics, as well as helping people develop and use their talents where they and the organization flourish.

To accomplish these goals, the book is divided into parts based on the developing leaders for leadership model (figure P.1).

Figure P.1. Developing leaders for leadership model

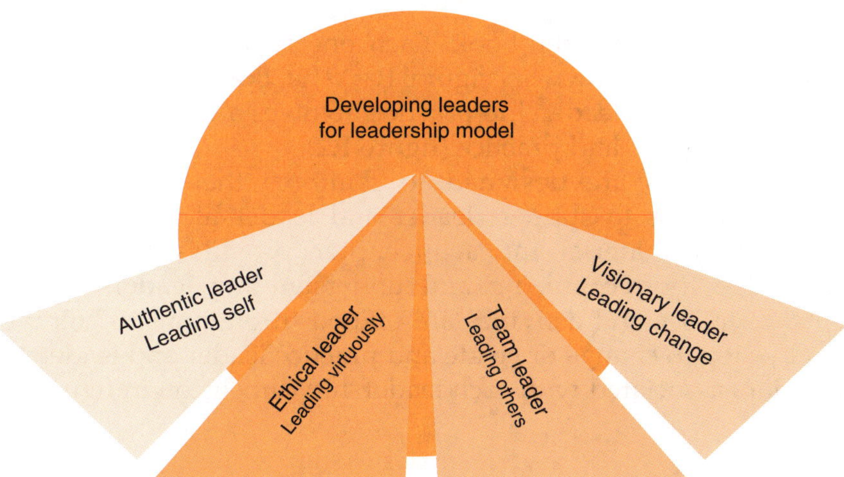

©Merida L. Johns

Part I: The authentic leader leads self by developing awareness of personal strengths, emotional intelligence, values, vision, and purpose and is able to leverage these for leadership practice.

Part II: The ethical leader leads virtuously by developing behaviors for appropriate conduct and taking personal action in creating standards of excellence, showing consideration and respect for others and treating them fairly, and modeling behavior for doing the right thing.

Part III: The team leader leads others by developing behaviors for collaboration and establishing coalitions, coaching others, and managing conflict.

Part IV: The visionary leader leads change by developing behaviors in appreciative inquiry for seeing future possibilities, changing the status quo, embracing change, optimizing decision making, and influencing and motivating others.

While each dimension of the model has specific, distinguishing features, there are overlaps among them. For example, features of the authentic leader, such as practicing values that support core virtues, overlap with those of an ethical leader. Likewise, features of the visionary leader, such as working for positive change for the common good, share characteristics with the ethical leader.

How the Book Is Organized

Four parts make up the book. Each one is devoted to a leadership dimension shown in figure P.1. The book assumes leader development and leadership practice involves a three-step process of learn, discover, and practice (figure P.2).

The chapters are designed to reinforce the learn-discover-practice process to support leader and leadership development. Introductory material in each chapter provides foundational knowledge for recognizing and understanding leadership concepts. Exercises and activities are offered throughout to help you step-by-step to change or create and practice leader and leadership behaviors associated with each leadership dimension in figure P.1.

Figure P.2. Learn-Discover-Practice model

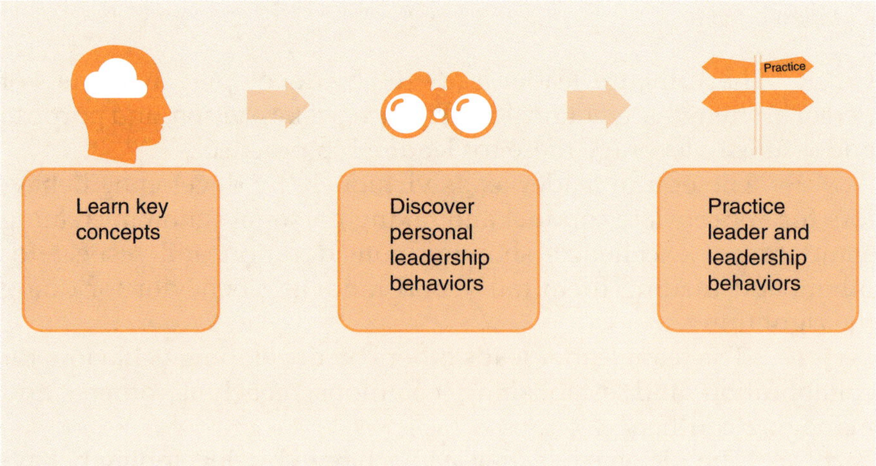

Learn key concepts → Discover personal leadership behaviors → Practice leader and leadership behaviors

Practice

©Merida L. Johns

Getting the Most from the Book

The book's subject matter and presentation are designed for professionals in the field as well as those preparing to enter the healthcare workforce. To get the most from the book, both professionals and students are encouraged to follow the learn-discover-practice process in each chapter and read and complete the exercises. Instructors may obtain guidance in the instructor's manual about subject matter presentation and ways of integrating it into a college curriculum.

Knowing, acknowledging, and appreciating who you are and what you stand for are leadership foundations that promote self-awareness, self-confidence, authenticity, and trustworthiness. Consequently the authentic leader section is the preparatory part of the book. Completing this section before the other sections is recommended. The remaining sections may be used in any order to support personal preferences in developing leader and leadership practice.

Acknowledgments

This book is dedicated to the role models in my life who have embraced the values and practiced the behaviors embodied in good leadership. They believed in a purpose beyond themselves and in every aspect of their lives demonstrated both moral and technical competence. Beginning with family members and extending to friends, teachers, and professional colleagues, their commitment to doing things right and doing the right thing is the guiding light in my leadership journey and in striving to be better myself. I am particularly thankful to my husband, Russell Johns, who has been my support in seeing this project and so many more to completion. Special appreciation to Marion Ball, EdD; Anne Durand, MCC; J. Michael Hardin, PhD; Patricia Hinton-Walker, PhD, RN, PCC; Denis Lambert, MBA; and Gayle Scroggs, PhD, PCC, who opened the door to my deeper understanding of leadership and have shown me a pathway for helping people, organizations, and communities to flourish. Special acknowledgment to my colleagues Leslie Gordon, MS, RHIA, FAHIMA, and Gretchen E. Jopp, MS, RHIA, CCS, CPC, whose insight and critique added perspective and quality to this work. To Megan Grennan and Pamela Woolf, for their patience in helping me navigate time constraints and deadlines and for their commitment and untiring support in taking a leap of faith in presenting a different approach for helping students and professionals fulfill their leadership potential.

Part I
The Authentic Leader

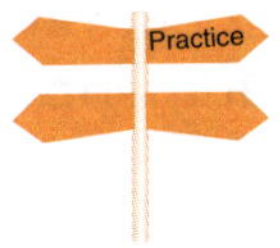

Authentic leadership is a recent and evolving leadership theory. This book views authentic leadership as more than a focus on knowing oneself, and instead views it as a combination of knowing oneself and applying that knowledge in establishing positive relationships and influencing others to achieve positive change. Using this perspective, the book defines authentic leadership as a process where a leader continuously develops self-awareness of her or his unique talents, strengths, sense of purpose, and beliefs and leverages these to create positive psychological capital such as building self-confidence, self-control, and resiliency—essential behaviors for good leadership. Leaders who know and apply their constellation of unique characteristics and couple these with psychological capital position themselves to carry out the purpose of leadership in cultivating a shared vision that inspires and motivates others to act ethically, embrace change, and develop and use their talents in creating an environment where people and organizations flourish.

The chapters in this section provide strategies for self-discovery and the application of this knowledge for developing good leadership behaviors. This book frequently uses the term *values*. Values in this book do not mean subjective personal preferences, such as a personal taste in clothing, food, manner of speech, or preferred cultural norms. Instead values throughout the book are defined in relationship to virtues that are certain ideals all people should strive to embrace that allow them to fulfill their human potential and lead a happy or flourishing life (chapter 8). Values are behaviors and indicators of those virtues. For example, the value of working hard to complete a task irrespective of the obstacles is an indicator of the virtue of courage (chapter 1).

Why Self-Awareness Matters

Self-awareness is the companion of good leadership. Leadership authorities concur that self-awareness and authenticity are the foundations to being a leader. For example, over two decades Kouzes and Posner (2007) have been studying how leaders mobilize others to accomplish extraordinary things. They have identified five practices of exemplary leaders. The first is being a good example or modeling the way for others. In other words, leaders must be models of the behavior they expect of others. To be a role model, a leader must be clear about his or her guiding principles, values, and ideals.

Likewise, Maxwell (1993), an internationally recognized leadership expert, says that knowing who you are and making sure your words and deeds match up no matter where you are or who you are with is the most important ingredient in leadership. Self-awareness and knowing what you stand for is your guiding north star and serves as the foundation for your values and beliefs, and helps maintain consistency in your actions. The more consistent the leader is in action and word, the more he or she builds the trust and confidence of their followers. "What people need is not a motto to say, but a model to see" (Maxwell 1993, 38).

Similarly, others cite self-awareness as the most important capability of a leader (George et al. 2011). People who are self-aware know who they are. They know their purpose in life and are passionate about it. They achieve results because they practice their values and leverage their strengths, establish meaningful and strong relationships with others, and set priorities that translate putting values into action.

This book integrates a variety of self-awareness strategies to help you apply the learn-discover-practice process and develop authentic leader behaviors. Each chapter covers a different strategy for developing self-awareness and is described briefly as follows.

Chapter 1: Identifying and Using Character Strengths

Character strengths are the positive components that describe what is best about a person. They are personality characteristics that make an individual authentic and unique. Knowing, embracing, and leveraging these will help make you a better leader. This chapter uses the Values in Action (VIA) Character Strength assessment to heighten your awareness of your strengths and provides supplemental exercises for assessing how you can leverage these in the practice of leadership.

Chapter 2: Enhancing Emotional Intelligence

Emotional intelligence (EI) is the degree to which an individual is emotionally self-aware and aware of the emotional composition of other people, is able to manage personal emotions, and can appropriately apply individual strengths and emotions in building successful relationships. This chapter explains the concepts of EI and provides exercises for helping to develop EI competencies.

Chapter 3: Leading with Confidence

Self-confidence is an individual's belief in his or her ability to accomplish things. Self-confidence provides the foundation for inspiring and motivating others. This chapter provides an overview of the underpinnings of self-confidence and offers exercises for acknowledging and appreciating yourself and building self-confidence.

Chapter 4: Defining and Executing Personal Life Vision

A personal vision and knowing one's purpose are standards that guide an individual's life. Vision and purpose provide the pathway for decision making, problem solving, working with others, and facing challenges. This chapter provides exercises for developing a compelling picture of your leadership that is rooted in your strengths, values, and aspirations.

Chapter 5: Amassing Social Capital

Social capital consists of networks and relationships among people that are based on trust and provide reciprocal value. Social capital provides value through a variety of channels such as information flow, mutual support, and access to resources. This chapter provides a guide to help you build a social capital portfolio in advancing your leadership.

Chapter 6: Developing Leadership Presence

This chapter focuses on developing mindful practice to support personal and organizational leadership. Mindfulness is a general state of engagement in the world. This chapter offers an overview of mindful practice and exercises to help you achieve clarity and a deeper understanding about your leadership and the world around you.

Chapter 7: Making and Keeping Goals

Vision without action is merely a dream. Leaders seek opportunities, set goals, and take action to fulfill their vision. This chapter leads you step-by-step through visioning exercises and provides a formula to help you set and achieve your goals.

References

George, B., P. Sims, A. McLean, and D. Mayer. 2011. Discovering Your Authentic Leadership in *On Leadership*. Boston: Harvard Business Review.

Kouzes, J.M. and B.Z. Posner. 2007. *The Leadership Challenge*, 4th ed. San Francisco: Josey-Bass.

Maxwell, J.C. 1993. *Developing the Leader Within You*. Nashville: Thomas Nelson.

1 Identifying and Using Character Strengths

Leadership is a commitment to excellence and leveraging personal awareness in cultivating a shared vision that inspires and motivates others to act ethically, embrace change, and develop and use their talents in creating an environment where people and organizations flourish. Leadership is rooted in who you are, not in you trying to be someone else. Recognizing, acknowledging, and appreciating your strengths and abilities, as well as knowing how and when to put these into action are key leadership characteristics. Character strengths are positive personality characteristics that define who you are. Bravery, perspective, honesty, judgment, and gratitude, for example, are considered character strengths. When character strengths are acknowledged and exercised appropriately they help the leader build self-confidence and take action consistent with his or her values, which models the way for followers and gains their trust. When embraced and used, they are the essence of authentic leadership.

Great leaders also recognize they have limitations. In other words, they do not view limitations as weaknesses or shortcomings. Instead they are prudent and offset these limitations by valuing and drawing upon the complementary character strengths of others to get things done. Knowing and using individual strengths and those of others is an essential part of leadership. For example, a health information management (HIM) director whose top strength is creativity and who generates novel ideas when solving problems may team up with someone who is better at organization and perseverance so that a new project idea achieves its goals on time and within budget.

This chapter introduces strength-based leadership concepts. It takes the step-by-step process of (1) learning key concepts about character strengths; (2) discovering your character strengths and how to identify the character strengths of others; and (3) practicing new ways to use and leverage your strengths to enhance your leadership. Each of these steps is highlighted with an icon throughout the chapter.

Character Strength Concepts

Character strengths are positive personality characteristics. The modern study of character strengths emerged with the development of the field of positive psychology and the research of Christopher Peterson and Martin Seligman (2004). Peterson and Seligman applied scientific methods to better understand the positive aspects of human nature and what is best in people. This research produced a classification called Values in Action (VIA), composed of six virtue categories and supported by 24 character strengths (table 1.1). The virtue categories classify the 24 character strengths into similar groups. For example, the strengths of creativity, curiosity, judgment, and love of learning are classified under the virtue of wisdom, whereas the strengths of bravery, perseverance, honesty, and zest are classified under the virtue of courage. The VIA is a grouping of people's positive traits and classifies what is good in us rather than prescribing what we should do to be good or to improve ourselves.

Character strengths are different from other types of strengths such as talents, skills, or interests. Talents are a person's natural abilities—for example, having a knack for playing a musical instrument. Skills are proficiencies a person develops over time—for instance, being an adept ICD-10-CM coder. Interests are activities a person enjoys, such as bird watching, gardening, or reading. While all of these strengths are part of a person's makeup, by themselves they do not define an individual. Character strengths, on the other hand, are components of an individual's core identity that explain a person's uniqueness.

Everyone to some degree possesses all 24 strengths. However, each individual has a set of certain strengths that are more naturally used than others—these are called signature strengths. Signature

Table 1.1. VIA classification of virtues and character strengths

Virtue	Character Strengths
Virtue of Wisdom and Knowledge: The acquisition and use of knowledge	Creativity (originality, ingenuity) Curiosity (interest, novelty-seeking, open to experience) Judgment (critical thinking, open-mindedness) Love of learning (mastering new skills, topics, body of knowledge) Perspective (provide wise counsel to others)
Virtue of Courage: The will to accomplish goals in the face of opposition	Bravery (valor) Perseverance (persistence, industriousness) Honesty (authenticity, integrity) Zest (vitality, enthusiasm, vigor, energy)
Virtue of Humanity: Tending and befriending others	Love (capacity to love and be loved) Kindness (generosity, nurturance, care, compassion) Social intelligence (emotional intelligence, personal intelligence)
Virtue of Justice: Civic strengths that support healthy community life	Teamwork (citizenship, social responsibility, loyalty) Fairness (notions of fairness and justice) Leadership (organization, seeing things happen)
Virtue of Temperance: Protects against excess	Humility (modesty) Prudence (careful about one's choices) Self-regulation (self-control) Forgiveness (mercy)
Virtue of Transcendence: Connections to the universe and provides meaning	Appreciation of beauty and excellence (awe, wonder, elevation) Gratitude (thankfulness) Hope (optimism, future-mindedness) Humor (playfulness) Spirituality (religiousness, faith, purpose)

Adapted from Peterson and Seligman 2004.

strengths represent the values that an individual views in the highest regard. When used appropriately signature strengths help people feel fulfilled and help them function at their best. When leaders use their signature strengths they put their values in action. When they put their values into action, leaders are authentic.

The VIA assessment, created by Peterson and Seligman, is a self-report survey that consists of 120 questions using a 5-point Likert scale to measure the degree to which an individual views the importance of each of the 24 character strengths in the VIA classification (Peterson and Seligman 2004). Using a variety of statistical techniques, the survey produces a report that provides a top-down ranking of an individual's character strengths.

The five highest ordered strengths of one's assessment results are referred to as an individual's signature strengths. These are the most dominant character strengths and those he or she prefers and uses naturally across many situations. When an individual uses these strengths he or she is energized and feels fulfilled. Like a main parachute that leads a skydiver safely to the ground, signature strengths are an individual's primary means for leading a flourishing life.

Signature strengths are a pathway for developing other strengths such as interests, talents, and skills. An HIM professional may use a signature strength like curiosity as a pathway for developing his coding skills, since performing quality coding requires inquisitiveness—for example, searching a patient's health record to find evidence to support a specific code. On the other hand, another HIM professional may have perspective as her signature strength. She may use this strength in developing problem-solving or decision-making skills. For example, when deciding whether or not to purchase a computer-assisted coding product, the HIM professional would consider several variables before selecting a product rather than making a snap decision based on limited input.

Even if a particular strength is not ranked in the top five strengths of an individual's profile, this does not mean the person does not have this strength. Strengths that are not rank-ordered as top strengths are called situational strengths. An individual possesses these strengths, but not to the same degree as the signature strengths. As their name implies, situational strengths are those an individual calls upon when required in a specific situation. They are like a reserve parachute that is used when needed. Take for instance Cary, a healthcare statistical analyst whose top strengths are gratitude, creativity, curiosity, persistence, and perspective. Cary's boss asks him to manipulate the results of a statistical report so that patient outcomes will look better than they actually are. Even though honesty and valor are not Cary's top strengths, these are situational strengths that he can readily call upon to help him take appropriate action in this specific situation. Cary draws upon his reserve or situational honesty and courage strengths by refusing to participate in tampering with the report results.

Character Strength Principles

Over the centuries, character has been interpreted in many ways. For example, one view holds that there are certain character traits that everyone should strive to achieve. Or some believe that what is defined as character differs from culture to culture. Other views contend that character traits do not occur in degrees; one either has or does not have a specific character strength (Niemiec 2013). The VIA conceptualization of character departs from these traditional views. For example, the developers of the VIA argue that the 24 character strengths exist across all cultures and do exist in varying degrees in individuals. Therefore to appropriately interpret and understand the use of the results of the VIA assessment it is necessary to be familiar with the underlying VIA assessment principles (Niemiec 2014). A number of these are described as follows.

First, an individual is not described by a single character strength. Character strengths are plural and work together. It is an individual's unique combination and the synergy of strengths working together that comprise one's character and what is unique and good about him or her (Niemiec 2014). For example, Diana is the vice president at a large healthcare system and her top strength is creativity. But it is the constellation of her curiosity, perspective, and judgment strengths coupled with creativity that work together and make her an excellent problem solver.

Character strengths are multidimensional. This means a strength has multiple aspects and is not defined by a one-word description (Niemiec 2014). For example, the strength of kindness has several dimensions such as generosity, nurturing, caring, and compassion. Therefore, kindness can be demonstrated in different ways by the same person in various situations and in diverse ways by different people. For instance, Jake is the manager of admitting services. He expresses the nurturing dimension of generosity through coaching his direct reports and helping them continually improve their skills and fulfilling their potential. On the other hand, Jake's generosity is expressed differently when he shows a caring attitude to people who come to the admitting services office with concerns about their upcoming hospital admission. Table 1.1 provides a partial list of the dimensions of each strength in parentheses following the name of strength.

Character strengths make up our spirit and personality that portrays us at our best self (Niemiec 2014). For example, when Anna is asked to describe an event where she performed at her best, she often gives an example of completing a difficult course in her college degree program. Anna refers to this time as performing at her best because even though she was tempted to give up on the course, she was able to collectively put into action her strengths of love of learning, perseverance, and hope to complete the class. Her love of learning helped her view the class as an opportunity to learn new things; her perseverance helped maintain her energy to complete what she started; and her hope provided her the optimism she needed to believe in herself and her control over events.

In addition, another important principle is that character strengths can be measured. This means that character strengths can be defined, categorized, and ranked (for instance, the 24 character strengths are categorized into six virtues). Because strengths can be measured they can also be quantified in profiles (Niemiec 2014). For example, Mark's profile of strengths can be quantified with some strengths ranked higher than others. And since strengths can be measured it means the validity and reliability of the VIA assessment can be evaluated through various statistical tests (Niemiec 2014). Validity is the extent to which an assessment measures what it is supposed to measure and reliability means the assessment results are repeatable. So if one takes the VIA assessment multiple times, it is likely to get the same results. The VIA assessment has strong reliability and validity and, therefore, the individual profiles produced measure the character strengths that a person views as important as well as the degree of importance relative to other character strengths.

Universality, which means character strengths are recognized across cultures, is another VIA principle. Character strengths are not culture-bound and associated with only a few or specific cultures. The researchers who developed the VIA categorization conducted an exhaustive historical survey of virtues across cultures and disciplines such as psychology, philosophy, and the social sciences, and by using empirical techniques concluded the character strengths represented by the VIA are universal (Niemiec 2014).

Character strengths are expressed in degrees and content; they are applied differently among individuals and among different situations. Two people may have bravery as their highest signature strength, for example. The expression of the strength, however, is likely to be different between them in its frequency, duration, and intensity and dependent on the situation in which it is applied. Individuals may also apply their strengths differently based on context. For example, the degree of curiosity an individual expresses at work or performing a hobby may vary from how the strength is expressed when interacting with friends or family.

Discover Your Strengths

Your strengths are a unique combination that defines who you are. They support you every day, in every challenge, in every circumstance. When acknowledged and used appropriately, these strengths provide a sense of fulfillment and make you a more authentic leader.

The VIA assessment helps you discover your strengths. Studies show that when you use your strengths you experience happiness in your personal and work lives, have a sense of authenticity, build confidence, and have a more rapid learning curve (Niemiec 2013). In this section you will complete the VIA survey and exercises to help you discover your strengths.

Identifying Your Strengths

Go to http://www.VIAInstitute.org and on the home page select "Take the Free VIA Survey." Once you register and complete the free 120-question survey, feedback about your 24 character strengths is provided. Your strengths will be ranked with your most dominant strengths listed first.

In the space that follows, write down your top five strengths. These are your signature strengths, which you naturally use across all situations.

Consider the following questions about your top five strengths:

1. Do these strengths come naturally for you, without any effort?

2. Do your friends, family, or co-workers say they observe these strengths in you?

3. Do you feel energized when you use these strengths?

4. Do you feel authentic when using these strengths?

Strengths Reflection 1: A Best Self Performance

This exercise provides you with the opportunity to reflect about a time when you performed at your best and to assess how your signature strengths may have supported your achievement.

1. In the following space provided, write about an event or period in your life when you were at your personal best. This could be a personal or work life event.

2. Assess how you used one or more of your top five strengths in the event you described. In the space that follows, write down what strengths you used and describe how these helped you achieve a best self in the given event.

3. What new discoveries have you made about your strengths? Write down your observations. Were there any surprises? What questions do you have?

Overuse, Underuse, and Misuse of Character Strengths

Character strengths can be overused, underused, and misused. The authentic leader is mindful of the appropriate use of his or her strengths in any given situation. Bonnie, for example, heads up a revenue cycle team. One of her signature strengths is creativity and she likes to find new ways of reducing non-billed accounts. She overuses her creativity by continually coming up with new ideas and projects, changing direction several times in the middle of a process. This overwhelms and frustrates her team because there is not sufficient time or resources to complete the process or make the necessary changes. Bart, on the other hand, underuses his creativity strength. His scanning job is process-bound, allowing him no opportunity to use his signature strength of creativity as he scans authorizations and consents all day into the electronic health record (EHR). If Bart cannot find opportunities to express his creativity—either at work or in his personal life—his motivation, fulfillment, and happiness will likely decrease. Finding the optimum balance where signature strengths can be expressed is essential for overall well-being.

Character strengths can also be misused when they are used for malicious purposes. Again using the strength of creativity as an example, think about how this strength has been misused by healthcare workers in designing fraudulent reimbursement schemes or hacking computers to obtain confidential patient information.

The authentic leader avoids underuse and overuse of his or her strengths and in uses them in the correct combinations depending on the context and situation.

Character Strengths and the Workplace

Studies show a relationship between the use of character strengths in the workplace and job satisfaction and worker engagement, motivation, goal attainment, and well-being. Workers who have a high awareness of their character strengths and are able to use these in the workplace are more likely to have high levels of emotional, psychological, and social well-being than those who do not have a high awareness of their strengths and thus do not use them (Hone et al. 2015).

It has also been found that workers who use their signature strengths in their job have a higher job performance level than those who do not use their strengths (Harzer and Ruch 2014). Similarly, when workers use four or more of their signature strengths they are more likely to have positive work experiences than those who use less than four of their top strengths (Harzer and Ruch 2012). The general conclusion from these and other studies is that specific character strengths are important in job performance and the use of signature strengths is a significant contributor to individual well-being and thriving in the workplace.

Many organizations, such as IBM, Westin Hotels, PricewaterhouseCoopers, and Allied Health, are using the VIA to help their employees identify and use their strengths in their jobs. Each of these organizations has examples about how the VIA has led to both organizational and worker success.

Strength Awareness

The authentic leader is able to recognize the use of character strengths in daily activities. The leader can identify whether these strengths are appropriately used in a given situation. Perfecting this recognition of strengths enhances one's awareness of how strengths are used and increases the possibility of using them more frequently and more appropriately. Some of the ways strengths can be identified include:

- Being energized or engaged when using a strength
- Losing track of time when using a strength
- Easily learning a new skill by using a strength
- Being repeatedly successful in an activity by using a strength (Linley 2008, 74–75)

In addition, a good leader is able to recognize the strengths of others. In other words, a good leader notices what strengths people are employing when they are at their best. Identifying the strengths in others and taking action to help them leverage their strengths is a leadership practice. There is a large body of evidence that shows people perform work activities better when they use their top strengths. Providing others with opportunities to use their signature strengths helps them grow and succeed. It also produces better organizational outcomes.

For instance, Bob is an HIM director and notices that Beth, one of his team members, consistently asks questions about work processes and likes to take the initiative in exploring alternative ways of doing things to improve her job. Bob recognizes that curiosity is one of Beth's natural strengths. So instead of becoming frustrated with Beth's questions and new ideas, Bob channels Beth's strength by making her responsible for process quality improvement in her release of information work area. Bob establishes a reporting structure ensuring that new ideas and processes Beth recommends are shared with and vetted by the entire team. Bob's actions provide Beth with an opportunity to grow and be fulfilled in her job. His actions also offer the potential for better organizational outcomes.

Identifying Strengths

Authentic leaders know their strengths and how to best leverage them for positive outcomes. The following reflections provide you with an opportunity to identify strengths in yourself and others.

Strengths Reflection 2: Recognizing Strengths in Yourself

Think about three activities you engaged in during the past five days. What signature and situational strengths did you use the most to perform these activities? Write these down.

Activity	Strengths Used

Review your results and answer the following questions.

1. Are there trends in the strengths you used? Do the same strengths show up? Were these strengths effectively used for the given activity?

2. Are there strengths you did not use? Which ones were they? Why did you not use them?

3. Were there times you overused a strength? If so, what happened to make you overuse the strength?

4. How can you avoid overuse in the future?

5. Identify missed opportunities this past week for not using your signature strengths. Why did you not use them?

6. How can you be more aware of opportunities to use your strengths in the future?

Strengths Reflection 3: Recognizing Strengths in Others

Select two people from your work, student, community, professional or student organization, or other team you work with and identify a time when each individual performed at his or her best. Write about this activity. What did each do? How did they do it? Why did you select this time as the time when each was at their best? Which strengths did they use in performing at their best?

Team Member	Description of Their Best Performance	Strengths Used

Answer the following questions after completing the *Strengths Reflection 3* exercise.

1. How did it feel to notice the best about someone?

2. How easy was it for you to recognize strengths of your team members?

3. Did the exercise help you better appreciate the value these individuals bring to the team?

Write down two to three ways you can engage in strength identification. Make a commitment to do these at least once a week.

1.

2.

3.

Practice Your Strengths

Knowing your strengths is only one part of developing as a leader. Using and leveraging your strengths to the best advantage in any given situation is where real leadership practice emerges. The more frequently strengths are used appropriately, the better the leader will perform, flourish, and be in a state of well-being. The more consistently signature strengths are used, the more authentic the leader is. This section provides you with two exercises to help you heighten your awareness of your strengths and practice them.

Identify Your Strengths Exercise

The purpose of this exercise is to heighten awareness (mindfulness) of the use of your character strengths and to identify potential overuse or underuse of strengths.

Instructions:

- At the end of each day for five consecutive days record the number of times you recall using a particular strength (be sure to change the dates on the spreadsheet to correspond with the dates you are recording).
- In the comments section record your recollections of the situations where you used the strengths: What was the outcome of strength use? What did you learn by the use of your strength? Did the use of the strength help you grow in anyway? Were there missed opportunities for using a strength you normally would not use?
- At the conclusion of the five days, review the bar chart on the Excel spreadsheet. Are there any surprises from the graph? What have you learned about yourself? Are there strengths you should use more often and less often?

Increasing the Use of Your Strengths Exercise

The purpose of the exercise is to increase the new ways you use your character strengths. When you use one of your signature strengths in a new way, you will experience benefits such as an increase in happiness for a sustained period of time.

Instructions:

For five days, take one of your signature strengths and use it in a new way each day. For example, if kindness is one of your strengths, try performing random acts of kindness such as complimenting someone, holding the door open, or offering to help someone. If love of learning is your strength, take some dedicated time and search the Internet to learn something new about a topic you are interested in. Or if creativity is one of your strengths, look at your work processes and find better ways of performing your tasks.

Each day journal one paragraph about how you used your strength. Write about what the experience was like. What did you learn? How did it make you feel? Examine how the exercise heightened your awareness of the use and value of your strengths.

Identify Strengths in Others Exercise

The purpose of this exercise is to help you practice and improve upon your ability to recognize strengths in others.

Instructions:

At your next work or team meeting or in a class you are attending open your mind to observing and listening to the people in attendance and note their strengths. Is someone asking a lot of questions (curiosity)? Is someone suggesting new solutions (creativity)? Is someone challenging the process (bravery)?

After the meeting or class spend 15 minutes assessing what you observed. Write down the strengths you noticed in others. What have you learned about them? Do you see them in a more positive light? Do you see them as performing their best?

The next time you see one of these individuals, tell them how much you appreciate his or her strength. Letting people know you notice and appreciate a strength they have helps them flourish. Scientists have found that people need three positive comments to combat every one negative comment they receive. People need this positivity ratio of good comments to function at a high level. (Niemiec 2014, 177). For example, you might say, "Breana, at our last meeting I was impressed with your ideas to solve that difficult problem. I admire your creativity." Or, "Jack, at our last meeting I noticed how thoughtful you were in helping us come to a decision. Thank you for your perspective."

Accountability Practice

The adage "practice makes perfect" does not just apply to skills like playing a musical instrument or perfecting a golf game. It applies to the development and use of your strengths as well. If you expect to develop into a leader who practices great leadership, then you must view your development as a journey of continually striving to improve.

A basic premise of improvement is setting accountabilities for yourself. Accountability is something specific that holds you responsible for doing what you say you are going to do or achieve. For example, if you promise to meet someone for dinner create accountability by naming the restaurant and designating a specific day and time you will meet. If you set a goal to improve your speed at running, your create an accountability that you will run for one hour from 7 a.m. to 8 a.m. every morning in order to meet your goal.

Accountabilities do not have to be huge. In fact, it is better to set small goals and take simple steps to achieve them. The following list displays a plan for establishing an accountability practice to enhance your use and leverage of your strengths.

- Set aside a specific time each week to plan how you will hold yourself accountable for practicing your strengths in the coming week. Mark the time in your calendar. For example, every Friday afternoon at 4 p.m., you will spend 15 minutes devoted to planning your strength practice for the next week. Then determine what action you will take during the upcoming week. You can repeat one of the exercises in this chapter, or you can develop your own exercises. Do not take on more than you can handle. Remember development is a journey; it is a marathon, not a sprint. Accountabilities should be stated in the first person. The following are some examples.
    - In each meeting I attend this week, I will recognize strengths of one of my co-workers and at the end of the meeting compliment them on what I observed.
    - This week I will purchase a journal so that I can write down my strength-based observations over the next year.
    - On Wednesday of this week, I will keep a journal of how I used my signature strengths throughout the day.
    - This week I will find one new way of using one of my signature strengths at work.

References

Harzer, C. and W. Ruch. 2014. The role of character strengths for task performance, job dedication, interpersonal facilitation, and organizational support. *Human Performance* 27(3):183–205.

Harzer, C. and W. Ruch. 2012. When the job is a calling: The role of applying one's signature strengths at work. *Journal of Positive Psychology* 7(5): 362–371.

Hone, L.C., A. Jarden, S. Duncan, and G.M. Schofield. 2015. Flourishing in New Zealand workers: Associations with lifestyle behaviors, physical health, psychosocial, and work-related indicators. *Journal of Occupational and Environmental Medicine* 57(9):973–983.

Linley, A. 2008. Average to A+: *Realising Strengths in Yourself and Others*. Coventry, England: CAPP Press.

Niemiec, R. 2014. *Mindfulness and Character Strengths: A Practical Guide To Flourishing*. Boston: Hogrefe Publishing.

Niemiec, R. 2013. VIA Character Strengths: Research and Practice (The First 10 Years). Chapter 2 in *Well-Being and Cultures: Perspectives on Positive Psychology*. Edited by Knoop, H.H. and A. Delle Fave. New York: Springer.

Peterson, C. and M.E.P. Seligman. 2004. *Character Strengths and Virtues: A Handbook and Classification*. Washington, DC: APA Press and Oxford University Press.

2 Enhancing Emotional Intelligence

Why do some highly intelligent and skillful people succeed as leaders while others with these same characteristics fail miserably at leadership practice? Recent studies suggest that intelligence and technical skills are only threshold capabilities and are not the only requirements for effective leadership. The distinguishing characteristic that separates effective from nominal performance is emotional intelligence (Goleman 2015).

Emotional intelligence (EI), also referred to as emotional quotient (EQ), includes a number of dimensions. It is comprised of self-awareness, self-management, social awareness, and building and maintaining a rapport with others. This chapter explores all of these facets and provides exercises to help you recognize emotional intelligence in yourself and others.

The Science of Emotional Intelligence

How much EI you demonstrate is related to how accurately you identify and manage your emotions in challenging situations. Allowing emotions, rather than reason, to dominate our actions may have regrettable consequences. For example, at a recent group meeting of healthcare information system project managers, someone inferred that Diane's team was responsible for delays in other projects down-stream. Diane's emotions flared at what she believed was an unfair accusation. She knew her team was behind, but this was not the team's fault. Resources her project needed from a subcontractor were overdue and these circumstances were out of Diane's control. Rather than addressing the comment with a rational response, Diane let her emotions take over. She took her colleague's comment as a personal affront and lashed out bitterly during the meeting.

This scenario demonstrates how the brain naturally responds in a challenging situation. Due to the brain's natural pathways, emotions kick in before rational thinking when people face difficult situations. This is often called the fight or flight response. When an individual perceives a threatening situation it triggers an emotional response in the brain. Physiologically this happens as an electrical signal that first enters the limbic system at the base of the brain before it passes to the frontal lobe. Emotional responses occur before rational ones because the limbic system (the first place the electrical signal travels) controls our emotions, while the frontal lobe controls our rational thought. In other words, rational thought can be easily hijacked by emotions if one is not self-aware. A significant part of EI is the ability to consciously monitor our emotional responses and control them when managing our behavior.

A Model of Emotional Intelligence

Several models of EI have been developed. The Goleman emotional intelligence model, which is one of the most popular, is described in this section. The model is based upon three processes of awareness, regulation, and motivation; and has five components that include self-awareness, self-management, social awareness, relationship management, and motivation (Goleman 2015).

Self-awareness of one's emotions in a specific situation is the foundation for managing personal responses. In the previous example, if Diane had been more self-aware that her emotions were controlling her, rather than her reason, she could have regulated her response more realistically by pausing to assess the situation in its entirety. Self-awareness and self-management put one in a better position to notice the emotions of others and to employ appropriate responses. Again using Diane's response as an example, if she had slowed her emotional response she could have created the necessary space for seeing the situation in a broader perspective and would be socially aware of her colleagues' concerns. She would understand that her co-workers were not personally attacking her, but were anxious because the project was falling behind schedule and this was adversely impacting them. Noticing their anxiety and fear, Diane could have responded more appropriately by stating the facts of the situation and then proposing to her associates that they work together to find workarounds to the subcontractor delays. In this last step Diana would be using her social awareness to maintain good relations with her co-workers. Figure 2.1 illustrates the model and its components are described in the following sections.

Figure 2.1. Goleman emotional intelligence model

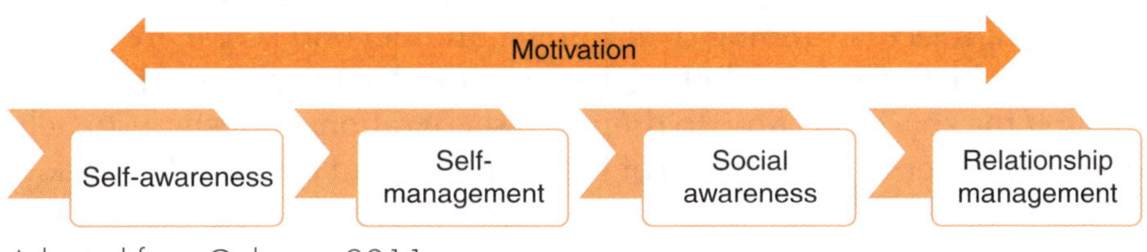

Adapted from Goleman 2011.

Self-Awareness

Self-awareness—the capacity to have a deep understanding of one's emotions, strengths, drives, and purpose—is the Goleman EI model's foundation. Self-aware people know what affects them positively or negatively, what makes them comfortable or uneasy, and what their strengths and limitations are. For example, a person who likes to investigate all aspects of a problem will wait to give an opinion until she is satisfied that all details of the problem have been gathered. An individual who likes to be on time to meetings will plan his or her schedule to allow for sufficient time between appointments.

Self-awareness is fundamental to leadership because it establishes self-confidence and authenticity. From a self-confidence viewpoint, people who are self-aware will play to their strengths, have confidence in their judgment, and take on assignments they know they can handle. They are able to realistically assess situations and use their judgment to avoid setting themselves up for failure (Goleman 2015). A self-aware person knows and can speak openly about his or her strengths and limitations. This is an individual with a realistic self-assessment and who provides an honest self-portrayal to those he or she works with and leads. Because this individual is self-aware and knows his or her capabilities, this person is confident in and discloses openly what he or she can and cannot do. Behaviors such as honesty and confidence build trust with colleagues and followers.

Self-Management

The model's second component is self-management, also called self-regulation. This is a person's ability to be his or her own emotional boss. The self-managed individual knows what triggers his or her emotional responses and is able to develop controls to responsibly manage these. For example, Betty is a high-achiever whose strength is excellence. Because she is self-aware, she knows that less than quality work is a trigger that increases her frustration and annoyance with others. When a project is running over budget and beyond scope, instead of berating her team and letting her emotions control her, she gives herself the space and time to prepare a set of rational questions to help the team determine the cause of the problems and get back on track.

Self-management supports acting in a responsible way in the face of change. When people are self-managing their emotions, they are able to control the fight or flight natural inclination. They are able to step back, look at the situation in a reasonable manner, and make decisions based on information and not emotion. Self-management is important for leadership practice in a number of ways. First, a person who has the ability to manage his or her emotions is consistent and reasonable. Consider how co-workers feel and respond toward a person who exhibits fluctuating emotions or who is fuming most of the time. Such behavior produces fear and distrust and reduces the motivation of others. Consistency and reasonableness resulting from self-management breed trust and loyalty among people—key hallmarks of leadership success.

Social Awareness

The third part of the Goleman EI model is social awareness, which is how adept people are at perceiving and empathizing with the emotions of others. Social awareness entails having the ability to listen to others and considering their perspectives when making decisions.

Leaders who are socially aware are able to pick up on subtle cues that tell them how others are feeling. For example, Lydia worked at the front of the health information management (HIM) corporate office where there was a lot of activity. She was energized by the continual hustle and bustle. However, because of space and reorganization reasons, Lydia's workstation was moved to the back of the corporate office. Sharon, the corporate director of HIM, notices that Lydia's mood seems subdued since the move and wonders if the more secluded space is contributing to Lydia's quieter temperament. Sharon, who has high social awareness, picks up on Lydia's change in demeanor. Rather than ignoring these changes, Sharon invites Lydia into her office for a cup of coffee and asks her how her new work arrangements are going. After a few probing questions, Sharon realizes that Lydia's mood change is not due to the new work arrangements, but due to concerns about a family member's illness. Sharon empathizes and acknowledges Lydia's feelings, telling Lydia she will support her in any way she can during this tough time. This awareness and openness to others' feelings lets people know that they (and their needs) are important.

Relationship Management

Relationship management is the fourth element of the Goleman EI model. Relationship management is the ability to maintain meaningful and positive relationships with others. It also involves taking responsibility for how we impact the feelings of those with whom we interact. For example, studies show that if a leader is in a good mood, the mood of the team is elevated as well; if the leader displays negative mood behaviors, then the negative mood is also assumed by the group. A leader's positive mood enhances group performance and a negative mood diminishes group performance (Goleman 2011).

Relationship management also includes managing conflict, seeking out new information and opportunities, influencing and motivating others, and helping others fulfill their potential. The definition of leadership implies a leader–follower relationship. The components of leadership, including cultivating a shared vision and inspiring and motivating others to act ethically and embrace change directly, rely on establishing and maintaining positive relationships with others.

Motivation

Motivation is placed in the center of the Goleman EI model because it drives all of the other model components. All motivation, however, is not the same. For example, some people are motivated by greed or only want to gain power and control. This is not the motivation of EI. EI motivation is a need for achievement that is driven by a deep desire to do things better. Unlike achievement motivated by external factors such as a higher salary, position, or winning an award, a person with high EI is motivated by internal factors such as passion in his or her work and the desire to do the right thing and do it well (Goleman 2015).

This kind of motivation requires knowing one's values and strengths and putting these into action. Without motivation of this type, it is unlikely a person would care about self-awareness or self-management or have a desire to develop social awareness and meaningful relationships. The effort would not be on how to do things better, but rather on a narrow focus to get ahead at any cost. For example, in a recent case of healthcare fraud a global pharmaceutical company failed to disclose safety data for a particular medication and used kickbacks to physicians and underpaid rebates under the Medicare Drug Rebate Program to increase their bottom line (US Department of Justice 2012). The motivation of the pharmaceutical company leaders was related to greed and certainly does not reflect EI motivation.

Emotional Intelligence in the Workplace

Emotional intelligence is translated in the workplace in many ways. All five components of the Goleman EI model are not necessarily executed in every situation. For example, a leader in one situation may only need to exhibit self-awareness and self-management, but in another case would need to utilize all components of the model. Regardless, personal motivation to do better and do the right thing is the fuel that propels EI and must be exhibited in all EI behaviors. The following examples provide insights and demonstrations of each of the components of EI in the workplace.

Self-Awareness in the Workplace

Amy is the corporate chief privacy officer for a large healthcare system. She frequently needs to develop policies that cut across organizational departmental boundaries. Amy is a take-charge person and likes to see immediate outcomes. Being self-aware, however, Amy realizes her focus on outcomes needs to be balanced by people who concentrate on the details of policy execution. Therefore, she puts together a team of colleagues to help her develop policies that are thoughtful and can be realistically implemented. She manages her frustration by tempering her emotions and changing her belief that immediate outcomes are not necessarily the best and calls on her colleagues to help streamline bureaucratic processes.

Amy's co-workers admire her steadfastness in pursuing outcomes that work. They also appreciate that she respects her colleagues' opinions and initiates soliciting and using different viewpoints to develop solutions that improve the organization.

Self-Management in the Workplace

Achieving results is a key motivator for Brian, a health information systems analyst who is easily exasperated with the large organization bureaucracy. For instance, he recently received a change order for an update to a drop-down selection box in one of the electronic health record applications. To Brian this seemed a relatively easy fix to implement, but policy required him to first submit the request to the data steward committee for approval. This would delay the change for another two weeks. Frustrated, Brian fired off an angry e-mail to the chairperson of the data steward committee and copied the chief data officer on the e-mail. Brian brooded and then angrily criticized the process to his colleagues at lunch.

This scenario demonstrates how Brian's emotions control him, rather than him controlling his emotions. Several alternatives are available to Brian for self-managing his emotions. Knowing he can become easily irritated, Brian can create a new habit of pausing when he feels frustrated and stepping away from a judgmental perspective. Rather than fuming, lashing out, and attaching blame to a person, he can calmly state the urgency of the situation and ask that the request be expedited.

There are several strategies that can be used to keep emotions in check. For example, emotional flares usually last only a few seconds if they are not engaged. Taking a time out or a break before reacting to emotion provides an opportunity to free oneself from emotions. The adage, "count to 10 before you act" really does work.

Once you are in control of your emotions, ask yourself the question: "Is this a calamity or an inconvenience?" Often the situations you react to are not disasters or a pending event with a catastrophic impact. In these instances consider taking the following actions:

- Put the situation in perspective.
- Make it a habit to pause and examine the situation and then decide on an appropriate response. For example, if someone is talking loudly by your work area and it is disrupting your work, rather than slinging a sarcastic remark at them or giving them a dirty look, respect them and communicate directly about the situation and its

impact, and ask, "I am working on a difficult task right now and am distracted by your talking. Could you talk a little more softly?"

Social Awareness in the Workplace

Lisa, a coding manager, depends on the insights and opinions of each of her team members in developing better coding processes. During a recent meeting with her team reviewing the new physician query process, Lisa noticed that Yvonne's body language and facial expressions indicated she had concerns about the process, yet Yvonne failed to speak up at the meeting. Sensing that others on the team might also have apprehensions about the process, at the end of her explanation Lisa used a round-robin input technique with the group. She asked each team member to write down one to three concerns they had about the process and put each of these on sticky notes. Each team member placed their sticky notes on the white board in the meeting room, and each concern was fully addressed by the team. Bottlenecks were identified and the team streamlined the process.

In this instance, Lisa was attuned to the emotions of each of her team members. She picked up on body language cues and noticed some members were not contributing to the conversation. Lisa's social awareness resulted in the development of a better process that all team members were able to support.

Relationship Management in the Workplace

As a vice president for a large long-term care company, Melanie relies on developing and maintaining positive relations with her team. To do this, Melanie makes herself available whenever her team members need her. One of Melanie's particular traits is that she is not afraid of healthy conflict. In fact, her peers often ask her to help them manage potential conflict. She does this by listening carefully, asking probing questions, and taking a nonjudgmental position. She uses all of these techniques to coach the parties involved in reaching a consensus. Melanie is also committed to helping all of her team members fulfill their potential. She helps their development by identifying their strengths and ensuring that their job functions coincide with their interests and values. Melanie builds enthusiasm within her team and offers feedback and guidance to each team member.

As a result of her behavior, Melanie is seen as a go-to and resource person. She has developed an excellent network of professionals who she can readily call upon for advice, information, resources, and other assistance.

What Does Your EI Look Like?

To develop your EI, assess your baseline EI by taking the Global Leadership Foundation Emotional Intelligence Test available at https://globalleadershipfoundation.com/geit/eitest.html.

Note your EI result and then complete the following activities and questions. Record your results from the EI assessment in table 2.1.

Review your EI scores and critically reflect on which areas you want to increase. Use the EI reflection tool in table 2.2 to help you identify areas of your EI that you are satisfied with and areas that you consider are a medium or high priority to improve.

Table 2.1. Your EI baseline

Self-Awareness	Self-Management	Social Awareness	Relationship Management

Table 2.2. EI reflection tool

	Satisfied	Medium Priority for Improvement	High Priority for improvement
Self-Awareness			
Ability to read and understand my emotions and recognize their impact			
Ability to recognize my strengths and limitations			
Possess confidence in myself and my ability to get things done			
Set goals for myself and achieve them			

(*Continued*)

Table 2.2. EI reflection tool (continued)

	Satisfied	Medium Priority for Improvement	High Priority for improvement
Self-Management			
Ability to keep my emotions under control			
Ability to be transparent and honest			
Manage my commitments and responsibilities			
Ability to adapt to change and overcome obstacles			
Ability to manage stress			
Social Awareness			
Ability to understand others, pick up on cues regarding the emotions or feelings of others			
Ability to take an active interest in the concerns or feelings of others			
Ability to engage others			
Relationship Management			
Ability to inspire and motivate others			
Ability to listen clearly to others without distraction			
Ability to work collaboratively with others			
Ability to handle conflict			
Ability to identify and cultivate professional relationships			
Increase my social capital			
Communicate with others in ways they can understand			

Identifying Your Emotional Triggers Exercise

The foundation of EI is self-awareness. A large part of self-awareness is being able to identify your emotional triggers. What are the situations or issues that get your emotions revved up to the extent that you feel stressed, frustrated, or angry? Remember your emotions might be expressed in different ways—for example as anger, sarcasm, or avoidance. Recall instances where you have lost control of your emotions and answer the questions in table 2.3.

Assess your responses in the given table. Do you see trends in the triggers? What are some things you can do to keep your emotions in check? Write these in the following space provided.

Table 2.3. EI triggers

What was the emotion?	What triggered the emotion?	What was the outcome?	What could you have done to rein in your emotion?

Enhance Your EI through Practice

Developing your EI takes practice. It is not necessarily easy or quickly accomplished. If you want to grow in leadership practice, developing your EI is a foundational and continuous activity. The following activities will help you implement two essential EI practices: self-reflection and goal setting.

Accountability Practice: Self-Reflection Journal

Every day for two weeks write about your emotional response to an event in a journal or in the student workbook. Use the following as a guide when writing in your journal:

- Describe an event that took place today that generated an emotion.
- Describe the emotion.
- Is this an emotion that is commonly trigged by an event like this?
- Did you handle the emotion appropriately? Describe how you handled the emotion (either appropriately or not).

- What was the outcome of the event? Was it positive or negative? How did the outcome impact you immediately and after some time had passed? How did the outcome impact other people or the organization?
- What did you learn from this event? How will this event help you grow?
- If you were not able to check your emotions, what future actions should be taken to be control your emotions? If you were able to keep your emotions in check, what future actions should you take to ensure you can continually develop this habit?

Accountability Practice: Develop an EI Action Plan

Use the results from your EI assessment and your EI reflection tool to develop an action plan to enhance your EI. Look at areas that have a lower score from your EI assessment and match these to the high priority areas you have identified in your EI reflection tool. Select no more than three areas to focus on. Use table 2.4 as a sample to construct your plan.

Table 2.4. EI action plan

Priority Area	What I Will Do	When I Will Do It	How I Will Evaluate My Actions
Ability to listen to others	I will limit my talking and increase my listening.	Each day for two weeks I will have one conversation where I primarily ask questions.	I will journal my reflections on this activity daily. I will note my reactions, what I have learned, and how the other person has responded.
Increase my collaboration working with others	I will speak up and offer opinions during meetings.	At every meeting I attend in the next month I will offer at least one suggestion during the meeting.	After each meeting I will note the suggestion I made and how this made me feel. I will also note how others responded to my suggestion.

(Continued)

Table 2.4. EI action plan (continued)

Priority Area	What I Will Do	When I Will Do It	How I Will Evaluate My Actions
Increase my self-confidence	I will create a success journal.	Before going home at the end of the work day I will write down three things I was successful at during the day.	At the end of the month I will review and celebrate my successes.

References

Goleman, D. 2015. What Makes a Leader? In *HBR's 10 Must Reads on Emotional Intelligence*. Boston: Harvard Business School Publishing Corporation.

Goleman, D. 2011. *The Brain and Emotional Intelligence: New Insights*. Northampton: More Than Sound LLC.

United States Department of Justice. 2012. GlaxoSmithKline to Plead Guilty and Pay $3 Billion to Resolve Fraud Allegations and Failure to Report Safety Data [Press Release July 2, 2012]. https://www.justice.gov/opa/pr/glaxosmithkline-plead-guilty-and-pay-3-billion-resolve-fraud-allegations-and-failure-report

3 Leading with Confidence

Confidence is the trust that one person has in another person. Before leaders can gain the confidence of others they must have confidence in themselves—self-confidence. Hibberd and Usmar defines self-confidence as "consisting of a cohort of variables that function together to produce a feeling of emotional security that comes from having faith in yourself," (2015, 12). With this definition in mind, self-confidence is the belief in one's judgment, skills, and abilities to accomplish things. Possessing self-confidence allows people to express their values, stand up for their convictions, and reach their goals. People with self-confidence view obstacles as challenges to overcome, rather than roadblocks preventing them from achieving their goals. Those with self-confidence are more likely to recover from setbacks quickly, have less anxiety, and have more energy than those without self-confidence. People are inspired and motivated to follow others who have confidence because they believe in their capabilities. In other words, an individual with self-confidence sets an example for others. This chapter provides an overview of the connection between confidence and leadership, explores gender differences in confidence levels, and suggests ways to build self-confidence to better lead oneself and others.

Defining Self-Confidence

Research links three variables that make up self-confidence (Popper et al. 2004). The first of these is trait anxiety, the degree and duration of anxiety an individual exhibits in response to a broad range of perceived threats. A person who has a low level of trait anxiety is more likely to function effectively when exposed to situations of uncertainty and to stressors than those with high trait anxiety. When confident people are faced with a perceived threat, they have more trust in themselves to confront the situation than those with less self-confidence.

The second variable is generalized self-efficacy, a person's belief in his or her capabilities and resources to meet the demands of a variety of tasks in different situations. People who have high self-efficacy are generally motivated, persistent, goal directed, and clear thinkers under pressure (McCormick et al. 2002). Those who believe in themselves and their ability to perform leadership tasks, for example, will likely take on leadership roles and function more effectively in these roles than those who have low self-efficacy.

The third variable linked to self-confidence is locus of control, the degree to which an individual believes he or she has the ability to influence or control the outcome of events. Locus of control is defined as either external or internal. People who believe they have little control over the events in their lives have external locus of control; those who believe they have the ability to control events in their lives have internal locus of control. Internal locus of control, closely associated with self-confidence, is the belief in one's ability to take charge of a situation, initiate action, and change the status quo. Individuals in leadership roles are expected to achieve better organizational performance by developing bold visions and implementing innovative strategies.

The following scenarios contrast the differences in the level of self-confidence between two individuals.

Scenario 1: Carol has a master's degree in health information management and is a registered health information administrator (RHIA). For 10 years she has been director of a health information management (HIM) department, responsible for 45 employees. Her scope of duties includes management, budgeting, monitoring, planning, as well as directing the functions of coding and reimbursement, release of information, document imaging, chart deficiency analysis, physician record completion, transcription, and master patient index (MPI) maintenance. Carol has avoided stretching herself professionally.

In the past when career advancement opportunities have risen, Carol always gets a sinking feeling in her stomach and believes she does not have the skills for success. Afraid of failing, Carol never takes advantage of advancing her career. A corporate director of HIM services position opened recently in her health system with oversight of four acute-care facilities and 200 employees. However, Carol doubts she can handle a larger scope of responsibility and is hesitant to apply for the job. She fears she does not have the capabilities to assume this level of responsibility or initiate changes to challenge the status quo.

Scenario 2: Kelly graduated two years ago with a bachelor's degree in health information management and is an RHIA. Since graduation Kelly has been an associate director of HIM operations at a large acute-care facility. She is responsible for the day-to-day operations of the clinical coding unit and oversees the clinical reimbursement managers ensuring efficient execution of key functions that align to projected operational and financial goals. Kelly is the key patient financial services liaison responsible for monitoring, adjusting, and prioritizing workflow to meet revenue cycle goals. Even though Kelly has just two years of HIM experience in a limited area, when she heard about the job opening for a corporate HIM director she jumped at the chance to apply for the position. Kelly believed her problem solving, organization, social awareness, and communication skills would make up for any deficit in broad HIM operational experience. Kelly considered the new position an extension of her already tested abilities and she was determined to apply and get the job.

These scenarios demonstrate differences in self-confidence. Although Carol has a more advanced degree and greater HIM experience than Kelly, her fear of rejection and failure hold her back. Kelly, on the other hand, believes in her capabilities and views the gap in her HIM experience not as an obstacle, but as a challenge she can overcome by leveraging her strengths and skills.

Self-confidence has been identified as a link to successful leadership performance (McCormick et al. 2002). Scholars have found that people who are self-confident are afforded a higher social status, are more admired and listened to, and have more influence in organizational decision making than those with less self-confidence (Anderson et al. 2012). In some cases having self-confidence has been found to matter more and to exceed competence. In other words, the self-confident individual appears capable and skilled even if this is not the case (Kay and Shipman 2014).

People who are in leadership roles and have self-confidence tend to exhibit behaviors termed *transformational* and that are generally recognized as needed for success. Transformational leaders (addressed in part 4) are visionary and see possibilities and opportunities by challenging existing assumptions. They build trust and initiate action by engaging in collaboration and empowering others. For example, those with self-confidence are more persuasive than those with lower self-confidence. They also prefer to solve problems by engaging others in face-to-face discussions instead of using administrative rules of standard protocols that those with lower confidence rely on. Confident leaders are viewed as personally secure and decisive as opposed to those with less confidence who are seen as unwilling to make tough decisions because they are afraid of being disliked (Kaplan 1986).

Gender and Self-Confidence

Differences in self-confidence and career ambition between men and women have been cited as factors that prevent women from moving into senior and executive positions. With women composing approximately 80 percent of the healthcare workforce it is important to highlight gender barriers that may hinder women from moving into leadership roles. For example, an Institute of Leadership and Management study (2011) revealed women often lack self-confidence which leads to less risk taking and more cautious career choices. Study results showed 70 percent of male managers had higher levels of self-confidence compared to 50 percent of female managers. The study also revealed that female managers are hampered in their careers by lower ambitions and expectations and by setting a lower career bar than male managers at the start of their careers. For even the most confident women, expectations for achieving a leadership position were lower than for very confident men—only 59 percent of these women had high expectations of assuming a leadership role compared to 67 percent of the men. A result of the confidence and expectation gap is that, on average, women lag three years behind in assuming management positions as compared to men who have higher career expectations and increased confidence.

The difference in women's confidence is also confirmed in other studies. Findings showed that 9 in 10 women did not feel confident asking for sponsors (92 percent), and nearly 8 in 10 women lacked confidence in seeking mentors (79 percent) or in asking for access to senior leadership (76 percent) (KPMG 2015). These results have an important implication for women's career advancement and leadership. Mentoring and sponsorship are critical for building a career pipeline. Without access to mentors who provide role modeling, advice, and social support, and sponsors who promote the skills and abilities of aspiring leaders to others in the organization, the chances of career advancement to leadership positions diminish significantly (Hewlett et al. 2010). In addition, the study revealed women were more hesitant in pursuing a job opportunity beyond their experience (73 percent), and 6 out of 10 women lacked confidence to request a job promotion (65 percent), salary increase (61 percent), or a new role or position (56 percent) (KPMG 2015).

Researchers provide several explanations for the confidence gap between women and men. For example, at an early age women are expected by cultural norms to be compliant, cooperative, and follow the rules, while boys are expected to engage in risky behavior. For girls, these expectations have a downstream negative impact on self-esteem and confidence. Girls believe their value lies in doing things the right way, which results in them avoiding taking risks and making mistakes—both critical behaviors for confidence building (Kay and Shipman 2014). Studies show that when a boy fails, he believes it is due to a lack of effort not his ability; but when a girl fails at a similar task, she views herself as lacking ability (Dweck 2006).

Another consequence of cultural expectations for girls' behavior is that girls learn early that compliance yields rewards and approval. This mindset can result in trusting people's assessments of them more than valuing their own self-appraisal. If approval of others is sought and not received, this also can result in self-doubt and lowered confidence. In addition, negative ability labels and stereotyping applied to women as well as implicit biases, such as girls are bad at science and math, hijack a female's true abilities and can also contribute to lowered confidence (Dweck 2006).

How to Measure your Self-Confidence

There are a variety of instruments for measuring the characteristics related to self-confidence. Many of these instruments are available through private companies that charge a fee for taking the survey, but there are also some available for no charge. You can measure your self-confidence using the tools discussed in this chapter or with the following free assessments:

- Rosenberg Self-Esteem Scale: Self-esteem refers to a individual's general feeling of self-worth or self-value. This is the most widely used self-esteem measurement used in social science research and is considered a valid and reliable tool to measure self-esteem. http://personality-testing.info/tests/RSE.php
- Locus of control test: Locus of control refers to the degree to which an individual believes he or she has the ability to influence or control the outcome of events. People with an internal locus of control believe they can influence events and obtain what they want. Those with an external locus of control believe that life's events are generally outside of their control. http://www.psych.uncc.edu/pagoolka/LocusofControl-intro.html
- Confidence Code Survey: This survey broadly measures confidence in women and was created with the help of Dr. Richard Petty of The Ohio State University, Dr. Kenneth DeMarree of the University at Buffalo, and Dr. Pablo Briñol at the Universidad Autónoma de Madrid. theconfidencecode.com/confidence-quiz/

After completion of one or more of the assessments answer the following questions.

1. What does the assessment tell you about your self-confidence? Be specific in your description.

2. Are there areas where you would like to improve (for example, self-esteem, locus of control, or self-confidence)? Be specific about what you would like to enhance. Then read the following section to learn how you can increase your self-confidence.

Increasing Self-Confidence

Because there is a collection of characteristics associated with self-confidence, there is no single approach or technique for building it. Usually a number of methods are used to develop specific characteristics. The following sections provide strategies for developing self-confidence.

Increasing Internal Locus of Control

Locus of control described earlier is how people interpret their successes and failures. When people believe they control events rather than events controlling them, they have internal locus of control. Facing the unpredictable makes people uncomfortable. An internal locus of control helps to reduce unpredictability because people believe they can control the outcome of events, thus making the events more foreseeable. Among the strategies that can bolster internal locus of control are reframing and controlling the inner critic, discussed as follows.

Reframing

Reframing is the process of realistically interpreting events for explaining one's personal success or failure. Examine the differences in the following scenarios for explaining personal control of events.

Scenario 1: Ruth recently completed an information systems project on time and within budget. When her manager asked her how she was able to accomplish this she explained: "It was a perfect storm and everything just magically came together."

Scenario 2: Barbara just earned a master's degree in informatics. When a colleague complimented her on this achievement, Barbara responded: "Yes, it was a tough program. Earning this degree is an example of my personal best. My love of learning and persistence carried me to the top."

In the first example, Ruth attributes her success to external forces, circumstances or factors over which she had no control. In the second example, Barbara credits her success to being under her control and due to her own abilities. When people consistently and unreasonably attribute their successes to outside forces and attribute their failures to personal weaknesses, the result is a diminished external locus of control related to low self-confidence. The attribution of the causes of successes and failures plays a major role in self-confidence. For instance, is it true that the project success was totally out of Ruth's control? Or did some of her abilities play a role in its success? Rather than accrediting all of her success to luck, Ruth could reframe the situation more realistically in the following way: "A lot of factors came together and I was able to use my skills to leverage these to make sure I got a positive result."

Control the Inner Critic

Sometimes called one's inner judge, the inner critic is a negatively slanted running discourse that plays out in a person's mind. This is the voice that criticizes an individual's every misstep, berates him or her for not being perfect, and derides that person. The inner critic's voice is represented by statements such as: Who do you think you are? You are not good enough. You are stupid. You will not be able to take this on. These negative automatic thoughts (NATs) disguise themselves as facts when they are actually distortions of information that conform to unfounded beliefs about oneself or unrealistic fears.

The first step in controlling the inner critic is to recognize the critic's commentary. Once recognized, the inner critic can be challenged by evaluating those thoughts and presenting an alternative point of view. Barry, a sales associate with a healthcare information technology company, for example, wants to ask for a salary increase but his inner critic is restraining him with a running commentary of, "Why would the company want to give you a raise? You do not have the talent to command that kind of an increase." Barry can question the validity of these negative thoughts by realistically evaluating the talent he possesses and the value it brings to the company. Challenging the inner critic, Barry replies, "In the past six months I have closed six new big accounts and have substantially increased the number of products each of my existing accounts has purchased. This is more than any other account manager in the company." Armed with controlling the inner critic, Barry confidently asks for a raise in salary.

Many times the inner critic's self-talk is so ludicrous that it can be pushed away immediately. For example, Terri just completed a presentation to the hospital's revenue cycle committee. During the presentation she recognized she had forgotten to include a key slide measuring coding productivity over the past month. Although flustered, she was able to provide the data from memory. After the meeting Terri's inner critic appeared in full force taunting, "What a complete failure you are for screwing up the slide deck. Everyone in the room saw how incompetent you are." The critic's voice was so ridiculous, Terri pushed it aside at once. She was not a complete failure. In fact, she showed how knowledgeable she was by presenting the information without a slide.

Increasing Self-Efficacy

Self-efficacy is a belief people have in their ability to perform a given task. Self-efficacy related to leadership would be an individual's belief in his or her ability to be successful in a leadership role. People develop a belief in themselves by interpreting information from four sources: mastery experience, vicarious experience, social persuasion, and psychological states (Bandera 1977). Each of these is explained in the following sections.

Mastery Experience

Mastery experience is the most influential source for developing self-efficacy. Mastery experiences are those experiences, tasks, and activities that an individual performs. How an individual interprets the success or failure of those experiences determines his or her belief about one's ability to engage in subsequent similar activities. When an individual interprets the results of these experiences as positive, self-efficacy is increased. One way of increasing self-efficacy is to identify successes in a particular task. For example, Kelly keeps a daily log of her successes as a manager. Examples of the successes she records include coaching a colleague, making a tough decision, leading a committee meeting, and creating a solid project plan.

Vicarious Experience

Vicarious experiences involve observing others as they successfully perform a role or task. Observing others who are successful and modeling their behavior helps to create self-efficacy beliefs. In effect, vicarious experience is learning by observing. For example, Ross is an HIM student who is learning how to use an electronic spreadsheet. The more he watches his instructor demonstrate the various spreadsheet commands, the more confidence he has in his ability to execute the same commands.

Role model and role modeling are terms frequently associated with vicarious experience. Role modeling becomes particularly powerful when the individual sees similarities between the role model and himself or herself. For example, a woman will increase her leadership role self-efficacy when she sees another woman successful in that role.

Social Persuasion

Social persuasion is the influence others have on an individual's self-beliefs. How others verbally express their view, judgment, or encouragement helps to cultivate one's level of self-belief. For example, Krista's manager recently assigned her as lead on a new data modeling project. The project was challenging and Krista was outside of her comfort zone taking the lead role. Krista's manager, however, told Krista she had all the confidence in world in Krista's abilities and knew Krista would manage the project successfully. Social persuasion like this encourages and empowers an individual and builds the capacity for increased belief in oneself. Likewise, if the persuasions are negative they weaken self-efficacy.

Psychological State

Stressful or challenging situations can cause emotional and physiological responses. These responses in turn can influence how one believes in his or her abilities. For example, when giving a presentation to a large audience, Mark's anxiety level increases and he experiences a sick feeling in his stomach. Mark's anxiety level raises his fears he will make mistakes and will not present well. On the other hand, Carrie is invited to speak at a state professional association meeting. Although her anxiety is increased, Carrie mediates it by emulating the behavior she has observed in her mentor. By readjusting her frame of reference, Carrie is able to build belief in herself and in her ability to do well in the presentation.

Enhance Self-Confidence through Practice

Developing and sustaining self-confidence takes attention and practice. Even the most self-confident and successful individuals experience times when self-doubt creeps in and their confidence wanes. Building self-confidence and having strategies in place that support an individual throughout the continuum of his or her experiences are necessary. For example, Marie is a successful chief information officer of a large healthcare system. During a recent meeting a member of the information systems strategic planning committee derided Marie as a complete failure because of some recent implementation short comings. Yes, Marie's confidence was shaken for a moment by this attack, but she was able to use reframing techniques to quash the unrealistic statement that she was a "complete failure." Marie reframed the comment by acknowledging her successes in implementing a $1 billion dollar electronic health record system and delivering the best financial results of any executive in the healthcare system. Anyone able to do that is not a complete failure, she correctly reasoned.

Self-confidence is a foundational block for authentic leadership. As results of studies support, people have confidence in leaders who have confidence in themselves (Kay and Shipman 2014). The following exercises can help you develop and sustain your self-confidence.

Documenting Your Successes

One of the ways to build self-efficacy is through mastery experiences. Mastery experiences can be defined as a series of tasks that are completed with success. Acknowledging past successes is one of the best ways to increase and sustain self-confidence. Maintaining a success journal is a way to keep track and remind yourself of your successes.

Start your success journal (a model is in table 3.1) by writing down one or more successes you have achieved each day. Document the strengths you used to achieve each success. For example, Bob, an HIM director in a 140-bed facility, reduced discharged not final billed accounts (DNFB) from 10 to 3 days. When Bob examined how he achieved this, he realized his strengths of curiosity and perseverance worked together to support his success. His curiosity helped him identify the major work obstacles and his persistence helped him to implement the needed changes.

After the first week of documenting in your success journal, continue it throughout the month and then extend it throughout the year. Constantly reinforcing the acknowledgment of your successes

Table 3.1. Success journal

Accomplishments/Successes	Strength Used
Day 1	
Day 2	
Day 3	
Day 4	
Day 5	
Day 6	
Day 7	

and the strengths you have used helps to support a positive self-belief. Use the questions that follow to reflect on your successes each week.

Reflect on your successes

Review your successes and strengths by answering the following questions.

1. Do you see any themes or relationships among your successes?

2. How did writing down and acknowledging these successes make you feel?

3. How did each strength help you achieve success?

Celebrate Your Successes

Celebration is another way of acknowledging your successes and accomplishments. Like the success journal, celebrations provide a reminder of your successes and elevate your success to another level. Celebration also enriches your life with passion and connects and recommits you to your purpose. Celebrate in public and invite others to celebrate with you. Consider how you will celebrate your successes each week.

For instance, Susan, a nursing director, meets every other week with a small group of other nursing professionals for the specific purpose of celebrating each other's successes and evaluating how the challenges they have encountered can be turned into growth opportunities. Public celebration announces your achievements to others, makes your achievements more visible, and demonstrates your commitment to your strengths and values.

1. In the following space provided write five or more ideas about how you can celebrate your weekly successes. The celebration can be personal like taking an hour off and reading a favorite book, or enjoying or starting a hobby; or it can be doing an activity with someone else like going out to coffee or having lunch or dinner with a friend.

2. Review your celebration idea list. Choose one of the ideas to celebrate your successes this week. Input the day and time you will celebrate in your calendar and hold yourself accountable for it.

3. Revisit your celebration idea list each week. You may want to add more options to your list or keep the ones you have. Each week choose one way you will celebrate your successes, note the day and time in your calendar, and hold yourself accountable.

References

Anderson, C., S. Brion, D.A. Moore, and J.A. Kennedy. 2012. A status-enhancement account of overconfidence. *Journal of Personality and Social Psychology* 103(4):718–735.

Bandera, A. 1977. Self-efficacy: Toward a unifying theory of behavioral change. *Psychological Review* 84(2):191–215.

Dweck, C. 2006. *Mindset: The New Psychology of Success*. New York: Ballantine Books.

Hewlett, S.A., K. Peraino, L. Sherbin, and K. Sumberg. 2010. The Sponsor Effect: Breaking Through the Glass Ceiling. Center for Work-Life Policy. http://wliut.com/wp-content/uploads/2015/09/The-Sponsor-Effect.pdf

Hibberd, J. and J. Usmar. 2015. *This Book Will Make You Confident*. New York: Quercus.

Institute of Leadership and Management. 2011. Ambition and Gender at Work. https://www.i-l-m.com/~/media/ILM%20Website/Downloads/Insight/Reports_from_ILM_website/ILM_Ambition_and_Gender_report_0211%20pdf.ashx

Kaplan, R. The Warp and Woof of the General Manager's Job. Technical report no. 27. Center for Creative Leadership, Greensboro. 1986.

Kay, K. and C. Shipman. 2014. *The Confidence Code*. New York: HarperCollins.

KPMG Women's Leadership Study. 2015. Moving Women Forward into Leadership Roles. http://womensleadership.kpmg.us/overview/announcement1.html

McCormick, M.J., J. Tanguma, and A.S. Lopez-Forment. 2002. Extending self-efficacy theory to leadership: A review and empirical test. *Journal of Leadership Education* 1(2):34–49.

Popper, M., K. Amit, R. Gal, M. Mischal-Siani, and A. Liask. 2004. The capacity to lead: Major psychological differences between leaders and nonleaders. *Military Psychology* 16(4):245–263.

4 Defining and Executing Personal Life Vision

"The instrument of leadership is the self, and master of the art of leadership comes from mastery of the self," (Kouzes and Posner 2007, 344). This quote conveys that one must be self-aware to be a good leader. In addition to characteristics like knowing and appreciating your strengths and values, gauging your emotional intelligence, and having self-confidence, a critical component of self-awareness is having a vision of where you want to go.

Vision is broadly defined in this book as the product of forward thinking, imagination, and discernment that describes a desirable future achievable state. A personal life vision describes what you hope to be and achieve during your life. To lead others you must first lead yourself. You cannot lead yourself unless you clarify your values and how these frame the direction you want your life to take. Therefore, the clarity of a personal life vision is the foundation for developing a personal leadership vision that describes the kind of leader you want to be and what you hope to achieve as a leader.

Unfortunately, when people in leadership roles are asked, "What is your life vision?" or "What is your leadership vision?" they frequently have no immediate response. Many people have not taken time to think about what they want for their personal legacy, let alone how such a legacy is incorporated in their leadership.

This chapter describes the interrelationship between personal life vision, purpose, and mission (figure 4.1). It highlights what constitutes a personal life vision, how it is operationalized and fulfilled, and how it provides the foundation and guidance for a personal leadership vision.

Relationship of Personal Life Vision, Purpose, and Mission

Knowing your personal life vision helps you identify your purpose, and knowing your purpose narrows down the specific paths or missions you embrace throughout a lifetime. Figure 4.1 displays how these three concepts are related.

Figure 4.1. Relationship of personal life vision–purpose–mission

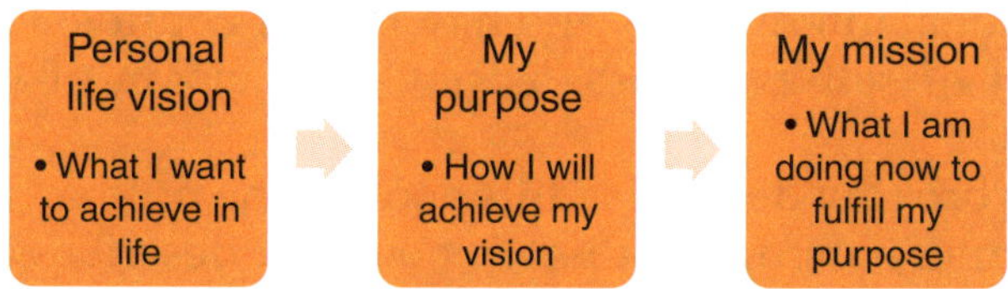

©Merida L. Johns

Personal life vision, purpose, and mission are sometimes used interchangeably. However, there are differences among the terms. Defining each of these as follows offers a framework for viewing one's life from the general to the specific.

- *Personal life vision* is a broad proclamation of what an individual wants to achieve in his or her life. It is usually expressed as an aspirational outcome and stated in the present tense. For example: I am a person who has a love of beauty and spreads beauty throughout the world.
- *Purpose* is how one operationalizes and achieves his or her personal life vision. It is usually expressed by identifying what personal strengths, values, and abilities are used to help achieve a personal life vision. For example: Using my strengths of appreciation of beauty, love of others, and perseverance my purpose in life is creating useful items of beauty that enhance the lives of others.
- *Mission* describes what an individual is doing in the present to fulfill his or her purpose and achieve one's personal life vision.

> It is usually expressed through a current job, community, or family activities and relationships. For example: My mission now is perfecting my artistic and musical talents by completing my master of fine arts degree.

In the examples given notice how personal life vision, purpose, and mission are related. The personal life vision is to spread beauty throughout the world. The purpose statement is more specific, describing that this individual creates useful and beautiful articles that enhance the lives of others. This could be the personal life vision and purpose statement of a person who is a furniture designer, potter, or song writer. The mission statement makes clear the individual's current efforts in fulfilling the purpose to achieve his or her personal life vision.

Vision, together with purpose, supports an individual and provides a measure for assessing how one makes decisions, solves problems, works with others, and generally faces life challenges. Once an individual's personal life vision and purpose are known, prioritizing life choices becomes simpler and more straightforward. Personal life vision and purpose also contribute to self-confidence. Standing up for oneself and using strengths in executing core virtues (chapter 1) feels more comfortable; and leading oneself and others becomes easier. The following example illustrates these points.

> Jennifer works as a statistician in a large healthcare data analytics department. Her personal life vision is: "I am making the world a better and happier place by helping others fulfill their potential." She believes her purpose is to use her courage, creativity, and organizational abilities to model a way that inspires and motivates others to live their lives to the fullest. In her current role she has little opportunity to fulfill her personal life vision. Recently a manager at a smaller facility presented Jennifer with a supervisory opportunity. The wage, however, would be a 10 percent decrease from her current salary. The new position would give Jennifer the chance to finally use her strengths and focus on creating a productive team. For many people, the choice of taking the new position may be challenging. They may be uncertain and not know whether or not to accept the job. They may be tempted by the money versus personal fulfillment. However, Jennifer, armed with her personal life vision and purpose as guiding principles, had clarity about her choice. She accepted the new position because she knew it would provide her with more meaning and fulfillment in life by mentoring others.

Research shows that finding meaning in life helps people select new paths and accept inherent risks involved in new paths. Having a personal life vision with purpose is associated with better job satisfaction, higher productivity, increased engagement, and longer happiness (Barsh et al. 2008). Leadership always begins with vision. Specifically, "Great leaders give real thoughts to the values, ideas, and activities they're most passionate about and those are the things they pursue, rather than money or prestige or options forced on them by someone else" (Ryan 2009). Certainly Jennifer's story fits this theme.

Writing Personal Life Vision, Purpose, and Mission Statements

People develop written personal life vision, purpose, and mission statements for several reasons. First, putting the effort into writing personal life vision, purpose, and mission statements helps an individual to think about one's strengths and values and clarifies what is important to him or her. All too frequently people do not give themselves the gift of time to think clearly or deeply about what they want to accomplish or how they want to live their lives. Without this knowledge, many people are aimless and often do not fulfill their potential.

Second, written statements take thinking about one's values and what a person considers important to a higher level of commitment. When values and aspirations are documented, it helps to motivate the individual to achieve what is important in his or her life. Written documentation also helps guide a person when making important decisions about choices in his or her life and filtering opportunities. In the earlier scenario about Jennifer, her life personal life vision helped her make a better decision about her career path. Finally, documenting one's personal life vision, purpose, and mission helps an individual to look positively toward the future and provides a means to measure successes. The following offer some examples of personal life vision, purpose, and mission statements.

Personal Life Vision Statement Examples

The folk singer, Joan Baez, said, "You don't get to choose how you're going to die. Or when. You get to decide how you are going to live now." Writing a personal life vision statement says how you have decided to live and provides you with a direction throughout your life. It keeps you in touch with what is important and meaningful to you, maintains your focus, and helps you set and keep important goals. Most importantly, your personal life vision statement tells the world where you are leading yourself and makes it easier for others to follow you.

Writing a personal life vision statement is challenging and usually is not done quickly. It involves reflection on your strengths and core virtues and requires self-awareness. Framing personal life vision another way—it is simply how you want others to know and remember you. If someone were to write a headline story about you in a newspaper or blog what would you want it to say?

There is no prescribed format for the vision statement but some examples are provided as follows. These are written in the present tense to describe yourself as if you have already achieved your personal life vision. Writing a personal life vision statement in the present tense conveys action that is ongoing and constant, strengthens an internal locus of control mindset, and increases positive momentum (Anderson and Anderson 2010, 172).

- I am a brave and courageous person and act on my convictions in making the world a better place.
- I am an artistic and creative person. I help make people's lives better with my creations.
- I am a person of courage who embraces excellence. My efforts are guided not only by doing things right, but by doing the right thing.

Each of these personal life vision statements is broad. They provide a convincing image of a plausible and desired future state. They encompass the values the individual views as intrinsic to his or her character.

Purpose Statement Examples

A purpose statement expresses how you use your strengths and talents to operationalize and achieve your personal life vision. There is no prescribed format for a purpose statement. Here are examples of purpose statements that explain how the previous personal life vision statements might be operationalized.

Personal life vision statement: I am a brave and courageous person and act on my convictions in making the world a better place.
Purpose statement: My life's purpose is to stand up for others and increase social justice throughout the world by using my strengths of bravery, kindness, and spirituality.

Personal life vision statement: I am an artistic and creative person. I help make people's lives better with my creations.
Purpose statement: By using my creativity and curiosity, my purpose in life is to conceptualize, design, and produce innovative items that create a safer world.

Personal life vision statement: I am a person of courage who embraces excellence. My efforts are guided not only by doing things right, but by doing the right thing.
Purpose statement: My purpose in life is to use my strengths of courage, fairness, and appreciation of excellence to promote the common good.

Notice how the purpose statements describe the way each personal life vision is achieved. In the first purpose statement, the individual tells us how bravery is executed by being specific about increasing social justice. This personal life vision and accompanying purpose statement could have been written by an attorney, a social worker, or community activist. In the second example, a personal life vision of creating items for a better world is defined more clearly in the purpose statement as creating items specifically to make a safer world. This could be the personal life vision and purpose of an engineer, architect, or a clinical researcher. Notice how the last personal life vision statement of action with courage is conceptualized in the purpose statement as promotion of the common good. These personal life vision and purpose statements could have been written by a public office holder or teacher.

Mission Statement Examples

Where a personal life vision statement describes a future state, a mission statement expresses what is happening in the present. It describes what the individual is doing now to fulfill his or her personal life vision and purpose. Examine the following mission statements, referring to the original personal life vision and purpose statements.

Personal life vision statement: I am a brave and courageous person and act on my convictions in making the world a better place.
Purpose statement: My life's purpose is to stand up for others and increase social justice throughout the world by using my strengths of bravery, kindness, and spirituality.
Mission statement: My mission is working as a social worker in a nonprofit community agency that advocates for the homeless.

Personal life vision statement: I am an artistic and creative person. I help make people's lives better with my creations.
Purpose statement: By using my creativity and curiosity, my purpose in life is to conceptualize, design, and produce innovative items that create a safer world.
Mission statement: My mission is completing my doctorate in engineering to prepare for creating innovative products in the clean energy sector.

Personal life vision statement: I am a person of courage who embraces excellence. My efforts are guided not only by doing things right, but by doing the right thing.
Purpose statement: My purpose in life is to use my strengths of courage, fairness, and appreciation of excellence to promote the common good.
Mission statement: My mission is working as a staff member to a state legislator to help my community grow and prosper.

Throughout life, people usually engage in different missions to fulfill their purpose. For example, Jackie states her purpose as using her abilities for modeling a way that inspires and motivates others to live their lives to the fullest. As a new college graduate, Jackie's first job was as a middle-school teacher. In that position, using her strengths of integrity, kindness, social intelligence, and creativity in the classroom, Jackie helped young people realize their potential. Later, Jackie ran for elected office and became a member of the city council. In that position, Jackie leveraged her strengths in improving her community and thereby fulfilled her purpose of helping citizens have a better life.

Developing Your Personal Life Vision and Purpose Statements

Developing and writing personal life vision and purpose statements takes time and is challenging. You may even draft and revise the statements numerous times over the course of several days, weeks, or even months. There is no prescribed format or length for these statements. What is important is that the statements represent what you want to do with your life and express what is important to you, what you want to contribute, and how you want to be remembered.

The following exercises can help you formulate your personal life vision purpose. Developing these statements is a highly personal endeavor; no two are alike. Do not become paralyzed on trying to find the most appropriate or exact words for your statements. Write the statements exactly as they come to mind; you can always keep refining them. What is important is the essence or meaning that these statements deliver. Figure 4.2 provides a summary of the exercises you will use to help develop your personal life vision statement.

Developing Your Personal Life Vision through Discovery

The following four exercises are experiential. This is a process where you obtain results from doing an activity and then reflect on the meaning of the outcomes produced. The exercises are structured so you can synthesize your reflections of each and develop a cohesive personal life vision statement.

Revisit Strengths and Values

An imperative of a personal life vision is that it is consistent with your core values. For example, if you highly value creativity and learning, and appreciate beauty, a personal life vision devoid of these would make life feel like a struggle and would not serve you well. The need for a personal life vision consistent with core values

Figure 4.2. Summary of discovery exercises

Revisit your strengths and values

- Evaluate your strengths and values and how using them helps you feel fulfilled

Quotes that inspire

- Identify themes important to you

Dream big

- Identify values that are important to you

Personal life vision exercise

- This uses the outcomes of the previous exercises to help you write your personal life vision

Your purpose statement

- This exercise helps you operationalize your vision

Your future story

- Write a story in the present tense of what your future story may look like

is supported by research indicating that using one's strengths in new and original ways increases happiness and helps an individual flourish in life (Seligman et al. 2005). Given this, reflecting on your strengths and how they represent core values and thinking about what ignites your passion and fulfills you is a first step in developing your personal life vision statement. The following questions will help you with this reflection.

1. List your top five strengths identified in the Values in Action (VIA) assessment.

1.	
2.	
3.	
4.	
5.	

2. How have you used these strengths in your life? Write a brief description of two or three situations that highlight where using these strengths made you feel fulfilled.

Strength	Situation
1.	
2.	
3.	
4.	
5.	

3. What are three or four key words or phrases you can take from these experiences as a foundation for describing an achievable future state for your life?

Identify Quotes that Inspire

People who inspire individuals usually have similar or shared values. They inspire by their actions and demonstrate their commitment to their values. Values are frequently reflected in what these people say, which is consistent with their actions; in other words they walk their talk. Eleanor Roosevelt famously said, "It is my conviction, too, that only the power of ideas, of enduring values can keep us a great nation. For where there is not vision the people perish." Certainly this quote is consistent with Roosevelt's actions throughout her life, which were based on the power of ideas and included working tirelessly for civil and human rights. Consider this as you answer the following questions.

1. Think about people you admire and why you admire them (these may be family members, associates, friends, or famous people). Find three or more quotes from each of these people that inspire you and write them down in the space provided.

2. Categorize these quotes by the themes they represent. What commonalities among them can you find?

3. Assess the degree to which you see similarities between the themes of quotes and your top five signature strengths. Describe these similarities in the space provided.

4. Assess what you have discovered about the quotes, their themes, and your strengths. Write one or two sentences summarizing the connectedness among them.

5. In the following space, write about what you discovered about the values you consider important and that you can incorporate into your personal life vision.

Dream Big

Our values are frequently reflected in dreams of a future state. For example, Susan, a director of quality management at a healthcare system, has had a dream of being a teacher since she graduated from college. Her dream reflects her love of learning and her desire to share her learning with others. Armed with this knowledge,

Susan evaluates if her value of love of learning and helping others is reflected in her current role or mission and certainly she sees similarities. Although not a teacher in a classroom, Susan's current role as director of quality management embodies her aspirations of sharing knowledge so that others can improve.

The following exercise helps you to identify and evaluate the key themes in your dreams.

1. Reflect on two or three of your biggest life dreams. Use the space that follows to describe these dreams in two to four sentences.

Dream 1	
Dream 2	
Dream 3	

2. Now evaluate each dream and make a list of words reflecting the essence of each. You can record your reflections using table 4.1 that follows.
   - What values does the dream embody that are important to you?
   - What causes are represented in the dream?
   - What impact or outcome does the dream have on you, other people, the community, and the world?

Table 4.1. Dream evaluation

Dream	Values Represented	Causes Represented	Impact
Dream 1			
Dream 2			
Dream 3			

3. Identify common threads, similarities, or themes among your life dreams and write these in the space provided.

4. How are your strengths and values represented in your dreams? Write about this in the space that follows.

5. How can you use your strengths to help you achieve your dreams?

Personal Life Visioning Exercise

This activity helps you to combine the outcome of the reflections from the previous exercises and provides the foundation for a draft of your personal life vision statement.

1. Make a list of the central themes that have emerged from the previous exercises and write them in the space provided.

2. What are the similarities among these themes? Write down these similarities.

3. What do these themes mean to you and how can they provide a foundation for developing your personal life vision?

4. Assess how your top five VIA strengths relate to, coincide with, and support the central themes you have identified.

5. Armed with this insight, develop a draft of your personal life vision statement that is your script for life and that will guide your leadership. When writing your personal life vision statement, it may be helpful to answer the following questions: Who am I? What do I want to accomplish? How will I accomplish it? Who will I impact?

Identifying Your Purpose

Recall that a vision represents a future achievable state. However, it does not outline how to achieve this future state; this falls under the purpose statement. The purpose statement expresses how an individual contributes to making his or her vision a reality. Vision expresses *what* one wants to achieve, purpose expresses *how* one is going to achieve it.

To help develop your purpose statement consider the example of Jennifer provided earlier in this chapter. Jennifer's personal life vision is "making the world a better and happier place by helping others fulfill their potential." Jennifer makes her purpose statement more specific and describes how her strengths help her to execute her personal life vision. Jennifer's purpose is: "Use my courage, creativity, and organizational abilities to model a way that inspires and motivates others to live their lives to the fullest."

In the space that follows write a draft of your purpose statement and explain how you will achieve your personal life vision.

Your Future Story

Writing a compelling story of your future encapsulates your personal life vision, purpose, and mission. A personal future story involves imagination and is written from retrospective point of view sometime in the future. It is like looking down from a mountain top at a panoramic view of what is below. On the left side of the panorama is the present and on the right side is the future. Looking at the big picture from left to right you can trace the steps taken from the present to get to the future.

In writing your future story, use words that connect you emotionally with your personal life vision and purpose and that make you feel like you have stepped into your future. Describe how you have used your strengths to fulfill your purpose and reach your personal life vision. Include your missions (for example, jobs, volunteer activities, and other work) that played a role in your future story.

The following is an example of a future story, written in the present but looking back as if it was 20 years into the future. Try to identify this woman's personal life vision and purpose and how she used a variety of missions and strengths to reach her personal life vision.

> As I reflect on my life from 20 years in the future, I see that I have made the world a happier and better place for thousands of people by empowering them to fulfill their potential. It has not always been an easy road, but I have made it an exciting one. I have used my strength of bravery working for causes that have helped people flourish. From helping victims of abuse to supporting community revitalization efforts, I have tackled every challenge as a chance to live my dream. I have been a staff member and later a chief executive officer of a large nonprofit organization. I have reached the top levels of policy making as a staffer in state government and now I am a successful congresswoman. I have used my strengths of exploration

> and creativity to model a way that inspires and motivates others to live their lives to the fullest. I am especially happy about my relationships with my family—that they are a central part of my life and that I have inspired them to pursue their dreams. I have used my leadership strengths to lead myself. I make sure that I have balance in my life and that I take care of myself. My leadership strengths have helped me bring people together to solve problems and implement solutions. Each day I live my personal life vision of making the world a better place by empowering people to take charge of their lives and create a better community. Life is terrific!

Use the following space to write your future story.

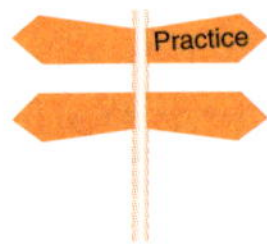

Connecting Personal Life Vision and Mission

Personal life vision and purpose statements are a guide for living and conducting one's life. But if these statements are not supported with action, they are empty exercises. The various missions throughout one's life connect an individual's personal life vision with how to lead his or her life. Setting specific goals to help select activities and missions that are aligned with your personal life vision and purpose is an important activity for maintaining focus on what is important in life. How to develop goals is covered in chapter 7.

Your mission is what you are currently doing or have done in the past to support your personal life vision and purpose. It may consist of your current or past job, volunteer activities, hobbies, or relationships with others. The following example illustrates this case.

> Claire's personal life vision is that she is a person of courage who embraces excellence and her life is guided not only by doing things right, but by doing the right thing. Claire's purpose in life is promoting the common good.

As a college student, Claire majored in health information management (HIM) because she believed that health information is the life blood of the healthcare system. Patients and their caregivers need good information to be well-served. During college Claire was a member of a campus organization that sponsored summer camps for underserved grade school students. Claire extended her volunteer service as a student representative on the board of her state's association for HIM. These missions, student and volunteer, were consistent with her life mission and purpose.

After earning her bachelor's degree, Claire sought out positions in quality management and furthered her education with a master's degree in jurisprudence. Claire held director positions in quality management in hospitals, requiring her to ensure that not only were things done right, but the right things were done. Many times she had to take a stand for doing what was right when confronting serious quality issues. In some cases she even had to battle higher authorities to ensure that the right corrective actions were taken. Claire felt her personal life vision could be best served by taking her career to the next level. As a vice president for quality healthcare and measurement leading a team of people who designed, implemented, and evaluated evidenced-based solutions to support policies and programs to improve healthcare, Claire believed she could have a larger impact on promotion of the common good. Claire's role as an executive also put her in a position where she influenced corporate culture, building an organization where employees flourished. Throughout her life, Claire had several missions and all were focused on achieving excellence and seeing that the common good was served through ensuring quality health care.

The following exercise helps you evaluate how your current and prospective missions work to fulfill your personal life vision and life's purpose.

Mission Possible

Table 4.2 illustrates how an individual's various missions can be contrasted with his or her vision and purpose. This table demonstrates how consistent Claire's missions were with how she envisioned her life. Notice that not all missions fulfill every vision theme, but taken together her life fully embraces her personal life vision and purpose.

To evaluate how the missions in your life support your personal life vision and purpose, take the results of the earlier activities in this chapter and write down the major themes of your personal life vision and purpose. Following these themes, write down your current activities and roles. For example, these missions might include roles such as being a student, an employee, or a volunteer; activities such as hobbies and interests; or relationship roles such as family member or friend.

Using the template in table 4.3, document how your current missions support your personal life vision and purpose for five consecutive days.

Table 4.2. Illustration of mission, personal life vision, and purpose

Personal Life Vision/ Purpose Themes	Student	Student Volunteer	Director Quality Management	Vice President Quality Management
Excellence	✓	✓	✓	✓
Courage		✓	✓	✓
Promote common good		✓	✓	✓
Do things right	✓	✓	✓	✓
Do the right thing	✓	✓	✓	✓

Table 4.3. Mission, personal life vision, and purpose themes template

Personal Life Vision/Purpose Themes	Day 1 Roles	Day 2 Roles	Day 3 Roles	Day 4 Roles	Day 5 Roles

1. In reviewing your chart, evaluate how your current mission(s) supports your personal life vision and purpose. Are there things that you can do associated with your current mission(s) that would help them better support your personal life vision and purpose? Do you need to seek other types of mission(s) to better support your personal life vision? Contemplate these questions in the space that follows.

Personal Life Vision and Leadership

A leader's personal life vision lays the foundation for his or her leadership. A personal life vision announces to the leader's followers not only what values he or she holds important, but also the leader's aspirations. For example, the personal life vision statements provided earlier included values such as love of beauty, bravery and courage, and creativity. Aspirations included making the world a better place to live, doing the right thing and doing things right, and helping people have better lives. Because one's personal life vision serves as the reference point for navigating life, it also serves as a reference point in executing leadership. The following scenario shows how personal life vision lays the foundation for leadership vision and leading others.

> After graduating from high school, Gayle was uncertain what direction she wanted to take in life. Her family wanted her to pursue a professional career that would earn her a large income and provide a stable life. Gayle attended a top-ranked university and did well in her coursework, however, she did not feel fulfilled. During the summer between her second and third year of college, Gayle secured a position working at a children's summer camp. Gayle loved her job—every morning excited to be with the children and enjoying her day helping the children fulfill their potential. Gayle realized that her real values lay not in the career she was pursuing in college, but in expressing her creativity, compassion, empathy, and social awareness identified in the VIA assessment. When she returned to college, Gayle changed her major to early childhood education. Her personal

life vision was to put her values to work by influencing better advocacy, care, and development of young children. She wanted to see a world where every preschool age child had access to a quality educational opportunity. Gayle's personal life vision informed her leadership vision and leadership. Gayle's first job after college graduation was working in an early childhood development center. But Gayle wanted to have a bigger influence beyond the local center. Her personal life vision for child advocacy informed her leadership vision and she used her creativity in founding and becoming the CEO of a nonprofit organization devoted to assisting local communities in developing educational opportunities for preschool children. Gayle used her passion for better education for children and put her values of compassion, empathy, and social awareness to work in creating a shared leadership vision with her followers and donors for educational equality for young children. Her leadership vision was inspired first by her personal life vision.

References

Anderson, L. and D. Anderson. 2010. *The Change Leader's Roadmap: How to Navigate Your Organization's Transformation*, 2nd ed. San Francisco: Pfeiffer.

Barsh, J., S. Cranston, and R. Craske. 2008. Centered Leadership: How Talented Women Thrive. http://www.mckinsey.com/global-themes/leadership/centered-leadership-how-talented-women-thrive

Kouzes, J.M. and B.Z. Posner. 2007. *The Leadership Challenge*. San Francisco: Wiley.

Ryan, J. 2009. Leadership Success Always Starts with Vision. http://www.forbes.com/2009/07/29/personal-success-vision-leadership-managing-ccl.html

Seligman, M., T. Steen, N. Park, and C. Peterson. 2005. Positive psychology progress: Empirical validation of interventions. *American Psychologist* 60(5):410–421.

5 Amassing Social Capital

Studies show successful leaders have certain characteristics in common, ranging from a few to 20 or more. Among those characteristics, honesty, visionary, and fair-mindedness are high on the lists (Kouzes and Posner 2007). From the perspective of what makes a leader successful one might jump to the conclusion that success rests solely on the characteristics of the individual with circumstances or environment playing no role in leadership success.

From a narrow view of examining an individual's traits these results are valid. However, a leader functions in a context and carries out his or her responsibilities within complex systems of components that interact to accomplish a goal. As one part of a complex system, the leader both affects and is affected by other parts of the system. For example, when a health information management (HIM) director implements a new process for coding inpatient health records, the decision potentially affects how other functional areas—such as the medical staff and billing and claims management—perform their work. In addition, policies developed by the revenue cycle management team, such as the length of time an account can be designated as discharged not final billed (DNFB), will have an influence on the HIM director's decision about how to conform to the policy.

This is where social capital—how it is created and how it is leveraged—plays a role in supporting the leader in his or her success. Broadly, social capital is a social network consisting of relationships with people built on trust and reciprocity, created and maintained by an individual to provide information, influence, and other resources necessary for leadership success. In the previous example, the HIM director's success relies on maintaining an effective social network with the medical staff, billing, and revenue cycle management departments.

This chapter describes social capital, the importance and benefits of acquiring social capital, and how to amass and leverage social capital for individual success and the success of the organization.

Social Capital as a Leadership Competency

While social capital has emerged as a hot topic in leadership literature in the last decade, the concept is not new. In fact, the expression "It's not what you know, but who you know that makes a difference" has been around for centuries and one can see the truth of it occurring in everyday life. For example, consider an interview with Benjamin Waller regarding how he achieved career success.

Waller, a noted Virginia judge, remarked that he owed his success to his father and to a man named John Carter. Curious, the interviewer asked Waller how Carter had contributed to his success. Waller explained that Carter, who was one of the wealthiest men in Virginia, took interest in him as a young man, offered him advice and encouragement, and helped him advance through his own connections. Through Carter, Waller was able to obtain a position as a clerk of the court, which led him to more important roles. Waller acknowledged that while you must always prove yourself through competency, the help of an influential person is indispensable to moving forward in a career and life (Crews 2014).

Although the interview was conducted in 1781 when Waller was 65 years old, the insights are as true today as they were over 200 years ago. While the importance of social capital has not changed, the degree to which it is being scrutinized today as an essential leadership competency has. As leadership is increasingly viewed as a social process, the relationship between social capital and leadership success is being studied. Findings show that creating and leveraging social capital are essential leadership competencies (McCallum and O'Connell 2009).

The next sections explore how social capital is defined, what constitutes the foundations of social capital, what benefits social capital provides to the organization, and how social capital contributes to leadership success.

Social Capital Defined

Most people are familiar with the term *capital* as it relates to finance, human resources, or physical materials. In a financial context, capital is used in reference to the wealth an individual or organization has in the form of money, credit, or other assets. Financial capital is owned, available, and contributed by a person or organization for a particular use, usually in pursuing more revenue. For example, "She has the capital to purchase a new business," means the individual has sufficient money or other financial assets to buy a business.

Similar to financial capital, social capital is wealth, but in the form of norms and trust associated with social networks that facilitate coordination, cooperation, and reciprocity (Van De Valk 2008). As a form of capital, an individual's social network should be viewed as an asset. However, to create value it must be managed. The wealth of the social network is measured by its focus, quality, and diversity.

Because of social capital's relational aspects, it is frequently viewed as relational wealth created within groups for the mutual benefit of its members. Some examples are relationships that provide social wealth of cooperation and collaboration within an organization such as a workgroup, community, or a professional body. Viewed from this perspective, social capital is not the property of a single person. It is a public good that is produced by social investments of time and effort (OECD 2001).

Some have argued the value of physical, financial, human, and environmental forms of capital are dependent on an organization's social capital (Zacharakis and Flora 2005). Assuming this viewpoint, social capital takes on an important role in leadership and organizational effectiveness, productivity, and efficiency. The better the individual's social ties (capital) are, both within and external to the organization, the greater the wealth generated for the organization.

Foundations of Social Capital

Social capital goes beyond a superficial idea of collecting business cards at a networking function or adding entries to one's digital contact database. The foundations of social capital are networks of people that are supported in their shared values, resources, trust, and cooperation (figure 5.1). Networks usually consist of one or

Figure 5.1. Foundations of social capital

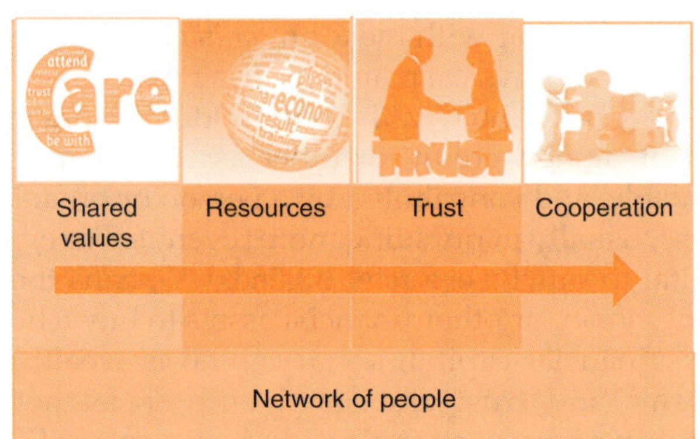

©Merida L. Johns

two types—internal and external. The first are connections between people within groups. For example, connections of people within the same work unit or company. This type of network is often referred to as an internal or bonding network. The second are ties that link different groups together. These types of networks are normally referred to as external ties or bridging or linking networks. An example of this type of network is the connection between different workgroups in the same company or between one company and another. Internal networks are usually considered to have stronger ties than external networks.

To qualify as social capital, social networks must include the components in figure 5.1. Without these, capital cannot be created. Shared values among the members of the network are imperative. In other words, the network generates unity (a type of wealth) because its members hold beliefs about what is and is not desirable and norms about what behaviors are acceptable. Embodied in the definition of capital is wealth, therefore resources that provide wealth are essential for social capital. Resources, whether in the form of information, referrals, intelligence, services, or some other wealth derived from social interaction, must be present for social capital to be maintained. Trust among members of the social network is imperative in order to create social capital. Trust entails a belief that members of the network will act in mutually supportive ways. The development of social capital relies on members of the network acting cooperatively. In other words, cooperation means being willing to engage in all aspects of creating social capital.

Social Capital Benefits for the Organization

The benefits derived from social capital related to organizational life are shared among the network and the company, not necessarily just by the individual. As the Benjamin Waller interview suggests, amassing and leveraging social capital has been found to positively impact individual income and job mobility (Stoloff et al. 1999) and has an economic impact equal to education and experience (Krebs 2008). Just as social capital benefits individuals, it also benefits organizations.

Organizations derive several benefits from relational networks and the social capital they create. Take, for example, two different information systems development teams at a healthcare facility working on the same project. Jack is the leader of the team that is developing a data dictionary in conjunction with the project. Jack has a professional relationship with Julie, the leader of the second team. Wanting to find out if there are any crossovers or potential duplication between the projects, Jack contacts Julie and discovers there is duplicative work. Jack and Julie work together to resolve the duplication issues. In this case the exchange of information and collaboration is the key resource of Jack's internal social capital. Jack's use of his social capital reaps benefits for both his and Julie's teams; duplication is reduced, which positively impacts costs, and productivity and potential conflict is avoided. But, as team leader, Jack also nets benefits because he more successfully leads his team, which is viewed positively by his manager.

In addition to the transaction benefits described, organizations gain other benefits. Social capital produces development of shared goals and common frames of reference, which in turn increases knowledge creation in the organization. Turnover is decreased and hiring, training, and severance costs are reduced because organizational membership is stabilized. In short, social capital increases financial return (McCallum and O'Connell 2009).

Building Social Capital

At the most basic level, building social capital is about cultivating strong relationships. Productive relationships are built through interpersonal competence. This involves social awareness and social skills that help "people understand how to relate to others, coordinate their efforts, build commitments, and develop extended social networks by applying self-understanding to social and organizational imperatives," (Day 2001, 586).

The first four chapters in this book help you develop self-understanding about your strengths, emotional intelligence, confidence, and how you apply your values to a personal life vision, purpose, and mission. To develop social capital, self-understanding is applied in building relational capacity in a specific environment. The following scenario is an example of the process of developing social capital in a new situation.

> Audrey recently accepted a position as an assistant vice-president for a healthcare system consisting of five acute-care hospitals, a hospice, a home-care agency, and several physician office practices. Audrey knows her success depends on gaining trust not only from her functional staff but also from the medical staff and the colleagues she interacts with across the organization. Since Audrey is an outsider to the organization, she does not have a built-in internal social network. Audrey has used her character strengths of perseverance, bravery, and curiosity in the past to build social capital. Leveraging these strengths throughout her career, Audrey has continually increased her social awareness of others and strengthened her listening skills.
>
> Audrey prioritizes scheduling meetings with key people with whom she can develop shared goals and common frames of reference for organizational success. She knows she needs these people for gathering insight and information about the organization and its culture and for building reciprocity among the groups she is dependent upon. Audrey's bravery helps her take the first step by initiating meetings with these key influencers. She has a strong desire to know about new things and applies this strength in identifying the needs of these key people and the departments they oversee. Audrey's strength of persistence helps her cultivate these relationships over time.
>
> Besides leveraging her strengths, Audrey's personal life vision and purpose and the context of her current mission guide her in building social capital. Her vision is to be a courageous person who embraces excellence in all domains of life and to live every day to its fullest. She views her life's purpose as helping others help themselves achieve personal excellence. She believes excellence helps develop a safer and more productive world. When things get tough, Audrey always reverts to the guiding principles of her vision and purpose: courage, excellence, and building relationships that work toward the common good. This frame of reference makes it easy for Audrey to approach and interact with people from a nonjudgmental viewpoint.

It also makes it easier for other people to understand the core values Audrey embraces, thus helping to build trusting relationships.

Audrey also recognizes her emotional intelligence strength and where potential gaps exist. In building her social capital, Audrey knows she must purposefully work toward awareness of others and use this knowledge in building relationships. Lastly, Audrey's self-awareness of her strengths, emotional intelligence, vision, and purpose are the foundations for her confidence. She believes in herself and her ability to be successful in executing leadership behaviors and developing a strong reserve of social capital.

Evaluating Social Capital

By definition social capital implies wealth, but like financial and human capital, it is the degree of wealth and how it is leveraged that determines its value. For example, one can say that Jim has financial capital. But the value and power of the capital is very different if it is worth $1,000 cash versus $500,000 cash. Certainly with $500,000 Jim can accomplish a lot more in business investments than he can with $1,000. Human capital, which includes an individual's skills, knowledge, abilities, and education, works in a similar way. Pat has a bachelor's degree and three years' experience as a supervisor. Rose has a master's degree, 10 years of department head experience, and several leadership positions in volunteer organizations. Both Pat and Rose have human capital, but Rose has accumulated more "wealth" than Pat. Like financial and human capital, social capital works the same way. Most people have some type of social relationships, but the key is whether the type and level are sufficient to produce the capital required for success.

The most effective leaders are those who have networks that are made up of high quality relationships that are select, diverse, and come from all levels of the corporate hierarchy (Cross et al. 2003). One characteristic of these networks is that they are deep relationships that are mutually beneficial, built on commonalities of interests and experiences among people. A second characteristic of strong networks is response and follow-through. In other words, acting in ways that fulfill the promise made to another is essential to cultivating and maintaining a social network that accumulates social capital. A third characteristic is reciprocity and uncalculated giving, meaning valuing strong social relationships as more than transactional (that is, "If I do something for you, you need to do something for me") relationships. The following sections provide a guide for assessing the quality of social capital.

Critical Features of a Social Network

Studies show strong social capital is acquired as the result of a social network consisting of six critical features (figure 5.2). These include having people in the network who

- Provide new information and expertise. These people can be internal or external to the organization whose factual and tacit information furthers critical thinking, decision making, opens new insights, and sparks innovation.
- Have influence. These are people who hold both formal and informal power or influence and who can provide networking, political

Figure 5.2. Social capital portfolio

©Merida L. Johns

support, and influence in securing resources, coordinating efforts, and gaining the support of others for specific initiatives.
- Offer feedback. These are people who give developmental feedback and challenge the leader's ideas.
- Provide personal support. These are people who are the leader's cheerleaders and keep the leader focused and on track.
- People who add purpose to life. These include family, friends, and colleagues who confirm the work they are doing has a broader meaning.
- Provide accountability for an integrated life. These include those who hold others accountable for activities that improve their physical health, mental engagement, or spiritual well-being. (Cross and Thomas 2011)

Having a social network is not by itself sufficient to reap social capital wealth. The grouping and variety of one's social assets consisting of the features listed is called a social capital portfolio. Just like a financial portfolio consisting of a variety financial assets, the social capital portfolio requires management. For example, with a financial portfolio, the investment mix and policies associated with investment are assessed with regard to current and projected circumstances. In the case of a social capital portfolio, the appropriate mix of people and how they contribute to the network are assessed with regard to current and projected circumstances. For example, the portfolio should contain a mix of people who can provide information, influence, feedback, personal support, and personal accountability now and in future situations.

Assessment of Social Capital

A common way to assess the social capital portfolio is to use a four-step sequential process: analyze, adjust, diversify, and leverage (Cross and Thomas 2011). Each of these steps is described as follows.

Analyze the Portfolio

Analyzing the portfolio is usually accomplished by doing three things. First, identify the people in the network including those internal and external to the workgroup, unit, and company. After listing these people, assess how many of these people function as bonding or bridging ties. This assessment can provide an immediate visual picture of potential gaps in the network.

Second, evaluate the degree of value each person adds to the relationship. Does the individual bring new ideas and solutions to the table? Or does the individual devalue the relationship by offering complaints rather than solutions. Research shows when the network includes people who bring value and see possibilities, there is a greater probability of success over time than networks that include complainers who frame problems as barriers as opposed to challenges to overcome. Studies show that about 90 percent of anxiety at work is created by 5 percent of people who zap energy (Cross and Thomas 2011).

Third, identify the benefits each individual brings by comparing the six critical features of a relational network (figure 5.2) to the network. The network should include every type of resource identified by the six elements. By conducting the assessment in this way, gaps and overlaps are defined.

Adjust the Portfolio

A financial portfolio is adjusted to eliminate poor investments, and the social capital portfolio is managed similarly. Adjusting the portfolio is the time to evaluate and remove people who are chronic complainers, negativists, and who take up time and energy without providing value. Steve, for instance, has a weekly lunch date with Joe who works in another business unit. After each session, Steve comes away feeling drained because Joe complains about his dysfunctional work unit, his incompetent peers, and how unhappy he is. Steve provides suggestions and ways for Joe to reframe his job, but Joe refuses to accept responsibility for improving things or making a change. Many times Steve believes Joe exaggerates events and wonders if much of the dysfunction is due to Joe. A relationship like this, which lacks trust and reciprocity, is toxic and is not building social capital. Steve needs to adjust his portfolio by reducing or eliminating his lunch meetings with Joe.

Adjusting the portfolio can also mean separating from an organization or group, not just individuals. For example, Leslie volunteers as a board member with a community organization. The board meets once a month; meetings are scheduled for 90 minutes, but customarily drag on for two to three hours. It seems that the same issues are rehashed at every meeting with no forward action. When Leslie leaves these meetings she is frequently angry and believes her time is wasted. This association depletes rather than builds Leslie's social capital. In this case, Leslie could adjust her portfolio by resigning as a board member of the organization.

Diversify the Portfolio

Like most portfolios, the social capital portfolio is strengthened through diversification. The key features of a social capital portfolio (figure 5.2) represent broad diversification, including people who support the individual both professionally and personally. Leadership success requires life integration. This means successful leaders balance what they do professionally with what they do personally. Notice that the six features of the social capital portfolio are a blend of both professional and personal support. The first three assist the leader professionally, while the others aid the leader personally. This promotes life integration or balance.

Because there are multiple factors and circumstances that contribute to a strong portfolio there is no formula or specific profile of what constitutes a balanced social capital network. In other words, balance does not mean that there must be the same number of people in each key area represented in the portfolio. For example, some individuals may be sufficiently self-motivated and participate in activities that enrich their lives outside of work and thus they need less support to hold them accountable for physical and mental well-being than others who are not as self-motivated. Or some individuals may require more people in one key area than another because of their job position. Take Paula, for instance, whose title is research and evaluation specialist. Her job consists of conducting evaluations on cancer prevention and includes doing literature reviews, environmental scans, and conducting focus groups and surveys. The data and information she gathers and manages is used by her manager and others in developing healthcare policy. Because her job requires access to information more than it does influence, Paula's network would likely reflect this balance. She would have more people available to provide her with information than people who are influencers.

Leverage the Portfolio

Portfolios exist to create value. Portfolios that leverage their capital create more value than those that do not. Consider the following two examples.

Lucy has a master's degree in health information management, 15 years of progressive management experience, and a volunteer track record. Lucy leverages her human capital (that is, education and experience) to advance her career. Lucy has also created a diversified social capital portfolio. She has fostered relationships with people who have influence and who can serve as sponsors for her. For example, she has maintained relationships with her former professors who are happy to provide her recommendations when needed. Through her volunteer efforts she has created relationships with nationally influential people both within HIM and other disciplines. These individuals offer information and knowledge about new job positions and serve as references for her. She has also cultivated relationships with the C-suite (higher level executives who have "chief" in their title, for example, chief executive officer or chief financial officer) in her organization with her can-do attitude and reputation for being a person who achieves results. Several individuals among the C-suite act as her sponsors—those promoting her work to others and who are willing to suggest her for promotions. By using her human and social capital, Lucy secures an executive position as vice president of a large healthcare system.

Barbara, a director of enterprise analytics who also has a master's degree, has a career that is stagnating because she does not rise to new challenges or advance new ideas and has not created a diversified social capital portfolio. She has failed to reach out to people of influence, people who can provide her with information or other support. In other words, Barbara's human capital just sits in her portfolio and does not produce value. The longer the capital sits unused in the portfolio the less valuable it is. The old adage "If you don't use it, you lose it," applies equally to skills and social capital portfolios.

Assess Your Social Capital Portfolio

The following exercise helps you assess the strength of your social capital against the key features of a strong portfolio.

1. In table 5.1, for each key feature of a social capital portfolio (figure 5.2) write down the person(s) who support you in each area in the table that follows. Determine if they are internal or external links. Identify how often you have had some type of interaction with each during the past three months. Then identify one or more benefits that you have received from your interaction with each during this time. Finally, find reciprocity on your part: what benefits you have provided each person on your list?

Table 5.1. Assess your social capital

	Individual	Internal or external linkage	How often you have had interactions in the last three months	Benefits you have received from interactions with the individual in the past six months	Benefits you have provided to the individual in the past six months
People who have information and expertise					
People who have influence					
People who challenge me					
People who provide support					
People who add purpose					
People who hold me accountable for balance					

2. Assess the data you have compiled in the previous table by answering the following questions.
   a. Are there gaps that need to be filled in any of the key features? If so what are the gaps?

   b. Does your network have a good balance between internal and external links? Remember internal links are usually stronger than external.

   c. How well have you cultivated your network? Are there individuals you have not interacted with in the past three months? If so, do you believe this has lessened the value of that relationship? Why or why not?

   d. What tangible benefits have you received from your interactions with each individual? On a scale of one to five, with five being the highest, how would you rate the benefits achieved?

e. What benefits have you provided to others in your network? How would you rate the reciprocity of your interactions with your network partners? Is the reciprocity equal or lopsided?

Make Your Social Capital Work for You

Armed with the data and analysis given, it is time to make your social capital work for you. To do this you must objectively and purposefully take action to adjust, diversify, and leverage your network. Use the following questions to help you do this. Then take action to make it happen.

1. Adjust
   a. List the individuals in your social capital portfolio who are not providing you the social capital you need.

   b. How do you plan to lessen your interaction with these individuals? When will you begin to do this?

c. Are there individuals with whom you have little interaction and who do not provide appreciable support? If so, should they be eliminated from your network?

2. Diversity
   a. As identified in table 5.1, what are the gaps in your network?

   b. For each gap identify at least one person you would like to include in your network. Then identify how you will establish a relationship with him or her. For example, arranging a lunch date to discuss mutual interests; inviting this person to a function of mutual interest, and such.

   c. Are there key areas in your network that are overloaded and not providing value? If so, does this area need to be pruned to those individuals who provide the best benefit to you?

3. Leverage
   a. Are there key people you have not leveraged in your network? For instance, people who provide value but with whom you have not had enough interaction? If so, who are they and how can you increase your interactions?

   b. Have there been lost opportunities where you could have leveraged your network? What were these opportunities? How can you prevent this loss of value in the future?

   c. How have you provided reciprocity to the people in your network? Are there areas and opportunities for increasing reciprocity? If so, what are they and how can you be of value to your network partners?

References

Crews, E. 2014. Meet Benjamin Waller. *The Journal of the Colonial Williamsburg Foundation* Autumn 2014:19–20.

Cross, R. and R. Thomas. 2011 (July-Aug). Manage Yourself: A Smarter Way to Network. *Harvard Business Review*. https://hbr.org/2011/07/managing-yourself-a-smarter-way-to-network/ar/1

Cross, R., T. Davenport, and S. Cantrell. 2003. The Social Side of Performance. *Sloan Management Review Magazine*. http://sloanreview.mit.edu/article/the-social-side-of-performance/

Day, D.V. 2001. Leadership development: A review in context. *Leadership Quarterly* 11:581–613.

Kouzes, J.M. and B.Z. Posner. 2007. *The Leadership Challenge*, 4th ed. San Francisco: Wiley.

Krebs, V. 2008. Social capital: The key to success for the 21st century organization. *IHRIM Journal* 12(5):38–42.

McCallum, S. and D.O'Connell. 2009. Social capital and leadership development: Building stronger leadership through enhanced relational skills. *Leadership and Organizational Development Journal* 30(2):152–166.

Organisation for Economic Co-operation and Development. 2001. The Well-Being of Nations: The Role of Human and Social Capital. http://www.oecd.org/site/worldforum/33703702.pdf

Stoloff, J., J. Glanville, and E. Bienenstock. 1999. Women's participation in the labor force: The role of social networks. *Social Networks* 21:91–108.

Van De Valk, J. 2008. Leadership development and social capital: Is there a relationship? *Journal of Leadership Education* 7(1):47–64.

Zacharakis, J. and J. Flora. 2005. Riverside: A case study of social capital and cultural reproduction and their relationship to leadership development. *Adult Education Quarterly* 55(4):288–307.

6 Developing Leadership Presence

Leadership presence is defined in this book as the condition of being mindfully present, nonjudgmental, free of mental distractions, and giving undivided attention to people and the leadership task at hand in the moment. The foundations of leadership presence are based on mindfulness behaviors and the key components of emotional intelligence (EI) discussed in chapter 2 that include awareness of self and others, self-management, and relationship management. This chapter provides an overview of leadership presence, the relationship of mindfulness and EI and leadership presence, and the steps for cultivating mindfulness to achieve leadership presence.

Leadership Presence

Presence is sometimes difficult to explain, but you know and feel it when you experience it. Leadership presence is the full and complete nonjudgmental attention in the present moment (Marturano 2015). People with presence, both famous and not, are those who grab and command our attention when they enter a room because of their focus in the present. There is a positive energy that surrounds them because they are not distracted and because of this people stop and notice them. Presence is notable when you have had a conversation with someone and feel as if you are the only one in the room because he or she listened to you and asked questions that reflected a genuine curiosity about what you said, such as in the following example.

A federal legislator conducted a book signing. What stood out in particular was not the short presentation the legislator gave before the book signing, but his full and complete nonjudgmental attention when an audience member spoke to him and offered information about her participation as one of his campaign volunteers. The legislator's authentic presence in the moment was palpable as he listened to her story. His questions made it evident that he had payed close attention to what she had to say about her experience.

Equally, the lack of presence can be quickly identified. Think of a time during a conversation when you felt that the person with whom you were talking was so distracted that he or she heard nothing you said, even though the person nodded his or her head several times, smiled, and uttered confirmatory phrases.

People with presence command the attention of others. Sometimes presence is confused with appearance, the sound of a person's voice, or the way a person walks. While all of these may be important in gaining attention, presence is more than the clothes one wears or the way one talks. Presence is a characteristic within a person. It is the ability "to connect authentically with the thoughts and feelings of others" (Lubar and Halprin 2003, 4). Presence is about how one connects, listens, and responds. When presence is applied in this way by people who fill leadership roles, this book refers to it as leadership presence. Presence is not necessarily innate; it can be developed. One of the principle ways presence is developed is through the practice of mindfulness.

Mindfulness

Mindfulness is an increasingly popular subject in areas such as social science, business, and brain science research. Over the past two decades hundreds of journal articles have been produced on the topic, as well as dozens of books. Mindfulness is gaining publicity because of its benefits such as supporting well-being, enhancing clear thinking, and reducing stress. Because of this it is important to understand the scientific foundations of mindfulness separate from the increasing pop culture development that suggests easy techniques for instantly evolving mindful behaviors. Development of mindful behaviors is a process of practice over time. For example, programs focused on stress reduction typically consist of 2.5 hours of single sessions focused on mindfulness over the course of 8 to 10 weeks in addition to an all-day program session (Grossman et al. 2004).

Simply put, mindfulness can be described as "the art of conscious living," (Kabat-Zinn 2005, 6). Expanding on this description, a group of mindfulness scholars consolidated key mindfulness concepts arriving at an operational definition of mindfulness consisting of two components: self-regulation and orientation to one's experiences (Bishop et al. 2004, 232). In this context, self-regulation means being aware of one's thoughts and feelings in the present moment and being able to sustain attention to the particular task at hand. Lettie, for example, is the manager of clinical documentation improvement (CDI). During a CDI staff meeting, she notices she is thinking about her next meeting instead of focusing her attention on the current discussion. Lettie is aware her wandering mind is not in the present and by practicing self-regulation she brings her attention back to the current meeting and conversation.

Orientation to one's experiences means being nonjudgmental, curious, and open to a present experience. For example, Bernard is director of health information management (HIM) at a community hospital. During a meeting of the privacy committee, a suggestion is made to allow the emergency department (ED) physicians of another local hospital access to the patient portal of the hospital where Bernard works. This would allow the ED physicians timely access to patient medications and other important information for emergency treatment and would be particularly useful during the night shift when Bernard's HIM department is not staffed. Bernard's first response is to judge the suggestion as ridiculous and reject the idea outright because he fears it does not comply with HIPAA (Health Insurance Portability and Accountability Act) standards. But using mindfulness, Bernard recognizes he is being judgmental and changes his position from judging to being curious and follows up with questions to other committee attendees about how such a policy can be implemented.

Both of these scenarios demonstrate the benefits of mindfulness. In Lettie's case, functioning without distractions allows her to focus on the present meeting, listening better, and being able to participate fully. In Bernard's case, a new practice that would support better patient care is more likely to be implemented. The next section discusses in more depth several benefits derived from mindfulness, contrasts mindfulness to mindlessness, and provides ways of developing mindfulness and mindful practice.

Benefits of Mindfulness

As interest in mindfulness has grown, scholarly research continues to find mindful practice has a positive effect on the human brain and psychological well-being. Mindfulness is being studied from multiple frames of reference including clinical and counseling psychology, neuroscience, medicine, education, and business. The results of these studies point to multiple benefits of mindfulness, including the following:

- Vitality, life satisfaction, and quality of interpersonal relationships
- Decreased anxiety and stress
- Increased accuracy in judgment
- Better insights related to problem solving
- Increased academic performance
- Increased job performance (Dane and Brummel 2013)

Researchers suggest that these benefits are achieved because mindful people view events more objectively, which in turn supports them in regulating their thoughts and physical reactions to situations (Dane and Brummel 2013). This would account for decreased anxiety and stress and a positive correlation to life satisfaction.

Recent brain science research suggests mindfulness physiologically changes the brain, enhancing cognitive flexibility and promoting executive functioning of the brain such as problem solving, decision making, and judgment (Rock and Schwartz 2006). Critical thinking, making sound judgments, dissecting complex problems, arriving at effective solutions, and making good decisions are primary functions of leadership. Improving these cognitive functions can be accomplished by using mindfulness that supports enhancing EI behaviors such as self-awareness, self-management, social awareness, and relationship management.

Scholars have found that mindfulness relates to developing leadership presence in several ways (Rezek 2012). First, those with leadership presence look to the future rather than the past. Mindfulness increases proactive behavior. Good leaders look for opportunities to achieve positive change. Mindfulness practice supports a leader's curiosity and open-mindedness in discovering new things. These provide the foundation for change and innovation that is discussed in detail in chapters 15 and 16.

Second, leaders show their leadership presence by responding rather than reacting to situations. Reaction is a characteristic typically associated with exercising emotions and self-protection rather than thoughtfulness and logic. Mindfulness increases the leader's ability to respond rather than react to circumstances. The following illustrates the difference between reacting and responding.

James is director of quality management at a large healthcare system. Results of a recent audit show the respiratory service has a mortality rate significantly higher than the national average. During a regular meeting of the quality management team, Ross, a member of the team, lashes out at the poor showing of the respiratory service, blames two specific individuals, and recommends disciplinary action for them. Instead of reacting and making a snap judgment like Ross, James is curious and responds by digging deeper into the statistical report to seek answers about what has contributed to the high mortality rate. Upon closer inspection, James finds the cause of the high mortality statistics is due to a glitch in the computer system that incorrectly assigned acutely ill cardiac patients to the respiratory service resulting in artificially inflating the mortality statistics for the respiratory service.

Third, leaders with leadership presence inspire others and support them in fulfilling their potential. They ask for and consider the input from their followers; they listen to their followers, identify their strengths and needs, and use supportive and compassionate behaviors to help their followers be the best they can be. Mindful practice cultivates the leader's social awareness ability, encourages leader resiliency and supports personal well-being.

Fourth, leaders with leadership presence are not distracted and they do not multitask. Freed from extraneous clutter in their minds, those with leadership presence have clarity about the leadership task at hand. As a result they are more equipped to grasp nuances and detect and observe details that might go unnoticed by others in solving problems, making decisions, or in foreseeing future possibilities.

Finally, those with leadership presence are able to step outside their own experiences and biases. They are able to approach situations non-judgmentally and therefore are in a better position to learn new things and imagine transformative ways to handle current situations.

The positive outcomes of mindfulness when combined with those from emotional intelligence practices of self-awareness, self-management, social awareness, and relationship management discussed in chapter 2 result in leadership presence.

Mindlessness

One way of describing mindfulness is to look at examples of what it is not. When you are not mindful, you are mindless. For instance, a common example of mindlessness is when someone drives themselves home from work and arrives at the destination wondering "How did I get here?" Many have experienced this type of mindlessness when going through the motions of an activity without tuning into one's internal experience. As another example, perhaps you go for a walk to take a break from work. Does your mind wander from what is on your to-do list to the events in the last meeting you attended, or to your plans for that evening? Do you glance at your phone to read your text messages or e-mail? At the end of the walk you are hard pressed to explain anything about the people you saw, sounds you heard, or even if there were clouds in the sky. Such mindlessness behavior is frequently referred to as our brain operating on autopilot. As famed psychologist and mindfulness authority Ellen Langer said, "We are sealed in unlived lives where mindlessness abounds," (Langer 2009).

The adverse impact of mindlessness on personal and organizational well-being is well-documented. For example, when performance is measured by the accuracy of an output, the accuracy drops as the multitasking and mindlessness increases (Adler and Benbunam-Fich 2012). Specifically in healthcare, for instance, multitasking and resulting mindlessness has been associated with increases in medication and diagnostic errors (Westbrook et al. 2010).

Developing Mindfulness

In a frantic, 24/7, fast-paced world, how can people move from a mind that is overwhelmed or working on autopilot to being mindful? Breaking down the definition of mindfulness, four criteria emerge as necessary for achieving mindfulness and are addressed in the following sections:

- Self-regulation and focus of attention
- Noticing and being open to and curious about new things
- Attending to your thoughts nonjudgmentally
- Compassion for yourself

Consider the face-to-face or virtual meeting as an example of how many of these criteria are not met. Studies have shown in a typical workplace meeting, up to two-thirds of attendees in face-to-face meetings and up to 100 percent in virtual teleconference meetings are mindfully disengaged or multitasking during the meeting (Lyons et al. 2005). Figure 6.1 shows how participants in a virtual meeting fail to meet the first mindfulness criterion for self-regulation and focus of attention. In the top left quadrant, the worker is on the teleconference call but is attempting to juggle six other tasks at the same time. In the next picture, a tired worker, with speakerphone on, is sleeping through the meeting. In the left lower quadrant another worker is daydreaming, and in the final quadrant another is trying to multitask while driving and on the phone.

Self-Regulation and Focus of Attention

The first criterion of mindfulness is self-regulation and focus of attention. In the virtual meeting example, workers can increase their leadership presence by purposefully removing the distractions that interfere with giving their attention to the meeting. For example, attendees can turn off alerts to arriving e-mails, remove all materials from their desks not pertaining to the current meeting, or clear their computer screens so they are not tempted to multitask.

Figure 6.1. The virtual meeting

Self-regulation is not easy, but studies show that it can be developed (Kabat-Zinn 2005). Like developing a muscle, the more you use it the better it gets (Halvorson 2010). Exercising purposeful action through "if-then" planning helps develop self-regulation. For example, stating a purposeful action like "If I am attending a virtual meeting, then I do not multitask," defines a specific action and result. Or, "When I am in a discussion with someone and my mind starts to wander, then I will bring my attention back to the present." Studies show that if-then planning achieves lasting results and helps to create new habits because it provides contingencies that the brain easily remembers (Halvorson 2010).

Noticing and Being Open to and Curious about New Things

When people focus on the present they are more likely to perceive and be curious about new things. Noticing different things is the second mindfulness criterion and has several positive consequences. These include achieving greater sensitivity to the immediate environment, being open to new information, being aware of things in multiple ways, and forming multiple perspectives or points of view (Langer and Moldoveanu 2000).

A common example of noticing and being curious about new things is during discussions with other people. Consider Patty, a nurse on the IT team, who is fully present when she engages in a discussion with an associate about a proposed software change to the patient portal of the electronic health record. The associate does not directly object to the change, but Patty picks up on the nuances of concern expressed in the associate's tone and body language. Curious about this, Patty acts on her intuition and probes the associate further for her input. From new information the associate offers, Patty discovers the proposed change would post radiology and other diagnostic reports to the patient portal before the ordering physician had an opportunity to review them. This procedure change would result in a violation of current policy that requires the ordering physician to review all diagnostic reports prior to patient access via the portal. In this example, Patty was attentive to the immediate environment, she picked up on the associate's subtle cues, and she curiously probed the associate for more information. Patty avoided creating a potentially negative situation by being present, noticing the associate's cues, and being open to new information.

Attending to Thoughts Nonjudgmentally

The third criterion in achieving mindfulness is attending to one's thoughts nonjudgmentally. This does not mean that you do not judge anything; rather, you step back and bring new perspectives to your automatic impulses (Goldstein 2013). How many times do people make quick judgments about a person, idea, or situation only to realize too late that the judgment was wrong? Our brains act on instinct and make judgments based on past experience, often initiating a fight or flight response to a stimulus. While a quick impulse to step out of the way of an approaching car may be the right choice, jumping to conclusions frequently leads to poor decisions.

Being nonjudgmental allows people to view things from different perspectives and frees them from past experience and implicit and other biases; and by doing this, they give themselves a choice. Using the STOP method is one way of focusing attention and stopping our mind from jumping to conclusions (Goldstein 2012). STOP is an acronym for: **S**top, **T**ake a breath, **O**bserve, **P**roceed. The following scenario illustrates how the STOP method can be employed.

Tim, a systems analyst, is attending a meeting of his hospital's computer network task force. During this meeting Chuck, a computer network engineer, offers an idea for applying an information technology in a new way to solve an interoperability problem. Several people at the meeting immediately judge and perceive that Chuck's idea is unworkable. Like the others, Tim's first impulse is to disregard Chuck's idea. Instead, Tim uses the STOP method before jumping to a conclusion. He refrains from making an immediate comment (stops), he pauses (takes a breath), recognizes his judgmental attitude (observes), and exercises his curiosity by asking questions about Chuck's suggestion (proceeds). Tim used the STOP method to help better evaluate Chuck's idea. The following are some other examples for using the STOP method to halt mindlessness or making snap judgments.

- You are in a conversation with a colleague at work concerning a budgeting issue and your mind wanders to thinking about the soccer match you plan to attend that evening. When you realize you are not in the present, take a breath, observe what is happening, and then return your mind to the present and deal with the situation at hand.

- You have just read an e-mail from an associate that makes your blood pressure rise. Your immediate reaction is to go into fight mode and fire off a nasty e-mail in return. Recognizing your automatic judgment response is activated, you use the STOP method to pause, observe, and then proceed. As you give yourself some STOP time, you realize you misread the e-mail.
- At the end of the day you receive a voice mail from your manager asking you to meet with her the next morning. As you drive home from work every imaginable negative thought goes through your mind and you contemplate the terrible possibilities in store for you at this meeting. Recognizing that you are in a judging mind frame, you use the STOP method. What you observe is that your thoughts are exaggerated and there is nothing you can do in the present about the unknown tomorrow. You proceed and push away these thoughts and focus on what is most important in the present—a safe drive home.

Compassion for Yourself

Compassion for yourself is the final criterion of mindfulness. Self-compassion encompasses acceptance of oneself and involves self-kindness rather than self-judgment. The concept of self-compassion includes three components:

- Being kind and understanding toward oneself rather than being harshly self-critical
- Perceiving one's experiences as part of the larger human experience
- Balancing painful thoughts and feelings rather than over-identifying with them (Neff 2003, 85)

When exercising self-kindness an individual is mindfully aware of the thoughts about oneself and does not automatically identify them as truths or facts. When one is self-compassionate he or she offers nonjudgmental understanding. Illustrating this concept, Beth, the director of revenue cycle management, was challenged by the chief financial officer about the accuracy of the statistics she presented during a recent meeting. The statistics she provided on denied claims were incomplete. For several days after the meeting Beth engaged in harsh self-criticism and berated herself as incompetent and stupid. To change over-identification with these thoughts and treating them as facts, Beth should use self-compassion and modify how she relates to herself. Rather than scolding and being overly critical, Beth could acknowledge her error and accept that she, like all humans, is fallible. In other words, Beth should forgive herself.

This is not to say that acceptance and forgiveness excuses a behavior or mistake or allows it to go uncorrected. Instead, research finds that genuine self-compassion allows an individual to better perceive and rectify dysfunctional patterns of thought, feeling, and behavior through awareness (Neff 2003). Putting one's mistakes in perspective and being nonjudgmental when the behaviors do not support unhealthy actions is part of exercising leadership presence.

Mindful Practice

Frequently people associate mindful practice exclusively with meditation. While meditation is one type of mindful practice, it certainly is not the only one. There are several types of mindful practice that can easily be incorporated into everyday routine. In fact, whenever you bring your attention to the present moment with focus, curiosity, nonjudgment, or compassion you are practicing mindfulness. Several forms of mindful practice are described as follows (Niemiec 2014).

- *Formal:* This practice involves setting aside a specific amount of time each day to exercise mindfulness. This could include a meditation or an activity such as a purposeful walk.
- *Informal:* This practice calls upon using mindfulness when you need it, such as when you feel stressed or overwhelmed. The STOP method described earlier is an example of informal practice.
- *In-the-Moment:* This practice threads mindfulness into daily activities. For example, eliminating multitasking or returning your mind to the present when it wanders during a conversation.
- *Cued:* This practice uses external cues to help you return to the present. For example, whenever you have a cup of coffee bring your mind to the present and savor the first five sips; or use the STOP method before sending an e-mail; or use the if-then method as a cue to practice mindful behavior.

Mindfulness Assessments

There are several validated and reliable mindfulness assessments that can be taken to discover one's level of mindfulness. The following are two assessments that are available online at no charge.

- The mindfulness quiz at the University of California Berkeley, Greater Good: The Science of a Meaningful Life. This assessment uses a mindfulness scale developed by researchers at La Salle University and Drexel University that measures an individual's level of present moment awareness and acceptance. It is available at http://greatergood.berkeley.edu/quizzes/take_quiz/4/e.
- The Five Facet Mindfulness Questionnaire developed by researchers at the University of Kentucky assesses an individual's degree of mindfulness from the perspectives of observing, describing, and acting with awareness and degree of nonjudging and nonreactivity to inner experiences. The assessment is available in paper form from http://www.ruthbaer.com/academics/index.html or available online at http://www.awakemind.org/quiz.php.

After completing one or both of these assessments, reflect on the following questions and write your responses.

1. What do the results of your mindfulness assessment tell you? How well do you believe the assessments measure your mindfulness?

2. In which areas can you improve? (For example, in observing the present, being nonjudgmental and self-compassionate, acting in the present, and being able to perceive emotions without becoming dysregulated.)

3. What goals would you like to set for increasing your mindfulness? What methods will you use to meet these goals?

Mindful Leadership

"A mindful leader embodies presence by cultivating focus, clarity, creativity, and compassion in the service of others" (Marturano 2015). The following scenarios illustrate leadership presence and that focus, creativity, clarity, and compassion applied to the leadership task at hand leads to optimal outcomes.

Focus

When an individual is unfocused, his or her mind is wandering from the present moment. Marian, for example, needs to complete a report and presentation for the board of trustees where she is chief information officer. The report will lay out a vision for how information technologies can be leveraged in meeting the knowledge economy demands. In preparing the report, Marion must gather data from a variety of sources. She has been working on the report for several days, but just cannot seem to maintain her focus. Reviewing the data sources, her mind wanders to operational issues. She is distracted by the content of the last e-mail she received; she thinks about the dynamics of the morning meeting with the technology staff; she is preoccupied and anxious about the number of e-mails and phone calls that are unanswered. Her mind is everywhere except on the report preparation. With the deadline nearing, Marion is increasingly stressed because she cannot seem to get any traction on completing the task. At the same time, when Marion is engaged in other activities—such as a performance review of one of her managers, at a department director meeting, or when having lunch with a colleague—her mind is sidetracked thinking about the unfinished report in her office.

Marion's story is experienced every day by most people in leadership roles. Lack of focus becomes a circular and unending event that results in productivity losses (Marturano 2015). Consider this formula for productivity: Productivity = Value created ÷ Input or resources consumed (Cullinan and Harmon 2014). As more resources are consumed—in Marion's case, time—the value of the report produced is reduced. In addition, the circular nature of mindlessness impacts other areas of Marion's work. For instance, what is the productivity loss in the meeting she attends, or the performance review she conducts, or any other task when her mind is distracted by the unfinished report in her office?

In addition to this effect, there are productivity losses associated with reset time. Reset time is the time it takes for a person to get back up to speed after being distracted from a task. It is similar to a car moving at 50 miles per hour and having to stop for a red light. The reset time is the time it takes for the car to make up the mileage it lost while waiting for the light to change. If you think about how many times a day you are in reset mode, you can begin to understand your productivity losses. Catching the wandering mind results in increased productivity, but it is only one benefit of mindful leadership practice.

Clarity

Clarity is the quality of easily seeing or hearing something, and then discerning or understanding what is seen or heard. Leadership presence requires both of these clarity qualities. Lack of focus in the previous scenario blocks clarity. Clarity is also blocked in other ways, as well. Consider Brenda, a hard-driving president of a large nonprofit healthcare organization who likes to see quick results. During a recent board meeting, Brenda argued for the funding of a bold new program. Several board members challenged Brenda's idea. As others on the board presented their views, Brenda kept thinking about her next move as her blood pressure rose. Brenda's impulse was to dig in even stronger and advocate her idea. However, in that moment, Brenda recognized her driving social style was getting in the way of listening and hearing the obvious distress of her board. Brenda paused her thinking about the next steps. She stopped and recognized her own behavior and how it was preventing her from being in the present. Once she stopped thinking about how she would defend her ideas, she was able to clearly hear and understand the board members' concerns. Flaws in her argument became more apparent, and she also noticed signs of change resistance in some of her board members.

In this scenario, Brenda moved through two steps of mindful leadership. The first was awareness by bringing her hopping mind to the present. The second was clarity when she accurately heard and understood the present situation.

Creativity

Creativity is the use of imagination and generating novel ideas. When the mind is packed with back-to-back tasks, thinking about to-do lists and how many e-mails must be answered, and checking for texts every two minutes, there is no room for creativity. When people habitually rely on applying old solutions to new problems, use emotions to respond to situations, or make snap judgments about a person, event, or situation based on biases and incomplete information, then they do not consider different views and perspectives and find new ways of doing things.

Presence of mind frees the brain to use imagination and develop better ideas (Marturano 2015). Examining the case of Marion, is it surprising she is having difficulty creating a vision for leveraging information technologies? Her mind is so full thinking about the past and worrying about the future that there is no room in the present to develop new ideas.

People often engage in self-talk that wraps language around snap judgments, emotions, and biases, and closes the door to their creativity. For example, phrases like "It isn't possible," or "It's always been done this way," or "If it's not broken, don't fix it," or "It won't work here," or "You can't teach an old dog new tricks," prevent the brain from looking at things in different ways, generating new ideas for solving problems, and creating better efficiencies or being more effective. The following case illustrates these points.

Monty is the director of information systems management for a large skilled nursing healthcare group. The organization has over 100 facilities nationwide. A consulting company hired by the healthcare group has completed a database inventory. One of the findings is that most databases lack documented data models. Not knowing the underlying structure of the databases makes it difficult to establish an enterprise-wide data dictionary, integrate or map data for business intelligence purposes, or determine how new systems can interface and exchange data with legacy systems. Therefore, the consulting group proposes a policy that all databases must have documented data models. Monty challenges this recommendation and is defensive, believing his abilities are in question. Monty says that in his experience data models are difficult to maintain, are frequently incorrect when they are developed, take too much time to construct, and slow down the development process. Besides these reasons, Monty says he does not have enough trained staff to implement the consultant's recommendation. This scenario demonstrates Monty's lack of leadership presence. First, he refuses to see a different perspective by reacting with his emotions. Then he blocks his creativity further by making snap judgments and over-relying on previous experiences.

New findings about the brain show that being present in the moment, remaining nonjudgmental, and giving undivided attention to the task at hand frees the brain from overreaction to previous experiences, biases, and emotions and allows the brain to be more flexible in arriving at new ideas and creating innovative solutions (Greenberg et al. 2012). When leaders fail to open space allowing themselves to be creative, they not only stifle their own creativity, but also hinder the creativity of those they lead. How leaders set and model standards for others is an important part of leadership. If leaders indicate that rigid thinking is the expected behavior then that behavior becomes the corporate culture and followers will imitate it.

Compassion

Compassion is a consciousness of a person's distress, suffering, or pain and a desire to alleviate it. In mindfulness, compassion involves consciousness of the distress of others and of oneself with the desire to relieve it. Suffering in others is not relegated to physical pain. Suffering can occur in many ways. For example, a co-worker may be in distress because he lacks self-confidence or self-esteem. A subordinate may be distressed because she was slighted by a peer. Or an associate may be distressed by being embarrassed when she was reprimanded by her supervisor in public. Leaders need to be aware of how they may create suffering in others through lack of social awareness and mindlessness behaviors such as judgmental remarks, insults, and rude behaviors. Compassion can only be exercised when there is awareness of the present.

Leaders need to be self-compassionate as well. They need to be aware of their own distress and take steps to relieve it through mindfulness. For example, Jill leads the auditing team for a coding outsourcing company. During a recent audit, a reporting mistake was made that cost the client several thousand dollars. Jill mercilessly beat herself up over the error, to the point where she could not sleep at night. Because her mind stays tangled in the past it is unlikely Jill can be effective in her job. It is also doubtful she opened up space to see the situation with clarity and take the corrective action needed to avoid future errors. Being aware of her feelings, observing and analyzing them, and employing self-compassion will more likely allow Jill to identify and proceed with actions to avoid similar future errors.

Practice Mindful Leadership

Use the following exercises to help you practice your leadership presence.

Use the STOP Method

For a full workweek, use table 6.1 to log how often during the day you have used the STOP method to bring your mind to the present.

Reflect on this experience.

- What was the outcome of using this method?
- What insights have you gained?

Table 6.1. STOP method log

Day	Event 1	Event 2	Event 3
Day 1			
Day 2			
Day 3			
Day 4			
Day 5			

Practice Focus and Clarity

Incorporate mindfulness throughout your day at work and at home by noticing when you are not focusing on the present moment or task.

- Use the following space to write down what cues you can use to avoid multitasking. (For example, turning off your cell phone during a meeting, turning off your e-mail alert on your computer when you are doing another task or in a conversation with another person.) How will you hold yourself accountable for these actions?

- Practice returning your attention to the present when your mind wanders during a meeting or conversation with another person. Use table 6.2 and each workday write down your observation about how this practice has provided a benefit to you or others.
- Commit to one formal mindfulness practice every day using the if-then technique. The following examples show how you might construct an if-then cue.
  - If I am driving home, then I will concentrate on driving, not on what happened during the day.

    - If I am walking down the hall at work, then I will focus on noticing new things.
    - If I am taking a walk outside, then I will focus on the sounds and smells, and experience the environment I am walking in.
    - If it is 6 a.m., then I will take a five-minute mindful pause, close my eyes, and stay focused listening to the sounds around me.
- Before you attend a meeting, shed expectations. Instead focus on how you will be a better listener in the meeting. Try this practice for one week and document your outcomes and benefits of this practice.

Table 6.2. Mindfulness log

Day	Reflections
Day 1	
Day 2	
Day 3	
Day 4	
Day 5	

Practice Creativity

Use the following activities to develop your creativity.

- *Journaling:* Carve out time each day from thinking about your e-mails, to-do lists, texts, or performing your routine tasks. Focus your attention in the present moment and journal about your vision of the future. The future can be about new product development, process improvement, more productive teamwork, or a more positive work culture. Use the following example or your own to start the visioning process.

A year from now I envision that my department will be the most productive of any department in our healthcare system. To make this happen, the first thing I will do is set aside a two hour innovation meeting with each of my teams.

- *Creativity Pause:* Each week take time out from your e-mails, texts, routine tasks, and all distractions. Use this time for thinking strategically and identifying areas for innovation. Develop an innovation and action board. Write your creative ideas on sticky notes and put them on the innovation board. For each innovation create a plan of action. Write these action steps on sticky notes, arrange them in sequence to be performed, and place them alongside your innovation on the board.

Practice Compassion

Use the following activities for practicing self-compassion.

- Use awareness to identify negative self-talk. Respond to the negative self-talk with self-compassion. For example:
  - I made a mistake, and I love myself in spite of it.
  - I could have done better, and I will strive to improve the next time.
  - It was an awkward thing to say, and I will be more aware next time.
  - I stumbled through my speech, and I will prepare better in the future.
- Use awareness to identify ways you have shown compassion to others during the week. Journal about these instances and how this made you and the person toward which your compassion was directed feel.
- Use awareness to identify times when you did not show compassion during the week. Reflect on the situation using the STOP method. Observe the situation in retrospect and think about how you might proceed the next time a similar situation arises.

References

Adler, R. and R. Benbunam-Fich. 2012. Juggling on a high wire: Multitasking effects on performance. *International Journal of Human-Computer Studies* 70(2):156–168.

Bishop, S., M. Lau, S. Shapiro, L. Carlson, N. Anderson, J. Carmody, Z. Segal, S. Abbey, M. Speca, D. Velting, and G. Devins. 2004. Mindfulness: A proposed operational definition. *Clinical Psychology: Science and Practice* 11(3):230–241.

Cullinan, R. and S. Harmon. 2014. Mindfulness: The Key to Productivity? *The Huffington Post.* http://www.huffingtonpost.com/renee-cullinan/mindfulness_b_5976864.html

Dane, E. and B. Brummel. 2013. Examining workplace mindfulness and its relations to job performance and turnover intention. *Human Relations* 67(1):105–128.

Goldstein, E. 2013 (July 3). What Is Non-Judgmental Awareness Anyway? http://www.huffingtonpost.com/elisha-goldstein-phd/non-judgmental-awareness_b_3204748.html

Goldstein, E. 2012. *The Now Effect: How This Moment Can Change the Rest of Your Life*. New York: Atria Books.

Greenberg, J., K. Reiner, and N. Meiran. 2012. Mind the trap: Mindfulness practice reduces cognitive rigidity. *PLoS ONE* 7(5):e36206.

Grossman, P., L. Niemann, S. Schmidt, and H. Walach. 2004. Mindfulness-based stress reduction and health benefits: A meta-analysis. *Journal of Psychosomatic Research* 57(1):35–43.

Halvorson, H. 2010. *Succeed: How We Can Reach Our Goals*. New York: Penguin Group.

Kabat-Zinn, J. 2005. *Wherever You Go There You Are: Mindfulness Meditation in Everyday Life*, 10th anniversary edition. New York: Hyperion.

Langer, E. 2009. http://www.ellenlanger.com/thoughts/

Langer, E.J. and M. Moldoveanu. 2000. The construct of mindfulness. *Journal of Social Issues* 56(1):1–9.

Lubar, K. and B. Halprin. 2003. *Leadership Presence*. New York: Gotham Books.

Lyons, K., K. Henry, and S. Nevo. 2005. Paying attention in meetings: Multitasking in virtual worlds. *First Symposium on the Personal Web, Co-located with CASCON*. 2005(7).

Marturano, J. 2015. *Finding the Space to Lead: A Practical Guide to Mindful Leadership*. New York: Bloomsbury Press.

Neff, K. 2003. Self-compassion: An alternative conceptualization of a healthy attitude toward oneself. *Self and Identity* 2:85–101.

Niemiec, R. 2014. *Mindfulness and Character Strengths: A Practical Guide to Flourishing*. Boston: Hogrefe Publishing.

Rezek, C. 2012. A mind to manage. *The International Journal of Leadership in Public Services* 8(1):33–38.

Rock, D. and J. Schwartz. 2006. The Neuroscience of Leadership. *Strategy + Business*. Summer 2006(43). http://www.strategy-business.com/article/06207

Westbrook, J., A. Woods, M. Rob, W. Dunsmuir, and R. Day. 2010. Association of interruptions with an increased risk and severity of medication administration errors. *Arch Internal Medicine* 170(8):683–690.

7 Making and Keeping Goals

Every social movement, invention, company, and organization begins with an idea or a vision for the future. However, if these are not coupled with purposeful action they remain merely dreams. Accomplishing an idea or fulfilling a vision relies on developing a plan of action. The foundation of an action plan is identifying, listing, and executing goals. Goals are specific targets that describe and provide a roadmap for how an idea or vision will be achieved. Though all too often goals are set but never reached. For example, many people make New Year's resolutions, set career objectives, or establish fitness targets but are unable to achieve them.

To fulfill the intended purpose of setting targets that are met, goals must meet a number of criteria and be supported by the right incentives and level of motivation. This chapter introduces the importance of anchoring goals with vision, purpose, and mission. When goals are out of alignment with an individual's personal life vision and purpose or mission, achieving them is more difficult, if not impossible. To support success in reaching goals, the chapter explores current perspectives on the science of goal motivation and achievement and presents several key criteria and principles for goal attainment. How goals are structured, the degree to which they support core values, and how an execution plan is designed all relate to the motivation for attaining goals. The chapter concludes with a step-by-step goal-setting process that ties together these important concepts to help you identify, organize, evaluate, prioritize, and take purposeful steps to execute and achieve your goals.

Goals and Vision, Purpose, and Mission

The definition of leadership supports the assumption that vision and action are intrinsically part of leadership. Vision is a broad proclamation of some desired future state. A purpose describes how vision is operationalized and the mission describes how the purpose is being fulfilled in the present (chapter 4). While purpose and mission describe how the vision is actualized, they do not establish a plan of action for how it is reached. How a vision is going to be achieved is defined by identifying, listing, and executing specific goals.

To illustrate these relationships, recall the example of Jennifer from chapter 4. Jennifer's personal life vision is "Making the world a better and happier place by helping others fulfill their potential." She believes her purpose is to use her courage, creativity, and organizational abilities to model a way that inspires and motivates others to live their lives to the fullest. Her current position (mission) is the leader of a statistical analysis team. To reach her personal life vision, fulfill her purpose, and succeed in her current mission, Jennifer needs a roadmap in the form of goals. How Jennifer's current goals support her personal life vision, purpose, and mission is illustrated in figure 7.1.

Jennifer lists her goals and for each goal, she identifies what she will perform and when it will be done or completed. For example, the goals she has set for health and well-being and are performed daily. Other goals have a target date for completion. To achieve her personal life vision of helping others, Jennifer believes she must first maintain good health for herself. Completing the leadership development certificate helps Jennifer improve her own self-awareness and provides opportunities to better fulfill her leadership potential and inspire and set the example for her team. Jennifer's goal to use her leadership abilities to help set policy and strategic direction for a health information management (HIM) college program directly impacts the education and opportunities for others to fulfill their potential. Finally, Jennifer's goal to be part of a formal mentor program will directly help others fulfill their potential.

Figure 7.1. Relationship of personal life vision and goals for Jennifer

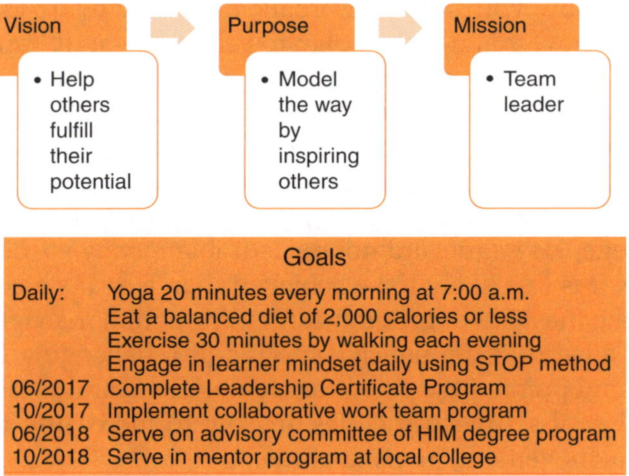

©Merida L. Johns

Studies show that setting goals is important for performance in several ways (Locke and Latham 2002). First, goals provide direction and help people focus on what is important. Goals essentially help people avoid focusing on irrelevant tasks. Consider Carrie, who sets the following goal: "Every week until I find a new job I will apply for at least one open chief privacy officer position that is located in the Midwest." This goal keeps Carrie on track, focusing her time on tasks that will specifically help attain her goal. In other words, she will be less likely to waste her time applying for jobs outside of the Midwest or that do not meet her job title criteria.

Second, because goals give people something to work toward, they motivate and energize people. In the previous example, Carrie will likely be more eager and interested in seeking new employment than if she had not set this goal. Goals also help people persevere. In Carrie's example, she will likely continue with her job hunt because she has set a specific goal.

Goals, Motivation, and Achievement

People frequently set goals or resolutions for the new year. Yet, when the year ends they often cannot remember the goals they set the previous January 1st, much less have achieved them. Scholars who researched the relationship between goals, motivation, and achievement discovered that motivation and achievement of goals is a function of how you state your goals, how they relate to your core values, and how you design a plan to achieve them (Grant 2011a).

Achieving goals is more likely when the goals are specific, can be measured, and are challenging. Studies show that setting challenging but possible goals, in contrast to easy and vague goals, increases effort, focus, commitment, and persistence in accomplishing them (Locke and Latham 2002). For example, a goal stated as "I want to go to college," is vague and not measurable by any specific criteria. Therefore, it is less likely to be achieved than a goal stated as "I will enroll in the master's degree in health information management program for Fall term 2018," which is specific and challenging, but achievable. The end point of the goal is easily identified and measurable.

Several goal-setting principles are key to increasing motivation and goal achievement. These include:

- *Commitment*. The degree of an individual's commitment to a goal determines its attainment. Commitment is highest when individuals feel they can achieve the goal and when the outcome of the goal is important to them. For instance, an HIM professional who wants to advance her career to an executive level might set a goal to complete a master's degree in HIM. Her commitment level would likely be high because the goal is attainable and the outcome is important for her career.
- *Feedback*. Summary information about progress toward meeting a goal is important in maintaining motivation. For example, if a coder's goal is to code 20 records a day, then knowing that the target is met provides the coder with motivation and a sense of accomplishment.
- *Complexity*. How challenging or difficult a goal is influences its attainment. If the task is either too difficult or too easy, motivation is lowered. In other words, people may give up if the task is too tough; for instance, setting up a threshold for coding 100 inpatient records a day for a new coder would likely be discouraging because it is doubtful the threshold can be met. Likewise if the task is too easy, such as setting a threshold of coding five inpatient records a day for a new coder, it may not be challenging enough and result in lowered interest or motivation. The key is to find the right degree of difficulty. (Locke and Latham 2002)

The following sections introduce key goal-setting criteria that support the principles for motivation and achievement of goals.

SMART Goals

The concept of creating goals that meet specific criteria was first introduced in 1981 with the development of SMART goals (Doren 1981). While there have been several variations of the meaning of SMART, the key concepts of the criteria as presented in this book are defined as follows.

- **S**pecific. Goals should be simple and specific and express what is done, why it is done, and how it is done. For example, a vague goal written as "I will exercise every day," turns into a specific goal when written as "Between 7 a.m. and 8 a.m. every day I will exercise by walking three miles." In this case, walking is the what; exercise is the why; and time of day is the how.
- **M**easurable. Goals should be measurable so that the end point is defined and so that progress can be monitored. Monitoring progress and success helps keep people motivated and engaged. In the previous example, the goal to walk three miles every day is measurable.
- **A**chievable: Goals should be challenging, but achievable. For example, a goal to walk 10 miles in an hour is likely unachievable for most people. However, a goal to walk four miles in an hour may be challenging, but achievable.
- **R**elevant: The individual should consider the outcome of a goal as important. For example, if exercise itself is not important to an individual, then it is highly unlikely that the individual will be motivated to achieve the goal. However, if losing weight is important, then rewording the goal to reflect this priority will likely increase motivation. For example, "To lose one pound a week, I will walk four miles every morning from 7 a.m. to 8 a.m." Here the important outcome is losing weight, not the exercise.
- **T**ime-bound. Goals should be linked to a time frame to provide a structure for completion, set accountability and establish urgency. In each of the examples in this section, time frames when the goal is to be performed or reached are identified.

Performance versus Learning Goals

Another key principle for goal achievement is the difference between performance or be-good goals and learning or get-better goals and how these influence goal motivation and attainment. Performance goals are ones that demonstrate a person can do something. For instance, setting a goal like "I am going to increase my ICD-10-CM coding rate by 10 percent this year," is a performance goal. In contrast, a learning goal focuses on developing mastery by enhancing skills and abilities (Grant 2010). A goal such as "Tomorrow I am going to spend a half an hour between 10 and 10:30 a.m. investigating techniques that will increase my ICD-10-CM coding rate," is an example of a learning goal because it focuses on developing a skill through new knowledge. Latham and Seijts show that discovery or learning something new is an effective method for mastering an ability or skill (2006).

Performance goals can be very motivating. After all, there are few people who do not want to prove that they are good at something. However, when performance goals are not easily or readily met, an individual may give up working toward the goal after a few failed attempts. Consequently, in certain cases performance goals can be as demotivating as they are motivating (Grant 2010). For example, not winning a specific sports competition might make a team feel like failures. Not being selected for the lead part in a play may make an individual feel she does not have talent or not achieving an A in a course, may make an individual feel like he is inept. All of these perceptions can adversely impact self-confidence and self-worth.

There are specific circumstances when performance and learning goals should be used. Typically when the desired outcome is to prove or validate oneself, performance goals are used; these are the ones frequently used in job performance reviews. On the other hand, when the desired outcome is a focus on learning new material, and increasing imagination and creativity that results in personal growth and mastery, then learning goals should be used. Studies show that when tasks are more complex and difficult to achieve, learning goals sustain motivation better than performance goals (Grant 2010).

Succeeding at Goals

"Successful people achieve their goals not because of who they are, but more often because of what they do," (Grant 2011a). Studies show people who are successful at achieving their goals commonly do nine actions, summarized as follows, which include some of the elements of SMART goals.

- *Make specific rather than vague goals*. "If it is 9 p.m. on a weekday evening, then I will read a professional magazine for 30 minutes," is better than the vague goal "I am going to read more in my professional journals." This criteria is in line with the S in SMART goal, but takes specific to a more granular level. In this case the exact time and day is specified.
- *Seize opportunities to work toward your goals*. Frequently people set goals, but then think they do not have time to work toward them. Think in simple, rather than large, steps to reach your goal. If you have 15 minutes in the morning, use it to take a small step toward your goal. The if-then goal-making technique works well to help you use your time effectively (chapter 6).
- *Monitor your progress*. Feedback on your progress is important for maintaining motivation and persistence. Every time progress is made, record the progress on a chart, write about it in a journal, or write it on a sticky note and paste it on your success board.
- *Believe you can achieve your goal, but know it may be difficult*. Having optimism that goals are reachable is fundamental to goal achievement. However, optimism without realism can be self-defeating. By their nature, challenging goals present obstacles to overcome. Realize that stretching is part of goal achievement and it may be difficult at times.
- *Focus on learning goals more than performance goals*. Learning goals help people grow, obtain knowledge, use imagination, and increase creativity. Thus, as your mastery continues, your performance will improve as well.
- *Commit to long-term goals*. Goals that are worthwhile and have a large impact on life are frequently long-term goals. Think about goals such as obtaining an advanced academic degree, becoming fluent in a second language, or becoming a master potter. All of these are long-term goals that require "grit" to achieve.
- *Build willpower and self-regulation*. Persistence is necessary for goal achievement. Work on advancing your goals even when you do not feel like it. For example, if a goal is to learn more about data analytics but the only time you have to devote 30 minutes of study is at 6 a.m. and you are not a morning person, then strengthen your willpower to start a new habit of getting up early to study.
- *Make goals that are achievable*. Do not overestimate your ability. Goals that are realistic and reachable are the ones that will be achieved.
- *Focus on what you will do, not on what you will not do*. Telling ourselves not to do something only makes the temptation

greater. Focusing on a positive action rather than a negative one makes goal attainment more likely. (Grant 2010)

These nine actions show that achieving goals is not rocket science; they are not difficult and everyone is capable of applying them into their everyday leadership practice. Each action by itself, however, is not enough to ensure success. For example, if you set specific goals but are not persistent, you are unlikely to succeed in achieving the goals. Or if you set long-term goals, but do not couple these with setting simple steps to progressively work toward the goals, then you are less likely to be successful. The conclusion of decades of research in motivation and achievement confirms that the power of each of these actions does not lie within itself. Rather the power for success rests in integrating all of the actions into leadership practice (Grant 2011b).

Discover Your Goal-Setting Behaviors

What are your goal-setting behaviors and how do they fit with the nine actions taken by successful people to achieve their goals? You can find out by taking the "9 Things Diagnostic" assessment at http://9thingsdiagnostic.com/. After completing the assessment answer the following questions.

1. From your assessment results, in which of the nine things successful people do areas can you improve best for setting your goals?

2. Which two or three of the nine things successful people do would you like to focus on first? Which ones would provide the most impact for improvement?

3. For each of the things you identified, write one goal that would help you improve. Be sure to make these SMART goals that are specific, measurable, achievable, relevant, and time-bound. For example, say you received a B on making your goals specific. An example of a goal that could help you improve on being more specific might be "When I write a goal, then I will include what I will do, why I will do it, and describe how I will do it." Or if you got a C on seizing opportunities for working toward your goals you might write a goal to improve this behavior like "When I write a goal, I will assign a time in my calendar to work on the goal every week."

4. Every time you achieve one of the goals you have made for improving your goal-setting behaviors, give yourself feedback and document your success. For example, draw a star next to the goal, or highlight the goal. You will be surprised how your stars or highlights will add up.

Developing Goals and Achieving Them

The previous exercises provide benchmarks for how to structure goals and apply specific actions that enhance motivation. Besides these strategies, goals should be consistent with your vision and purpose. It is unlikely you will achieve your goals if they do not synchronize with your values and the big picture of what you want to accomplish in life. When developing goals, each should be measured against the following criteria (figure 7.2).

- Is the goal meaningful in helping me achieve my vision and purpose?
- Why is the goal important in helping me achieve my vision?
- Is the goal specific and clear? Does it say what is done, why it is done, and how it is done?

- Is the goal measurable? How will I know when I have accomplished it?
- Is the goal achievable? What resources may I need to achieve the goal?
- Is there a reasonable and achievable time frame to accomplish the goal? (Johns 2013)

Figure 7.2. Goal evaluation criteria

Source: Johns 2013.

A six-step goal-setting cycle (figure 7.3), aligned with one's personal life vision and purpose, is used to identify, organize, evaluate, prioritize, take action, and reset and repeat in achieving goals (Johns 2013).

The following sections guide you through the cycle. As you move through each step, remember to incorporate the principles of SMART goals and the nine actions successful people do to achieve their goals. You should plan on taking several weeks to identify your goals; the time needed for subsequent action and achievement of the goals will depend on the goal itself. Also remember that developing goals is a repetitive process. Due to a variety of circumstances, goals sometimes need to be revisited and changed or readjusted. For example, Kurt had a goal to finish his master's degree within a four-year period. Due to an illness, Kurt needed to delay earning the degree for an additional year.

Figure 7.3. Goal-setting cycle

Source: Johns 2013.

Identify Your Goals

In the first step of the cycle you want to identify as many goals as you can. The purpose is not to evaluate the goals in this activity. You will categorize, prioritize, and evaluate the goals in subsequent activities. Use your personal life vision and purpose statements developed in chapter 4 as guides and identify 30 or more goals that you would like to achieve.

Think about *big* goals. For example, rather than stating "I will obtain a new job in healthcare privacy this year," replace it with "In 10 years, I will be the corporate vice president and chief privacy officer of one of the top 10 healthcare systems in the United States." The latter is a big goal. As noted earlier in this chapter research shows big, but achievable goals, helps to sustain motivation.

Because these are lofty goals, give yourself a realistic time frame to achieve them—say, one year, two years, or five or more years. The following is a suggested method to carry out this activity.

- You can limit your goals to your career or you can have a broader set of goals that demonstrate work–life integration. For example, you may have goals for education, building social capital, personal health, personal finance, and such.
- Write each goal on a large sticky note. Do not hesitate to write many goals. Thirty or more goals is a good start. Keep the sticky notes—you will organize these in the next activity.

- Keep a pad of sticky notes with you during the week. As you think of a goal write it down.
- Use your personal life vision and purpose statements as guides. Post a copy of each where you can see them to constantly keep them in the forefront of your mind. Think about or look for inspiring quotes and pictures that fit with your personal life vision and purpose and use these for motivation and to help identify meaningful goals.

Organize Your Goals

After you have written 30 or more goals it is time to organize them. Trying to work on all of these goals at the same time would be overwhelming, if not impossible. To manage your goals, organize them by theme. For example, put all career goals together, all health goals together, and so on. See what themes emerge. Give these categories interesting, exciting names that fit with your personal life vision and purpose. For example, The Information Governance Leader, The Mindful Professor, The Pulitzer Prize Winner, and so on. Giving descriptive names like these for the outcomes you desire provides a mental picture of what success looks like and supports motivation toward goal achievement.

After sorting and categorizing your goals, arrange them on a vision-action board. A vision-action board is a tool that helps you see how your goals are aligned with your personal life vision and purpose and is a way to organize and clarify your goals and keep you focused. The vision-action board can be a magnetic white board, poster board, a cork board, a large sheet of paper or felt, or anything on which you can arrange your goals. An example using a magnetic white board appears in figure 7.4.

Use about one-quarter of the top of the vision-action board to post pictures, quotes, or other images that graphically describe your personal life vision and purpose. Leave the rest of the board available to post your goals by category. Place your vision-action board in a prominent place in your home or office where you and others can see it every day. Doing this signals your commitment to your goals and keeps you focused on them daily.

After putting your goals in categories, ask yourself the following:

- Are some goals within the category duplicative? If so, combine them.
- Can any of the goals be arranged in a natural sequence within each category? If so, arrange them.

- Are there goals among the categories that have a relationship or synergy? If so, you might want to draw a dotted line between them, or place a piece of string or yarn between them to show their connectedness.

Figure 7.4. Vision-action board example

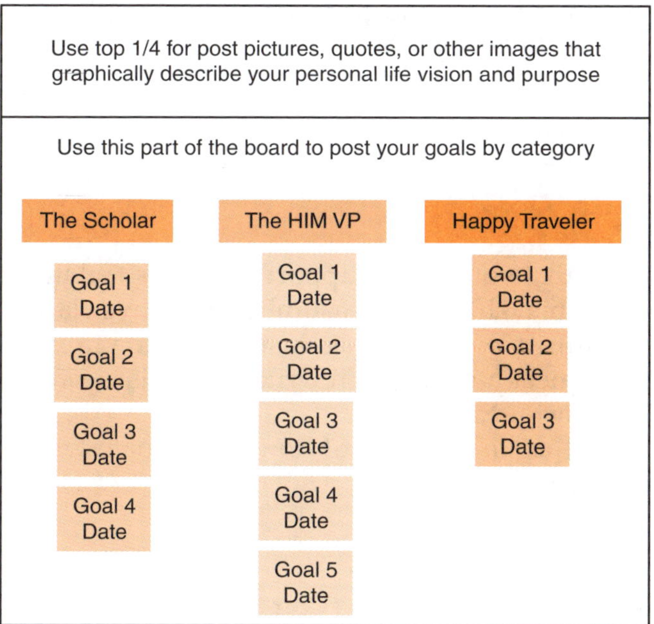

©Merida L. Johns

Evaluate Your Goals

After you have identified and categorized your goals, you are ready to evaluate them. In this step you will assess how your goals align with your personal life vision, purpose, and your current mission and ensure each meets SMART criteria.

- In the space that follows write down what you see emerging from this process. Do you see synergy between your goals and your personal life vision and purpose? If yes, write about this synergy in the space provided.

- If you do not believe there is synergy between your personal life vision and purpose, this is a good time for reflection. Evaluate why your goals, personal life vision, and purpose are not aligned. Is the personal life vision off? Are the goals off? Write down the actions you need to take to align the goals with your vision and purpose. Perhaps you need to revisit your personal life vision and purpose and make some changes or identify additional goals.

It is important that your goals support your personal life vision and purpose, are achievable and measurable, and have clarity. For each goal you identified, evaluate it against the criteria in figure 7.2. If a goal does not meet a criterion, rewrite it so it is clearer, and more measurable or achievable.

Use table 7.1 as an example of how to evaluate whether a goal meets each criterion.

Table 7.1. Goal Evaluation

	Goal: _____	Goal: _____	Goal: _____	Goal: _____
Is it relevant?				
Why is it relevant?				
Is it important?				
Why is it important?				
Is it specific?				
Is it measurable?				
Is it achievable?				
Does it have a realistic time frame?				

Prioritize Your Goals

All goals cannot be achieved at the same time. Prioritizing goals is essential to identifying which goals are most important to you. In many cases, while prioritizing you will discover a natural sequence of goals, where one goal must be accomplished first before another one can be achieved, such as completing educational requirements before seeking a new career path.

Spend time prioritizing goals in each category you have identified, placing goals that are most important to you at the top of the list. Are there goals that should be sequenced or are sub-goals of others (for example, you cannot achieve a master's degree until you have completed all the required coursework). Prioritize your goals by giving them a number on the sticky note and arranging the notes in numerical order within each category.

Use the vision-action board you developed to help you with this activity. This is also a good opportunity to review and determine if all the goals are relevant and important to your personal life vision and purpose. You may decide to discard some goals at this point.

Take Action with Simple Steps

Now you are ready to take action. Work on a few goals—say, one to three—at a time. Working on too many goals simultaneously can lead to goal fatigue and the inability to give the appropriate attention to each goal. In that case, you usually decrease your productivity as well as the quality of the work on the activity. You might want to develop a separate action board for the goals on which you are currently focusing.

Goals are rarely achieved by one swift stroke but rather through a series of consistent, meaningful, and purposeful actions. Take the goals you have selected to work toward and identify simple actions that can be repeated on a daily or weekly basis that will advance your progress. For example, if your goal is to "Gain professional visibility by having two articles I have written published in professional journals in the next 12 months," what simple actions would you need to take to accomplish this? One simple weekly action might be: "Each week, for the next three weeks, I will identify, contact, and arrange a phone call with the editor of a professional publication for which I would like to write. I will allocate time to do this each Thursday afternoon from 4 to 5 p.m."

Notice in this simple action statement the action is specific, the outcome is identified, and a specified time is designated to perform the action. Assigning a specific time to perform simple actions is important. Using vague time allocations like "sometime next week" will usually ensure that an action will not get completed.

The following is an example of a get-better goal and simple action. The goal is: "Increase my personal communication skills and visibility by engaging in conversation more often with people with whom I work." The simple action for this goal is: "Each day that I attend a meeting, I will turn off my cell phone and engage in purposeful conversation with at least one meeting attendee immediately before the meeting." Notice the specificity of the simple action and when the action will occur.

A description of the process for developing simple actions for the goals you will work toward is as follows.

- Choose a goal to work on.
- Identify one or more simple actions for the goal and write these actions on sticky notes, placing them under the goal on your vision-action board.
- Prioritize the actions for each goal. Note if some of the actions need to be sequential.
- Choose what you feel is the most important simple action and start performing it.
- Each week reflect and journal on your progress. Assess if the simple action is getting you where you want to be or whether you need a course correction adding to or halting the current action.
- When the anticipated outcome of the simple action is accomplished, celebrate! Give yourself the gift of time to acknowledge that you have successfully completed a milestone toward your goal.

Reset and Repeat

Identifying and acting on goals is a repetitive process. The process described in this chapter is one you can use throughout your life. Goals are like rungs in a ladder. Once you have climbed one rung, there is yet another one to climb. Goals should be reevaluated at least yearly to ensure they are still appropriate, fit with your personal life vision and purpose, and support your current life circumstances. To reevaluate your goals begin with the first step in the goal-setting cycle in figure 7.3.

References

Doren, G. 1981. There's a S.M.A.R.T. way to write management's goals and objectives. *Management Review* 70(11):35–36.

Grant, H. 2011a (February 25). Nine Things Successful People Do Differently. *Harvard Business Review*. https://hbr.org/2011/02/nine-things-successful-people/

Grant, H. 2011b. *Nine Things Successful People Do Differently*. Boston: Harvard Business Review Press.

Grant, H. 2010. *Succeed: How We Can Reach Our Goals*. London: Penguin.

Johns, M. 2013. *52-Week Game Changer: How She Leads*. Raleigh: Lulu Press.

Latham, G. and G. Seijts. 2006 (May/June). Learning Goals or Performance Goals: Is It a Journey or Destination? *Ivy Business Journal*. http://iveybusinessjournal.com/publication/learning-goals-or-performance-goals-is-it-the-journey-or-the-destination/

Locke, A. and G. Latham. 2002. Building a practicably useful theory of goal setting: A 35-year odyssey. *American Psychologist* 57(9):705–717. https://www.researchgate.net/publication/254734316_Building_a_Practically_Useful_Theory_of_Goal_Setting_and_Task_Motivation_A_35Year_Odyssey

Part II
The Ethical Leader

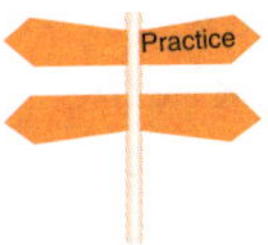

Phrases such as ethical leadership, ethical leader, ethical intelligence, and leadership ethics appear frequently in professional journals, magazines, and books. Often these terms are used interchangeably, although they may have different meanings. The chapters in this part of the book examine the similarities and differences among many of these terms and focus on the concepts and associated behaviors of an ethical leader from an applied ethics perspective. An ethical leader is defined here as a leader who does things right (is committed to excellence), does the right thing (acts ethically), does things for the right reason (creates an environment where people flourish), and motivates others to do these things as well. This definition acknowledges that leadership is relational, meaning the ethical leader develops and maintains a relationship with his or her followers.

The following chapters introduce the emerging field of leadership ethics and examine ethical challenges related to leaders, followers, and leadership. Each chapter provides exercises or activities that offer insights into developing ethical leader behaviors.

Why Ethics in Leadership Matters

The corporate and political landscape is awash in adverse consequences arising from unethical decision making. In the 1970s Ford motor company was in tight competition with overseas car makers of new compact cars. Ford rushed the Ford Pinto—its version of the compact car—into production, knowing there were design problems that could produce disastrous results in rear-end collisions. More than two dozen people were killed or injured in fiery rear-end collisions when Pinto fuel tacks ruptured before Ford recalled the cars (Bazerman and Tenbrunsel 2011). And consider the consequences of the biggest fraud scandal in United States history perpetrated by Bernard Madoff who conned people out of their life savings by falsely convincing them they would receive profits in return. Madoff swindled people out of $65 billion with few able to reclaim their losses. Think about the ramifications of the fraudulent accounting schemes by natural gas giant Enron that resulted in the company's bankruptcy where pensioners and shareholders lost everything (Silverstein 2013).

In each of these cases leaders made a narrow decision to increase revenues at any cost without any moral decision-making component. What their myopic cost-benefit approach failed to consider is that business does not exist to serve just itself and to make extreme profits. Business, as part of a larger system, exists to serve people and support—not squash—their interests and rights.

Unethical missteps are found in healthcare as well where fraud is big business. For example, Mercy Medical Center in Sioux City, Iowa, violated the False Claims Act by inflating charges for heart patients' care and paid a $400,000 settlement to the United States government. In another instance of fraud, Pfizer unit Pharmaceutical & Upjohn was fined $2.3 billion for illegal marketing of a drug for extended usage and higher doses that was not approved by the Federal Drug Administration and posed serious safety concerns for patients (AHIMA Foundation 2010). These decisions by healthcare organizations, like those cited previously, were narrowly focused on obtaining higher revenues devoid of any ethical considerations. Unfortunately, these kinds of cases are only the tip of the iceberg, where healthcare fraud in the United States is estimated at over $270 billion yearly (*The Economist* 2014).

While cases like these receive a lot of publicity, unethical decision making and behaviors extend well beyond fraud. Leaders face specific ethical challenges associated with temptations of power, ego, self-interest, and assuming responsibilities for groups and organizations (Ciulla 2014). A classic case of the use of power in relation to sharing or withholding information is Merrill Lynch, a financial company, whose CEO failed to inform its Board of Directors of the extent of the company's financial losses (Hollander 2014). This behavior along with other questionable practices resulted in the firing of the CEO, but the damage had been done as the company suffered a downward spiral.

Ethical lapses also occur when leaders fail to include or pay attention to appropriate input and advice. For example, an administrator of the Transportation Security Administration (TSA) made a policy decision to allow small knives to be brought onto aircraft. A primary constituency consisting of pilots and flight attendants had not been consulted about the soundness of the policy. The administrator's action resulted in protests by the affected parties and the policy was subsequently delayed until feedback was received by an advisory group. In this case, the TSA administrator had an ethical responsibility to consider the interests of the parties involved before developing the policy (Hollander 2014).

Ethics in leadership does matter. Unethical decisions and their subsequent actions directly or indirectly result in adverse consequences by suppressing the interests and rights of people involved and eventually hurt the larger ecosystem of communities, organizations, and nations. Ultimately, "leadership is always about self and others" (Gini and Green 2014, 58).

What is an Ethical Leader?

This part of the book provides an overview of the principles of ethical leadership and leadership ethics and considers what causes ethical lapses in leadership. The learn-discover-practice process gives you an opportunity to learn about the foundations of leadership ethics, increases your self-awareness of ethical behavior, and provides a framework to help you put behaviors that will enable you to be a good leader into practice.

Chapter 8: Ethics and Leadership

This chapter introduces a discussion about ethical theory and ethical leadership and establishes the foundation for understanding what constitutes the applied area of leadership ethics. It includes assessments for measuring good leadership in others and yourself.

Chapter 9: Facing and Handling Ethical Challenges in Leadership

This chapter offers examples of specific ethical challenges leaders face and how a framework for ethical practice can be used in meeting these challenges.

Chapter 10: Advancing Diversity

This chapter discusses and provides ethical frameworks for diversity management.

References

American Health Information Management Association Foundation. 2010 (November 4). A Study of Health Care Fraud and Abuse: Implications for Professionals Managing Health Information. https://www.ahimafoundation.org/downloads/pdfs/Fraud%20and%20Abuse%20-%20final%2011-4-10.pdf

Bazerman, M. and A. Tenbrunsel, A. 2011 (April). Ethical Breakdowns. *Harvard Business Review*. https://hbr.org/2011/04/ethical-breakdowns

Ciulla, J., ed. 2014. Introduction in *Ethics, The Heart of Leadership*, 3rd ed. Santa Barbara: ABC-CLIO, LLC

Gini, A. and A. Green. 2014. Moral Leadership and Business Ethics. Chapter 2 in *Ethics, The Heart of Leadership*, 3rd ed. Edited by Ciulla, J. Santa Barbara: ABC-CLIO, LLC.

Hollander, E. 2014. Further Ethical Challenges in the Leader-Follower Relationship. Chapter 3 in *Ethics, The Heart of Leadership*. Santa Barbara, CA: ABC-CLIO, LLC.

Silverstein, K. 2013. Enron, Ethics and Today's Corporate Values. *Forbes*. http://www.forbes.com/sites/kensilverstein/2013/05/14/enron-ethics-and-todays-corporate-values/#4a3e603d7688

The Economist. 2014 (May 31). The $272 Billion Swindle. http://www.economist.com/news/united-states/21603078-why-thieves-love-americas-health-care-system-272-billion-swindle

8 Ethics and Leadership

Ethics—whether it is business ethics, health information management (HIM) ethics, healthcare ethics, or leadership ethics—are based on the same fundamental principles of distinguishing between right or wrong, or good and evil in relation to people's actions, decisions, and character (Ciulla 2014). Ethics always involves a relationship with others. This relationship includes protecting the rights and satisfying the needs of an individual balanced against the needs and rights of others (Gini and Green 2014). For example, the leader may be in the position of making a decision where he or she must balance protecting and satisfying his or her own needs with the needs of others. Or the leader may be faced with taking an action where the rights and needs of a specific individual must be balanced against those of another person or a group of people. Whatever the situation, the leader must distinguish between right or wrong in relation to his or her actions, decisions, and values.

This chapter focuses on these ethical principles as they relate to leadership, provides a brief overview of classic ethical theories, and then introduces two different perspectives about how ethics is applied to leadership. The first is the construct of ethical leadership, describing what leaders do from a social science perspective. This view contends that ethical leaders are moral persons and moral managers. The second perspective is leadership ethics and, based in philosophy, describes what leaders should do when making decisions, taking action, and making choices, not what they do. Leadership ethics is an applied field of ethics that looks at the ethical challenges of leaders, followers, and leadership. This perspective asserts that ethics applied to leadership includes being a moral person, a moral manager, and an effective leader.

Ethical Theories

To understand how ethics is applied in leadership, it is important to know the classic and modern ethical theories that form the foundation of the study of ethics. Ethical theories are not a step-by-step explanation of how to make ethical decisions or behave in an ethical manner. Rather, they are a set of statements that define a concept and help people know the proper way of determining right or wrong. There are many ethical theories, such as utilitarian theory, Kantian ethics (deontological ethics), virtue ethics, gender theory, justice theory, rights theory, and egotism. A discussion of all of these is beyond the scope of this chapter. The following sections highlight utilitarian, Kantian, and virtue ethics theories—the three major theoretical approaches in normative ethics, a branch of ethics that seeks to determine what actions are right or wrong or which character traits are good or bad.

Utilitarian Theory

The utilitarian theory of ethics postulates that decisions about right or wrong should be based on the consequence of the decision and whether the consequence is useful in helping the greatest number of people or maximizing human welfare. In utilitarian theory, the interests of one individual do not supersede the interests of another. For example, the interests of the child, parent, or friend of decision maker do not outweigh the interests of any another person.

The utilitarian theory is often used in healthcare for justifying medical confidentiality. If patients are not assured that their medical information will be kept confidential, then as a group they may be less likely to seek medical care or share important medical information with providers. Having appropriate controls in place to ensure confidentiality will maximize the welfare of the greatest number of people because they will seek medical care (Jones 2003).

The consequences of moral decisions cannot always be accurately predicted because decisions are usually based on inherently imperfect or incomplete information. Therefore, accurately predicting the results of an action in all circumstances is difficult, if not impossible. One challenge to utilitarian theory is whether there are individual rights that cannot be overridden by the goal to achieve the best outcome for the most people. For example, are individual rights to freedom, pursuit of happiness, and privacy ever outweighed by the goal to achieve the best for the most people? For instance, HIPAA (Health Insurance Portability and Accountability Act) privacy regulations allow health professionals to communicate with law enforcement when the patient presents a serious or imminent danger to others. In this case the individual right to privacy is outweighed by what is best for society.

Kantian Theory

Kantian theory is one of the most cited rule-based ethical theories founded on an individual's duty or obligation. This type of theory is called deontological, from the Greek word *deon* meaning one's duty. Kantian theory proposes that decisions about what is right or wrong should be based on reasoning using rules, rather than based on reasoning that considers the consequences of decisions like the utilitarian theory. In Kantian theory, an individual's reasoning is guided by these rules, called maxims, that he or she believes and follows when making decisions and taking action. If an individual believes a rule to be true, he or she must apply the rule universally to everyone without exclusion. This is often referred to as a type of universal Golden-Rule analysis. But unlike the Golden Rule that is based on self-interest (treat others as you would treat yourself), Kantian ethics requires that a maxim is followed without consideration of self-interest. In other words, an individual may not do anything he or she would not allow everyone else to do. Kantian ethics is based on several formulations and principles. Three of these—universal rules, duty and respect, and respect for persons—are examined next.

Universal Rules

To be considered a universal rule, the rule must follow two criteria. The first criteria is the rule must be applied to everyone without exception. Consider Bella, for example, who believes the rule that "people must always keep the promises they make." If Bella believes that all promises made to her must be kept, then she must also accept that it is wrong for her to break any promises she makes to others. In other words, the rule is applied to everyone without exception.

The second criteria is that a universal rule can be applied without a contradiction or inconsistency occurring. For example, if Bart believes it is okay for him to break promises, then the rule must be applied to everyone else and Bart must accept that everyone can break promises made to him. If everyone can break promises, then promises would have no value in society and the practice of making promises would cease to exist. This contradiction makes it impossible to hold the universality of the rule that it is acceptable to break promises.

Duty and Respect

Kantian theory holds that ethical behavior is based on following a universal rule out of duty or obligation. Right or wrong action is determined by a duty, obligation, or law to follow universal rules. For example, Christy believes that contributing to society by paying taxes is a moral action (the right thing to do). Whether or not Christy is considered ethical or moral, however, depends on her intent or motivation in following the rule. For instance, "I pay taxes because it is my duty," demonstrates that Christy's motivation is based on a duty or obligation. Therefore she is judged as morally worthy (ethical). If her motivation is based on emotions or desires, such as "I pay taxes because I do not want to be punished," then she is considered morally unworthy (unethical).

Respect for Persons

A major premise of Kantian theory is that people have an absolute value and therefore cannot be treated as a means to an end. Everyone is obligated to act in ways that respect people's moral rights such as the right to dignity, right to autonomy, and the right to safety, among others. Thus, individuals should never be used unjustifiably or manipulated to achieve an outcome. For instance, Jan works as a systems analyst in the clinical laboratory department. She repeatedly manipulates her co-workers with passive aggressive behavior. She consistently is late to team meetings or does not show up for them and she promises to meet deadlines but fails to do so. Due to her tardiness and lack of preparation, she manipulates her co-workers to pick up the slack so that the team's project timelines are met.

Virtue Ethics Theory

Contemporary virtue ethics theory is founded in the work of Aristotle who advocated that ethical virtues (such as courage, temperance, and honesty) and intellectual virtues (such as wisdom) were necessary for a happy or flourishing life. Virtue ethics emphasizes virtues or the moral character of an individual. Unlike utilitarian and Kantian theories that emphasize what people should do, virtue ethics focuses on what people should be.

Virtue ethics is based on the premise that there are certain ideals all people should strive to embrace that allow them to fulfill their human potential and thrive in life. There is no definitive list of virtues. The Values in Action (VIA) assessment, for example (chapter 1), identifies the six virtues of wisdom, courage, humanity, justice, temperance, and transcendence that are applied through the practice of 24 character strengths. Aristotle, on the other hand, identified 12 virtues and various religions and others offer different perspectives on what ideals people should strive to embrace.

Just as athletes and musicians improve their skills through practice, as people practice and develop their virtues they become habits that define an individual's character. Virtue ethics asserts that people who are virtuous are disposed to act in an ethical way. However, virtues can be overused or applied with too much intensity or in the wrong situation. For example, courageous people may make reckless decisions resulting in negative consequences because they have not fully considered the potential risks of their actions. Or they may seek to engage in increasingly risky behaviors because of the adrenaline rush they get from such activities. In situations of overuse or misuse, the individual is lacking or underusing other virtues. In the case of high risk-taking, an individual is not exercising the virtue of wisdom or knowledge. To engage in ethical practice people must apply virtues appropriately in any given situation.

Applying Ethical Theories

Given the number of ethical theories, how are they applied in the real world? Is one theory better than another? Many philosophers have concluded that it is a mistake to view any one ethical theory in isolation of others or as mutually exclusive. Rather, each theory should be viewed as a contribution to a comprehensive ethical vision (Glover 2017). Ethical theories are not absolute. Instead they should be used to guide people in making moral decisions. The following scenario shows how one might approach a moral decision using utilitarian, Kantian, and virtue ethics theories.

> Laurie is the director of a nonprofit healthcare foundation located in the northern part of the United States. The foundation focuses its efforts on providing grant funding to other nonprofit healthcare organizations that specialize in providing healthcare services to senior adult populations in a four-county area. The nonprofit also provides assistance with business plan development, collaborative marketing, as well as workshops and seminars on topics of various interests to these nonprofit organizations. Recently there was a natural disaster that affected a large portion of the southeastern part of the country. Laurie asked the board of directors of the nonprofit group if they should consider donating some of their services and providing grants to senior healthcare nonprofits that were struggling with recovery from this natural disaster. Offering such services would normally be considered outside the scope of the mission of Laurie's organization. How might the board of directors make a decision about offering support to these nonprofits that were affected by the natural disaster?
>
> - Applying the utilitarian theory, the board of directors would consider the consequences of their actions and ask the question, "Would providing services maximize helping the greatest number of people?" In determining if they should provide assistance, the nonprofit would weigh the interests of its own constituency against the interest of those living in the affected area to determine the best possible outcome for the greatest number of people. The board may determine that providing assistance may be an inconvenience to its local group for a short period of time, but the effects of providing services to the struggling nonprofits in the southeast would better maximize help to the greatest number of people.
> - Applying the Kantian theory, the board of directors should hold the maxim that helping others in distress is a duty and must be applied universally, without exception, to everyone.
> - Applying virtue ethics, the board of directors may determine that providing assistance would exemplify the virtue of humanity.

Ethical Leadership

Ethical leadership is defined as "the demonstration of normatively appropriate conduct through personal actions and interpersonal relations, and the promotion of such conduct to followers through two-way communication, reinforcement, and decision making," (Brown et al. 2005, 120). The ethical leader engages in behavior that is considered normatively appropriate. Normatively appropriate in ethical leadership means that leaders do the following:

- Treat others with respect, do not have favorites, and make fair choices (fairness).
- Allow input from subordinates, listen to their input, and allow them to share in decision making on issues that concern their tasks (listen).
- Clarify expectations and communicate openly so followers understand what is desired and expected of them (role clarification). (Kalshoven and Den Hartog 2009, 104)

The dimensions and benefits of ethical leadership are described in the following sections.

Dimensions of Ethical Leadership

Ethical leadership has two dimensions that include the ethical leader as a moral person and a moral manager. As moral persons, ethical leaders are characterized by demonstrating specific characteristics in both their personal and professional lives. These characteristics include

- Honesty and trustworthiness
- Fairness and principled decision making
- Altruism (care about people and society) (Brown and Trevino 2006)

As moral managers, ethical leaders influence the ethical behavior of their followers. They expect their followers to behave ethically and communicate these expectations through role modeling, written and oral communications, and codes of ethics. They reinforce these expectations through rewards and discipline and hold followers accountable for their behavior (Brown and Trevino 2006). For instance, Joanne, a coding manager at a midsize community hospital had copies of the AHIMA Standards for Ethical Coding printed and laminated on cards for each of her coding staff. Fifteen minutes of each weekly virtual coding staff meeting that Joanne facilitates is devoted to discussing an example of how to apply one of the ethical standards. Joanne's leadership behavior is one example of a moral manager who communicates ethical expectations by not only providing a code of ethics, but in actively engaging her staff in discussions of ethical issues.

Researchers suggest that certain traits are more closely aligned with ethical leadership than others (Brown and Trevino 2006). The strongest of these is agreeableness, which is the tendency to be trusting, kind, and cooperative. Leaders who exhibit these qualities have been shown to be more effective as role models because they attract and maintain the attention of followers better than those who are not as agreeable (Brown and Trevino 2006). For example, Chet is the privacy officer at a critical access hospital. Chet works directly with several functional managers in other departments such as health information management, risk and compliance management, business office, clinical documentation improvement, and patient registration and admissions, and has gained the reputation for being energetic and an effective problem solver. What his associates appreciate about Chet is his willingness to listen to them and trust their opinions, share information with them, and his consistent practice of looking for alternatives to problems that will benefit the most people in the organization. Chet's associates know that he has no hidden agendas. Chet's cooperativeness and trust inspires his associates to assume these behaviors and make the hospital a trusting and respectful place to work.

The second characteristic is conscientiousness. Leaders who are conscientious exercise more self-control, are more dependable, and are more organized than those who are not conscientious (Brown and Trevino 2006). Leaders with these qualities are more likely to set clear standards and principles and apply them to themselves and their followers. Jackie, for instance, is a registered health information administrator (RHIA) and the chief financial officer (CFO) for her healthcare organization. Jackie has a long to-do list, but makes sure that it is organized from highest to lowest priorities. Each evening before leaving work, Jackie reviews her to-do list and examines whether or not she needs to makes changes in priorities for the next day in response to changes in circumstances. Jackie's cardinal rule is she will not commit to additional assignments or add to her to-do list if she believes she cannot meet time or quality requirements. Jackie's tenacity in keeping her to-do list well-managed and balanced has given her the reputation among her peers and followers as a person who makes and keeps commitments.

Finally, ethical leaders have low neuroticism. This means they are less likely to exhibit negative emotions such as a grandiose sense of self-importance, anger, fear, and anxiety, and are unlikely to be hostile to others. Therefore, ethical leaders are able to develop and maintain positive relationships (Brown and Trevino 2006).

Benefits of Ethical Leadership

Several positive outcomes are the result of ethical leadership due to the leader role modeling ethical behaviors, maintaining fair and caring relationships with employees, and expecting employee ethical conduct, ethical decision making, and accountability. Employees of ethical leaders are

- Likely to engage in ethical conduct such as honesty, trustworthiness, and respecting others
- Likely to make decisions based on ethical theory rather than on self-interests. This could include weighing the consequences of decisions, following a duty or obligation to do good, or embracing a specific virtue
- Likely to hold themselves and others accountable for ethical conduct
- Likely to demonstrate prosocial behaviors such as trust, gratitude, and commitment
- Less likely to engage in counterproductive and negative behaviors
- Likely to exhibit satisfaction and motivation (Brown and Trevino 2006)

A central part of leadership defined in this book is that leaders act in ways that motivate their followers to embrace ethical behaviors. When leaders set the example for ethical behavior their followers are likely to respond in a reciprocal manner by acting ethically themselves. The benefits of ethical leadership noted previously have positive consequences for the individual, organization, and ultimately the larger community. For example, when associates trust and respect each other there is less unhealthy conflict. The absence of unhealthy conflict in the workplace has a positive impact on an individual by creating a work environment where the employee exhibits less stress, anxiety, avoidance, and anger. These effects have a further impact on the organization. In a work environment free of unhealthy conflict, there is less employee turnover, decreased employee absences, higher productivity, and greater revenue. Organizations without unhealthy conflict also maintain better reputations and higher customer satisfaction than organizations with such conflict (Buss 2011).

On the other hand, when leaders act unethically, research shows that followers tend to imitate unethical behaviors opposed to followers whose leaders and organizational culture and structure encourage ethical behavior (Bandura 2002). For instance, if leaders engage in bullying and disrespectful behaviors, it is likely that their followers will engage in the same practices with co-workers and customers (Gilbert et al. 2012).

Assess Ethical Leadership Behaviors

Use the questionnaire in table 8.1 to assess how you have practiced ethical leadership behaviors in the past. When answering the questionnaire think about a time when you were in a leadership role.

Table 8.1. Ethical leadership behaviors

Leadership Behaviors	Always	Frequently	Sometimes	Infrequently	Never
I can be depended upon to complete tasks I promise to do.					
I can be trusted to tell the truth.					
I listen to others' ideas.					
I ask others for their input.					
I set a good example for others.					

(Continued)

Table 8.1. Ethical leadership behaviors (continued)

Leadership Behaviors	Always	Frequently	Sometimes	Infrequently	Never
Before I make decisions I consider how others' needs and rights will be affected.					
I try to do things in the right way.					
I try to do the right thing, thinking about the consequences of my decisions.					
I hold my temper when people disagree with me.					
I hold other people accountable for their ethical behavior.					
I make fair and balanced decisions.					
I share my views with others on ethical behavior.					
I acknowledge and take responsibility for my mistakes.					
I act according to my values.					
In tough decision-making situations, I balance my needs and rights with the needs and rights of others.					
In tough decision-making situations, I balance the needs and rights of an individual with the needs and rights of others.					

This could have been as a leader in a student group or association, team leader for a course project, team leader in a sport or at work, a supervisor or manager, or leading a volunteer or community organization or group. After you have finished the questionnaire answer the questions that follow.

1. Reviewing your answers, what do you observe or notice? What are areas of strength for you? In which areas can you improve?

2. Choose two areas where you can improve and for each one write down what action you can take in the next week to boost your ethical leadership. For example, if you want to improve your listening skills, you could commit to something like the following: "When I am in a discussion with someone, then I will listen to them without interrupting for at least 60 seconds." Or, "When I am in a discussion with someone, I will listen to them and ask follow-up questions rather than offer my opinion."

Leadership Ethics

All ethics are concerned with human relationships. Leadership ethics is an applied field of ethics, which means it uses ethical theory in a specific discipline to describe what a person is obligated or permitted to do. Leadership ethics focuses on the relationship between leader and followers and what a leader should do (Ciulla 2014). Among the special characteristics of the leader–follower relationship are power, influence, vision, obligation, and responsibility. The relationship in turn has its own set of ethical challenges. These center around personal challenges such as being authentic, balancing self-interest with the interests of others, and being disciplined, consistent, and executing moral obligations related to justice, duty, competence, and the greatest good (Ciulla 2004). The following sections describe foundational principles of leadership ethics by defining and contrasting good and effective leadership and providing examples of each.

Good Leadership

Leadership ethics incorporates the concept of the good leader. The good leader is both an ethical leader described earlier (moral excellence) and an effective leader (technical excellence). Technical excellence is effectiveness defined by having ethical intentions for bringing about change that is good, and accomplishing change through ethical means. Combining the dimensions of moral and technical excellence offers a more complete perspective of what good leadership should be and surpasses ethical leadership as discussed earlier. Adding effectiveness to the requirements of a good leader is important because a leader can be ethical but not effective. For example, consider a leader who oversees the merger of two companies. The leader demonstrates characteristics of moral excellence by being committed to creating a thriving company that will better benefit the local community; being honest in the merger transactions and fair in decision making; and modeling ethical behaviors for his followers. But three years later the merged company ends in bankruptcy; obviously the goal of a prosperous company has not been met. This individual would not be considered a good leader because while he was an ethical leader, the criteria for technical excellence was not met.

On the other hand, a leader can be effective, but not ethical. For instance, a healthcare administrator effectively meets budget every year and has an excellent relationship with the board of trustees, medical staff, and hospital associates, but takes money in exchange for influencing the decisions of the board of trustees in granting contracts to vendors (bribes). In this case the administrator is effective by meeting budget constraints, but does not rise to the moral excellence standard. So the administrator has not met both the criteria of moral and technical excellence and therefore is not a good leader.

Or consider a healthcare corporate director who receives excellent performance reviews. Previously she had worked for a vendor that provided housekeeping outsourcing services. In her current position she now provides contracts to that vendor without going through a competitive vetting process. While this director is effective given her performance reviews, her practice of awarding outsourcing contracts to her previous employer without performing due diligence is not the ethical practice. Good leaders must not only do things right (technical excellence), they must also do the right thing and for the right reasons (moral excellence).

Examples of good leaders who possessed both the qualities of moral and technical excellence are Martin Luther King, Jr., and Mahatma Gandhi. Both King and Gandhi created change that was good and that supported social justice and the civil rights and interests of others. Their intentions were not motivated by accumulating personal wealth or celebrity, but were focused on creating a common good. And they both accomplished change through nonviolent and ethical means. Thus, one measurement for determining the effectiveness of a good leader is to evaluate the answers to the following questions: What were the leader's intentions? Was change accomplished? What were the means by which the change was achieved? Was the change good? (Ciulla 2004).

Effective Leadership

An underlying question in leadership ethics is whether or not a leader must always be effective. For example, some leaders act ethically in all circumstances, but because of a convergence of circumstances are sometimes unsuccessful in achieving their goals. Take the chief information officer (CIO) of a healthcare system, for example, who is applauded for her successful installations and upgrades to the electronic health record over the past five years. In a major overhaul of the current system, costing several millions of dollars, the upgrade had to be stopped in the middle of the project because the vendor was significantly behind in delivering specific applications of the product. This caused the system to be delayed for over a year, costing the healthcare system additional millions of dollars, disrupting the efficiency of services, and causing frustration among clinical and administrative personnel. The CIO's peers and followers deemed her performance as ineffective. In this case, a number of questions should be answered to determine whether the project failure was due to a convergence of circumstances that could not have been foreseen by the CIO or whether the failure was due to not reasonably anticipating the vendor issues. For example, should the CIO have known that the vendor's promised deliverable was "smoke and mirrors" that was misleading or an exaggeration when she made the decision to purchase the product? Did the CIO use due diligence gathering and assessing information about the vendor in making her decision? Did the CIO appropriately consult with others in the organization before making her decision?

For the most part, leaders make decisions that are risky because the information they use is inherently either incomplete or imperfect. Furthermore, leaders rarely have complete control over all variables that could possibly affect the outcome of their decisions (Ciulla 2004). In this instance, the CIO likely pursued the system upgrade for the right reasons of increasing the safety of patient care and may have done due diligence in gathering and assessing vendor information. The vendor may have had an excellent reputation for delivering its products on time in the past. But the CIO did not have control over the vendor's internal project management, so failing to achieve results wasn't necessarily due to the CIO's ineffectiveness, but to unforeseeable circumstances outside her control. Thus, leaders who act with deliberate care and for the right moral reasons, but who nevertheless fail in achieving results, can be exonerated (Ciulla 2004, 309).

Assessing Good Leadership

Choose two leaders you know personally. They could be your manager, the CEO of the company where you work, a community leader, a minister, a teacher, or anyone you consider to be a leader. Use table 8.2 to determine how each meets criteria for moral and technical excellence. Put a check by each criteria that the leader meets, then answer the questions that follow.

Table 8.2. Assessing good leadership practice

Criteria	Leader 1	Leader 2
Moral Excellence		
Treats others with respect		
Does not show favoritism among subordinates		
Makes fair decisions, balancing needs and rights among people		
Is trustworthy		
Exercises self-control		
Follows through with promises		
Is a role model for subordinates and others		
Is organized		
Sets clear expectations for good behavior		
Holds people accountable for their behavior		
Establishes and maintains positive relationships		
Technical Excellence		
Successfully implements change in the organization		
The change implemented is good		
Intention for change is motivated by service to others and common good rather than for greed, power, or celebrity		
Uses moral methods to achieve change		

1. Examine your results for one of the above leaders. For each criteria the leader has met, provide a specific example of how that person fulfilled the standard. For instance, if you checked the leader is trustworthy provide a brief description of when you have seen his or her trustworthiness. Use the space that follows to give an example of each checked criteria.

2. What observations can you make from your assessment? To what degree can you determine if either leader is a good leader?

3. Do you believe that a leader has to meet all of the listed criteria all the time to be considered a good leader? Why or why not?

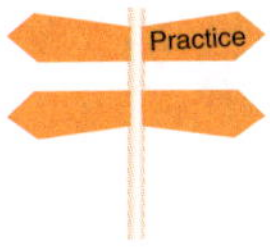

Applying Leadership Ethics

Think of a time that you were in a leadership role; it could be a position you currently hold or a previous position such as a team leader, officer in an organization, or other leadership position. Use table 8.3 to determine how you met the criteria for moral and technical

Table 8.3. Applying leadership ethics

Criteria	Met	Example
Moral Excellence		
Treated others with respect		
Treated all subordinates and team members the same		
Made fair decisions, balancing needs and rights among people		
Was trustworthy, could be depended upon to follow through on commitments or tasks		
Exercised self-control		
Kept promises		
Was a role model for subordinates and team members		
Organized and prioritized work tasks and commitments		
Set clear expectations for positive behavior of subordinates and team members		
Held people accountable for their behavior		
Established and maintained positive relationships		
Technical Excellence		
Successfully met the goals of the project or organization		
The change implemented was good for the organization		
Intention for change was motivated by service to others and common good rather than for greed, power, or celebrity		
Used moral methods to achieve change (that is, did not lie, cheat, misrepresent information, and such).		

excellence. Put a check by each criteria you believe you met and give an example in the third column that explains how you met the criteria. Then answer the questions that follow.

Reviewing the assessment, what are your observations? In which areas can you improve? Write down the areas in which you want to improve in table 8.4 and the actions you will take to do so.

Table 8.4. Actions for improving

Areas for Improving	Actions I Will Take to Improve

References

Bandura, A. 2002. Selective moral disengagement in the exercise of moral agency. *Journal of Moral Education* 31(2):101–119.

Brown, M. and L. Trevino. 2006. Ethical leadership: A review and future directions. *The Leadership Quarterly* 17:595–616.

Brown, M., L. Trevino, and D. Harrison. 2005. Ethical leadership: A social learning perspective for construct development and testing. *Organizational Behavior and Human Decision Processes* 97:117–134.

Buss, H. 2011. Controlling conflict costs: The business case of conflict management. *Journal of the International Ombudsman Association* 4(1):54–60.

Ciulla, J., ed. 2014. Introduction. In *Ethics, The Heart of Leadership*, 3rd ed. Santa Barbara: ABC-CLIO, LLC.

Ciulla, J. 2004. Ethics and Leadership Effectiveness. Chapter 13 in *The Nature of Leadership*, 1st ed. Edited by Antonakus, J. Thousand Oaks: Sage Publications.

Gilbert, J., N. Carr-Rufino, J. Ivancevich, and R. Konopaske. 2012. Toxic versus cooperative behaviors at work: The role of organizational culture and leadership in creating community-centered organizations. *International Journal of Leadership Studies* 7(1):29–47.

Glover, J. 2017. Ethical Decision-Making Guidelines and Tools. Chapter 2 in *Ethical Health Informatics: Challenges and Opportunities*. Edited by Harman, L. and F. Cornelius. Burlington: Jones and Bartlett Learning.

Gini, A., and A. Green. 2014. Moral Leadership and Business Ethics. Chapter 2 in *Ethics, The Heart of Leadership*. Edited by Ciulla, J. Santa Barbara: ABC-CLIO, LLC.

Jones, C. 2003. The utilitarian argument for medical confidentiality: A pilot study of patients' views. *Journal of Medical Ethics* 29(6):348–352.

Kalshoven, K. and D. Den Hartog. 2009. Ethical leader behavior and leader effectiveness: The role of prototypicality and trust. *International Journal of Leadership Studies* 5(2):102–119.

9 Facing and Handling Ethical Challenges in Leadership

Similar to other applied ethics that address ethical challenges in specific domains such as law, health, and health information management (HIM), leadership ethics address specific challenges in leadership. Ethics involves questioning what is right and wrong, and what are duties and obligations. It also exercises fairness, justice, and responsibilities in human relationships and with other living things (Ciulla 2014). Therefore, the ethical challenges leaders face ultimately are related to leaders and their relationship with the aspirations, needs, and well-being of their followers.

Ethical challenges can be categorized broadly as centering on personal and moral challenges. Personal challenges involve such things as authenticity, balancing self-interest with the interests of others, and being disciplined and consistent in leadership behaviors. Moral challenges are usually related to such things as justice, duty, competence, and concern for the greatest good. These challenges are not exclusively about making decisions regarding what is right or wrong. Frequently the struggle is between opposing goods. For instance, balancing showing compassion for an individual and being fair to a group of people when making a choice between two alternatives.

This chapter first examines a group of behaviors leaders can exercise to establish an environment that is more likely to support ethical leadership. Creating an ethical environment where people and organizations can flourish is a primary leadership goal and also reduces the opportunity for unethical behavior. The chapter then explores what contributes to ethical challenges and ethical traps and offers insights on how leaders can face and handle these.

Creating a Climate for Ethical Practice

The leader–follower relationship is based fundamentally on the exercise of power and influence. Leaders usually have more power or influence than followers and how leaders choose to use their power frequently gives rise to ethical challenges (Ciulla 2005). Good leadership (chapter 8) relies on developing loyalty and trust in the leader–follower relationship. Honesty and trust are based on fairness, principled decision making, and communication. When the leader's reason for using influence or power is unjust (such as promotion of self-interest), or when the use of power is unjust (such as administering unfair punishment), then the environment is not conducive to building trust. Participative practices between leaders and their followers that build trust and honesty, encourage communication, and promote the ethical use of power are likely to create a climate for ethical behavior (Hollander 2014). Some of these practices such as inclusive leadership and followership are discussed next.

Inclusive Leadership

Inclusive leadership (IL) is a participative process where the leader includes followers in the decision-making process. The leader encourages followers to voice their ideas and opinions in matters that concern them and listens to these ideas. This is a departure from leader-centric leadership where the leader is the sole decision maker, directing people rather than including them at the decision-making table. Being an inclusive leader means "doing things with people, rather than to people," (Hollander 2012, 3). Including followers in the decision-making process in matters that affect them not only helps followers participate in leadership, but also improves the likelihood of achieving desired outcomes (Hollander 2014).

In IL the leader–follower relationship is based on four key elements (figure 9.1). These include the following:

- *Respect:* Listening to others
- *Recognition:* Acknowledging another's input can make a contribution to the decision-making process
- *Responsiveness:* Engaging in discussion and consideration of the input of others
- *Responsibility:* Accountability for practicing respect, recognition, and responsiveness (Hollander 2012, 3)

Figure 9.1. The four Rs of inclusive leadership

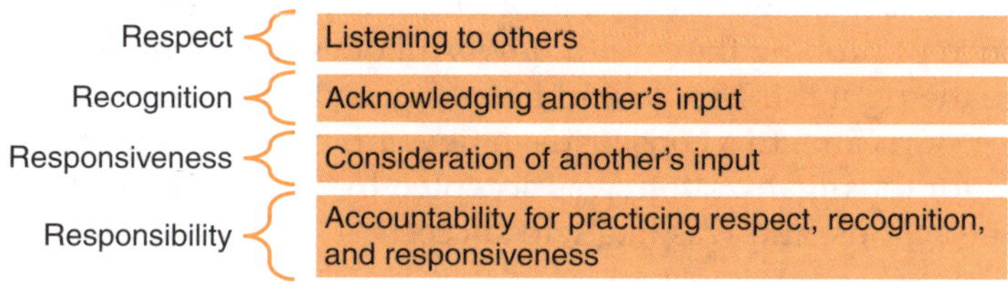

Source: Hollander 2012, 3.

Practicing these four Rs is required of both the leader and the follower if IL is to be successful. All of these behaviors rely on two-way communication between leaders and their followers. The following scenario demonstrates how IL might work.

> Lynn is corporate director of HIM services for a nine-hospital healthcare system. She has 12 managers who directly report to her and each is responsible for various aspects of health information services at one of the nine hospital centers. Recently the healthcare system hired an outside consulting firm to study efficiency and workflow problems in revenue cycle management. When Lynn reviewed the consultant's evaluation and recommendations, her first impression was: "There are a lot of challenges here and the recommendations cross organizational, departmental, and functional borders. These are likely to cause a lot of opposition from staff, but because the consultants have recommended these I am not going to be held responsible if they are not well received when they are implemented." However, Lynn continued to think about the implications of the recommendations before proceeding with them. Ultimately she was as concerned about doing what was right for the organization and staff as she was about doing things right. To be successful, Lynn recognized that the input from her staff was important to determine next steps. Lynn respected the perspectives her staff could provide and arranged for an all-day session with them to review the consultant's report and determine what action was appropriate and how it should be implemented. During the session Lynn asked questions like the following to engage her direct reports:
>
> - What do we know to be true?
> - What is difficult here?
> - What could we do better?
> - If we do not do this, what are the consequences?
> - If we do this, what are the consequences?

> The assembled group grappled with these questions, offering their opinions and insights. Often they did not agree with each other, but Lynn kept probing them with powerful questions about what actions were the right thing to do and how they could be best implemented. The group came to a consensus in developing an action plan that was right for the organization, was accepted by those who were affected by the actions, and was likely to succeed.

This scenario demonstrates how the four Rs of IL are implemented. First, Lynn showed respect for her followers by soliciting their input. She showed her staff recognition by engaging and listening to them. She demonstrated responsiveness by taking their opinions and crafting an action plan that was practical. Both Lynn and her followers fulfilled their responsibilities acting reciprocally by respecting, recognizing, and being responsive to each other, even when there were disagreements among them.

Inclusive Leadership Experience

Use the list in table 9.1 to assess the extent to which you have experienced an inclusive leadership environment in two organizations where you have worked. Think about times where you felt committed, motivated, and recognized in your job. Then check the column that applies for each statement and answer the questions that follow.

1. What are the similarities and differences between the two managers? Describe their areas of strengths and areas in which they can improve.

2. For each statement where you checked "sometimes", describe a specific instance where the manager displayed inclusive leadership behavior.

Table 9.1. Inclusive leadership assessment

Inclusive Behavior	Manager 1			Manager 2		
My manager:	**Always**	**Sometimes**	**Never**	**Always**	**Sometimes**	**Never**
Respect						
Listened to my work concerns						
Was interested in how I was doing at work						
Was interested in receiving my input						
Treated me with courtesy						
Recognition						
Asked for my input on policies or procedures						
Solicited input from me and my workgroup members before making decisions affecting myself or the workgroup						
Recognized my contributions to the organization						
Responsiveness						
Gave me opportunities to make decisions about how I did my work						
Was fair and consistent with how he or she treated me						
Addressed work concerns or problems I had						

3. How did you respond in situations where your manager did not practice inclusive leadership? How did this impact your motivation, commitment, loyalty, and self-esteem? Explain.

4. Pick one occasion where your manager could have changed his or her behavior and been more inclusive and describe possible results.

Followership

Because leadership involves a leader–follower relationship, leaders and followers are dependent on each other and their fortunes (success) rise and fall together (Burns 2012, 489). Inherent with this relationship are ethical challenges particularly in relationship to how leaders use their influence and power. For example, leaders can use their influence and power to advance or thwart various forms of distributive, procedural, and interactional justice discussed later in this section.

Followers can either support or impede a leader. For example, followers can embrace a leader's vision and take action to achieve it. On the other hand, in cases of situational power (namely, power that has been granted by holding a position) and in a leader-centric environment where respect, autonomy, identify and certainty are lacking, followers may sabotage a leader's vision and goals. Examples of this are deliberate nonperformance, not speaking up when there is an obvious process problem that will adversely affect an outcome, or stealing or maliciously destroying digital assets. Thus, there is almost universal consensus that mutual reciprocity must exist between leaders and their followers if leadership is to be successful (Hollander 2014). Leaders need to understand their followers to be successful. The concept of followership contests the notion that the sole aim of a leader is gaining personal power. As discussed in the following sections, followership involves understanding and supporting the needs and rights of followers, and advancing various forms of organizational justice.

Followers' Needs

There are a variety of motivation theories used to describe why people act in certain ways. These theories describe the degree of motivation based on assumptions about people's needs and how well these are met. For example, Frederick Taylor's motivation theory is founded on the premise that workers' performance is directly related the degree to which their need for a reward is being met. Therefore, Taylor's theory suggests that people are motivated by a reward, such as money, to work more productively. Elton Mayo's theory of motivation, however, challenges the notion that workers act in a certain way based solely on the need for a reward. Mayo's theory proposes that meeting the social needs of workers, such as providing humane working conditions, are motivators for workers' productivity. Others such as David McClelland classify people's needs somewhat differently. McClelland's theory suggests that people's behaviors are motivated by three drivers—needs for achievement, affiliation, and power. Achievement is defined as a need to accomplish something; affiliation is a need for belonging to a group; and power is a need to control others or organize people.

Another theory of motivation, developed by Abraham Maslow, focuses on explaining people's behavior in relation to the extent that physiological and psychological factors such as safety, social, and ego needs are met (Maslow 1943). Using Maslow's hierarchy of needs as a basis, followers' needs beyond physiological and safety needs are divided into four categories: belonging, self-esteem, self-actualization, and transcendence needs. Each of these is described briefly as follows.

- *Belonging*. This need is described as an individual's desire for social acceptance and feeling he or she is part of a group. When a follower feels isolated or not appreciated for who they are and what they contribute, then their needs for belonging are not met.
- *Self-esteem*. This need is described as individuals believing in themselves and receiving the respect and recognition of

others. Self-esteem needs are met when others value and validate the individual, listen to him and her without judgment, and recognize the individual's personal achievements.
- *Self-actualization*. This need is associated with an individual reaching his or her full potential and includes the autonomy to make choices and decisions and engage in challenging and creative work.
- *Transcendence*. This need involves a person wanting to identify with or experience something beyond the individual self or provide services to others outside of service to oneself.

The real role of leadership, like business, is not just to generate a product for extreme profit but to also help people fulfill their potential (Hollander 2014). Leaders can help people fulfill their potential by knowing what motivates their behavior and acting in ways that help meet their needs. In building an environment of followership, leaders not only satisfy this criterion but also create an atmosphere conducive for ethical conduct. For instance, a leader can help meet a follower's need for belonging by practicing inclusive leadership and valuing different cultural viewpoints (chapter 10). Or a leader can help meet a follower's self-esteem needs by practicing mindful leadership behaviors such as listening and responding to follower's concerns (chapter 6).

Organizational Justice

Creating a leader–follower relationship involves recognizing followers' rights—including the right to privacy, autonomy, dignity, and justice—and ensuring these are met. Organizational justice is examined in this chapter because it is closely associated with these other rights.

The right to organizational justice consists of three concepts: distributive, procedural, and interactional justice (figure 9.2).

Studies confirm the practice of organizational justice builds follower trust and commitment, improves follower job performance, and fosters follower citizenship behaviors such as doing more than what is expected and having concern for the welfare of others. The citizenship behaviors cultivated through organizational justice have been shown to have direct effect on both employee relationships and customer relationships, where customers are treated with respect and feel valued and thus are loyal and satisfied (Cropanzano et al. 2007).

Figure 9.2. Organizational justice

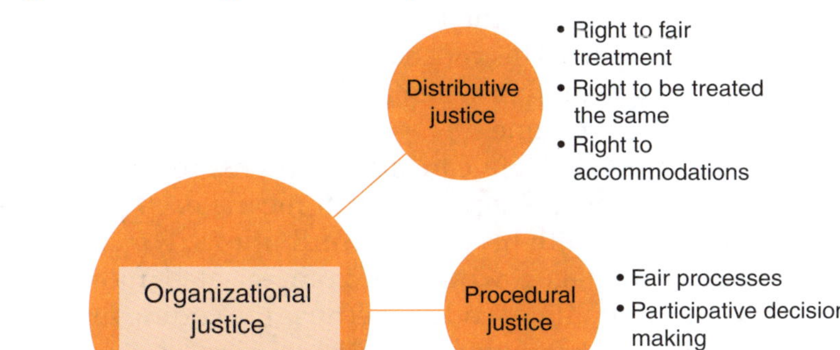

©Merida L. Johns

Each of the rights of organizational justice is summarized as follows.

Distributive Justice

Distributive justice ensures the appropriateness of outcomes (Cropanzano et al. 2007, 36). Distributive justice is related to equity theory that asserts individuals have the following rights:

- They are rewarded based on their level of contributions (equity)
- They are provided the same compensation for the same work (equality)
- They are provided a benefit based on one's needs (need) (Cropanzano et al. 2007, 36)

Distributive justice suggests followers have a right to fair treatment and an expectation that leaders treat everyone the same. Equity right requires a fair balance between follower inputs and outputs. Inputs are work quantity and quality, commitment, cooperation, loyalty, and their skill level, for example. Outputs consist of salary, benefits, job security, and recognition. Leaders, therefore, have an obligation to ensure that follower inputs are appropriately balanced for the individual and among individuals. The leader has a responsibility to ensure that the reward-to-effort ratio is consistent among all individuals. This means that one person should not be rewarded more than another when their value and contribution to an organization are the same.

There are three rules leaders can follow to ensure distributive justice. The first rule ensures equity, which means each person is compensated consistent with his or her contributions. For example, Michelle, a coding manager, would be compensated more than either John or Cathy, outpatient coders, because the coding manager has more responsibility than either outpatient coder.

The second rule guarantees equality, meaning each person is treated the same for the same contribution. For example, John and Cathy are both outpatient coders and are expected to meet the same quality and quantity criteria. The work of John and Cathy, therefore, will be evaluated the same, fulfilling the equality rule.

The third rule makes certain each person is treated in accordance with his or her personal requirements. For example, Cathy has physical needs requiring a quiet workplace and is accommodated by a separate work cubical, whereas John works in a common workspace because he does not have these needs.

Procedural Justice

Procedural justice is concerned with the processes used to determine outcomes, such as pay, benefits, and other compensation or recognition. Fair processes in work evaluation and handling employee complaints are two examples of procedural justice. Leaders can achieve procedural justice by using accepted and ethical best practices that are free from bias or discrimination and are applied consistently. Participative decision making is an additional component of procedural justice, where leaders provide opportunities for followers to have input on decisions that impact them. Studies show that procedural justice is related to building trust and loyalty with followers and increasing follower motivation (Cropanzano et al. 2007).

Interactional Justice

Interactional justice involves the leader's interpersonal behavior with followers. Interactional justice and has two components: informational justice and interpersonal justice. Informational justice refers to truthfulness and fairness in providing explanations for policies, decisions, and procedures that affect the follower. Interpersonal justice refers to treating followers with courtesy, dignity, and respect. Examples of interactional justice include exchanges such as giving a follower appropriate explanations for decisions, listening and paying attention to a follower's concerns, and showing empathy in difficult situations (Skarlicki and Folger 1997).

Contributors to Ethical Challenges

The leadership process is laden with many ethical challenges. Ethical challenges arise from the convergence of three dimensions activated by a trigger event called a critical incident (Chandler 2009). The first two dimensions that must be present in a leadership ethical challenge include the presence of a leader and a leader's follower. The third dimension is the situational context or the circumstance impacting the leader–follower relationship (figure 9.3).

Each of these dimensions includes several variables contributing to development of an ethical challenge. For example, leader variables

Figure 9.3. Dimensions of ethical challenge

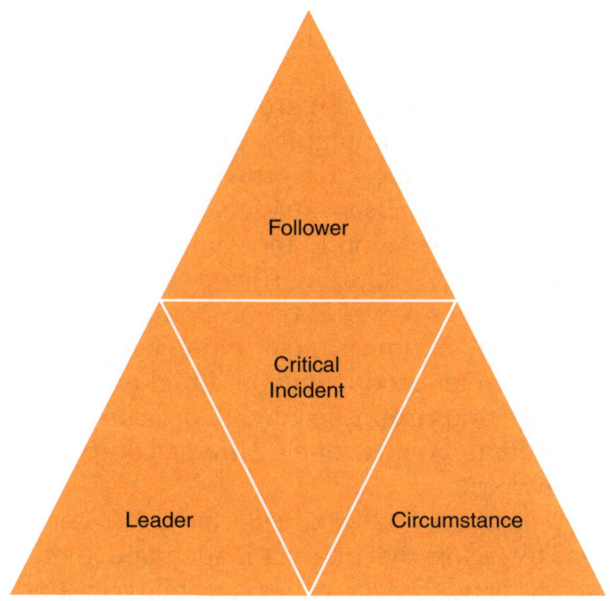

Adapted from Chandler 2009

may include healthy or unhealthy self-esteem issues, moral values or character weaknesses, personal stressors, or effective or ineffective personal skills. Follower variables include follower needs, rights, values, attitudes, and beliefs.

Studies show follower variables can influence leader behavior. In other words, leaders can be susceptible to follower judgments that contribute to leader unethical practices. For example, knowing that a work team dislikes one of its members, the leader fails to stand up for the rights of the member fearing a backlash from the rest of the team. On the other hand, followers are also susceptible to a leader's unethical behavior. For instance, followers can passively support unethical behavior as bystanders or can actively support leader unethical behaviors by condoning and participating in the unethical behavior. Support of the Nazi regime includes examples of both bystanders and active supporters of unethical behavior (Chandler 2009). In the healthcare realm, followers might passively support unethical billing practices.

The third dimension of an ethical challenge is the situational context or circumstance that influences the leader–follower relationship. The common factors include the amount of environmental uncertainty that exists, the degree of competitive drive, effectiveness of organizational processes and oversight, and previous organizational success (Chandler 2009). Each of these is explained as follows.

- *Environmental uncertainty*. Environmental uncertainty is caused by factors that create ambiguity. These include such things as organizational transition or growth, financial instability or duress, or weak or absent leadership. For example, a CEO misrepresents information to the company's board of directors when the company is faltering financially.
- *Extreme competitive drive*. Extreme competitive drive can be caused by overly optimistic goal setting and tight deadlines, or pressure for higher productivity and higher profits at any cost. Recall the previous example where Ford rushed to production of the Ford Pinto because of an extreme competitive drive and profit at any cost.
- *Ineffective processes or oversight*. Ineffective processes and oversight are caused by factors that produce inadequate feedback and communication channels, lack of responsibility and accountability mechanisms, insufficient checks and balances, and incomplete or

incorrect information. Healthcare contains numerous examples of accounting fraud due to inadequate monitoring of processes (oversight) and the lack of checks and balances within the organization.

- *Previous organizational success*. Previous organizational success can produce organizational complacency. This may lead to neglecting to update processes and organizational structures or lacking awareness of and response to environmental changes.

Ethical behavior exists within a complex environment and is determined by multiple factors. The interplay among these dimensions, each with their variables, contributes to the development of an ethical challenge requiring the leader to make a decision between the right and wrong actions in a specific circumstance.

Ethical Traps and Incidents

Awareness of the interplay among forces that create an ethical challenge is one of the first steps in grappling with ethical challenges. But the convergence of leader, follower, and situational variables only make the environment ripe for a critical ethical event or trigger. The variables do not by themselves cause the incident; what launches an ethical challenge is sometimes referred to as a critical incident, stimulus, or tipping point. The critical incident is "a thought, condition, intention, or event, which prompts unethical behavior," (Chandler 2009, 71). Sometimes the critical incident is an external stimulus (like an overly competitive environment), but it can also be internal to the individual (such as an intention to serve self-interests).

A critical incident can be viewed as a social-psychological trap that together with leader–follower and situational variables causes an individual or organization to take an ill-fated action. Critical incidents or ethical traps can fall into three categories: primary, defensive, and personality (Hoyk and Hersey 2008). The following sections provide a description and an example of each.

Primary Ethical Traps

Primary ethical traps are external situations that entice the leader to move in a direction without regard to the leader's ethical principles. These include obedience to authority, competitive drive, and self-interest. Consider the following example of the obedience to authority trap (AHIMA 2013).

> The HIM director of a regional health center is preparing for a Joint Commission review. The Commission has selected 20 closed records to review. The HIM director reviews each of them and finds several where the orders include the date but not the time they were ordered. The director reports this to the hospital Joint Commission coordinator who is also her manager. The manager berates the director: "Why was this not caught by HIM before now? You are going to take the fall for this one—not me! Go back to the physicians and get these orders timed." What is the ethical challenge for the HIM director and how might the director proceed?

An ethical challenge is created when leader, follower, situation, and the critical event variables converge. In this case, a leader–follower relationship exists within a hierarchical structure where there is an expectation the follower (the HIM director) will obey the authority figure (her manager). Follower variables include follower needs, rights, values, attitudes, and beliefs. In this case, the HIM director's obedience to authority conflicts with her value of honesty. The Joint Commission standards clearly require that the authentication of the date and time of physician orders must occur at or near the time of the event. The HIM director's value of honesty requires that she not follow her manager's directive to now add times to the orders. However, if she disobeys her manager her job, future promotion, or salary increase are potentially in jeopardy. The HIM director's ethical challenge is balancing her need for job security, her value of honesty, and doing the right thing.

The situational context converges with these other variables and plays a role in the developing ethical challenge. In this instance, appropriate processes that could have prevented the authentication failure did not exist or were not applied. A competitive environment to succeed at any cost may be an instrumental variable as well. For example, what would happen if the hospital was denied accreditation, or would be required to undergo a follow-up survey due to the authentication failure? The critical incident pulling these forces together is the manager's command to alter patient health records. In addition to the ethical challenge between needs and values, the social-psychological trap for the HIM director is blind obedience to authority.

Defensive Traps

Defensive traps are attempts to find easy ways to undo a wrongdoing that has occurred. They are traps that attempt to preserve one's self-interests. Frequently defensive traps involve trying to lessen guilt or shame (Hoyk and Hersey 2008). For example, excusing wrongdoing by falsely assuming the wrongful act is something everybody does, minimizing the wrongful act by comparing it to something that is worse, renaming the act (that is, "just a white lie"), or transferring blame to another. In the previous scenario there are several defensive traps the HIM director could fall into. If she altered the health records, she might justify her action as "everybody does this," or "in the big scheme of things this is a little transgression," or "I am just following orders," or "It is my boss's responsibility." In all cases, the defensive traps are attempts to hide or minimize the unethical behavior and actions.

Personality Traps

Personality traits—such as low self-esteem, or overuse or misuse of personal strengths—and social style such as competitiveness, need for control, and conflict avoidance are particularly susceptible to outside forces and make a leader more vulnerable to unethical behavior. The following scenario offers an example of a personality trap.

> Christine, a nurse, is a quality coordinator at a large health system. Her tasks include data collection and analysis and performing audits against specific quality measures. In a recent audit she notices that one physician consistently has more level 4 and 5 billing codes on his encounter form. Upon further inspection of the patient health records, her audit reveals that the codes were not justified in many of these instances. In the past this physician has praised Christine's work and she is now hesitant to speak to him about overbilling and reluctant to submit the current audit results. Christine fears that the physician will lower his opinion of her if she confronts or reports him. This is a case where Christine's low self-esteem (needing the approval of others) places her in a potential personality trap that may lead to unethical behavior.

Unethical behaviors can also result from the interaction of more than one ethical trap. For example, Julie works the evening shift in the clinical laboratory department with her co-worker Anne. One evening Anne has a family emergency and has to leave work early. She asks Julie if she will punch her time card for her at the end of the shift. Even though Julie empathizes with Anne, she knows she will be acting dishonestly if she punches Anne's timecard. Julie falls into a primary ethical trap and goes against her values and punches the time card for Anne. Because productivity levels were not met during the shift, the laboratory director asks Julie if she and Anne were on duty for the entire shift. Falling into a defensive trap, Julie lies and takes the easy way out to cover up her own dishonesty, compounding the ethical failure.

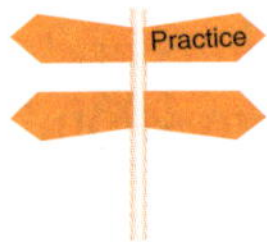

Apply Key Ethical Behaviors

In this chapter, *practice* means to apply ethical theories and to improve your development of ethical leadership behaviors in a leader role (for example, leading a class team, student organization, or community organization; or as a supervisor or manager in another capacity). Use the assessment in table 9.2 to cross-check your behavior and actions against some of the key concepts presented in this chapter. After your analysis, answer the questions that follow and identify where you can improve and set personal goals to do this.

1. Reviewing the assessment, what are your observations? In which areas can you improve?

2. Write down the areas in which you want to improve and the actions you will take to do so.

Table 9.2. Assessment of ethical leadership

Inclusive Leadership				
Inclusive Behavior	**Current Actions**			**How I can improve**
As a leader I :	**Always**	**Sometimes**	**Never**	
Listen to the concerns of my followers				
Ask my followers for input on policies or procedures that affect them				
Am interested in receiving feedback from my followers				
Treat my followers with courtesy and respect				
Give my followers autonomy to make decisions about how they do their work				
Solicit input from workgroup members before making decisions affecting the workgroup				
Recognize my followers' contributions to the team and organization				
Provide clear work goals to my followers				
Show interest in my followers progress and well-being				
Am fair and consistent with how I treat my followers				
Address the concerns of my followers				
Followership				
Attend to my followers' need to belong				
Validate the value of my followers				
Recognize the achievements of my followers				
Help my followers reach their full potential				
Allow my followers appropriate autonomy to make decisions				

(*Continued*)

Table 9.2. Assessment of ethical leadership (continued)

Inclusive Leadership				
Inclusive Behavior	**Current Actions**			**How I can improve**
As a leader I :	**Always**	**Sometimes**	**Never**	
Communicate to my followers that they contribute to a bigger purpose				
Organizational Justice				
Fairly balance inputs and outputs of followers in compensation considerations				
Ensure that followers are equitably compensated for the work they do				
Fairly evaluate the work of my followers				
Fairly and consistently apply policies to all my followers				
Am truthful with all my followers				
Provide clear explanations to my followers for decisions I make that affect them				
Provide clear goals and expectations to my followers				
Show my followers empathy when they are in difficult situations				
Ethical Traps				
Am aware of primary ethical traps such as blind obedience to authority, solely acting in my own self-interests, and winning at any cost				
Am aware of defensive ethical traps such as attempts to hide or excuse my wrongdoing				
Am aware of personality traps where I may overuse or misuse a personal strength or style				

References

American Health Information Management Association. 2013. Reality Check 2013: Ethical Issues in HIM. *Journal of AHIMA*. http://journal.ahima.org/2013/10/01/reality-check-2013-ethical-issues-in-him/

Burns, J. 2012. *Leadership*. New York: Open Road Media.

Chandler, D. 2009. A perfect storm of a leader's unethical behavior: A conceptual framework. *International Journal of Leadership Studies* 5(1):69–93.

Ciulla, J., ed. 2014. *Ethics, The Heart of Leadership*. Santa Barbara: ABC-CLIO, LLC.

Ciulla, J. 2005. The state of leadership ethics and the work that lies before us. *Business Ethics: A European Review* 14(4):323–335. http://www1.worldbank.org/publicsector/anticorrupt/LeadershipEthics/CuillaBEER06.pdf

Cropanzano, R., D. Bowen, and S. Gilliland. 2007 (November). The management of organizational justice. *Academy of Management Perspectives* 21(4):34–48.

Hollander, E. 2014. Further Ethical Challenges in the Leader–Follower Relationship. Chapter 3 in *Ethics, The Heart of Leadership*, 3rd ed. Edited by Ciulla, J. Santa Barbara: ABC-CLIO, LLC.

Hollander, E. 2012. *Inclusive Leadership: The Essential Leader–Follower Relationship*. London: Taylor and Francis.

Hoyk, R. and P. Hersey. 2008. *The Ethical Executive: Becoming Aware of the Root Causes of Unethical Behavior*. Stanford: Stanford University Press.

Maslow, A. 1943. A Theory of Human Motivation. *Psychological Review* 50(4):370–396.

Skarlicki, D. and R. Folger. 1997. Retaliation in the workplace: The role of distributive, procedural, and interactional justice. *Journal of Applied Psychology* 82(3): 434–443.

10 Advancing Diversity

In this book, *diversity* is defined as the presence of "a mixture of differences in age, religion, culture, gender, ethnicity, education, and more amongst a group of people within the same environment," (Rahim 2013). Diversity management can be defined as an organization's voluntary efforts for developing policies and practices designed to generate the inclusion of employees from different backgrounds into the formal and informal organizational structures and networks (Gotsis and Kortezi 2013). In today's global environment, organizational diversity—whether in the form of employees, customers, or stakeholders—is a fact. For example, breaking down the US workforce by ethnicity, 64 percent are white non-Hispanic, 16 percent are Hispanic, 12 percent are African American, and 5 percent are Asian. From a gender perspective, approximately 47 percent of the workforce are women and by 2020 the number of women in the workforce is expected to be greater than the number of men (Berns et al. 2012).

More than ever before, diversity management raises important ethical questions for leaders regarding equity and inclusion. Equity is the fair treatment of individuals and inclusion is the valuing of each individual's differences and contributions and practicing behaviors that support fairness and belonging. Several examples of ethical questions of equity and inclusion are provided in chapters 8 and 9.

Organizations have customarily taken a narrow perspective of diversity management limiting it to implementation practices that protect the organization from discrimination lawsuits and instituting job positions, such as diversity officer, to oversee mandatory equal employment practices. But such a superficial treatment of diversity has not solved issues of discrimination. It has not increased inclusive behaviors in leadership—accepting and valuing individuals for their unique characteristics and talents or including them in formal and informal processes for information access and decision making. For instance, women and racial and ethnic minorities remain underrepresented in board rooms, senior positions, and in certain key sectors despite diversity management initiatives. There has been debate whether this phenomena is due to lack of qualifications or discriminatory barriers. Studies have confirmed that while factors such as education and job training account for some of the gap, discrimination is also a key factor even though deliberate expressions of bias are constrained by anti-discrimination laws (Egaly and Chin 2010). In addition, taking a narrow perspective of diversity management as solely consisting of meeting legal requirements has not created inclusive and valuing organizational cultures.

This chapter examines diversity management beyond compliance and business imperative issues. It contrasts traditional perspectives of diversity management with contemporary thought about inclusive organizations and presents criteria by which an organization can measure its degree of inclusiveness. The chapter presents ethical frameworks for diversity management that provide an ethical foundation for supporting diversity and inclusion in the workplace and introduces the concept of implicit bias that is a frequent barrier to the practice of inclusive behaviors.

Traditional Perspective of Diversity Management

Equal opportunity legislation and affirmative action laws in the United States and many other countries require companies to follow nondiscriminatory hiring practices in regard to gender, race, and religion. Traditionally diversity management has been viewed as a compliance issue managed by an organization's human resource management (HRM) department. Company diversity management goals have frequently focused more on categorization of individuals and achieving specific numbers within a category rather than on developing an inclusive work environment that builds a culture of valuing and respecting differences (Gotsis and Kortezi 2013).

Beyond meeting legal requirements, companies have looked at the functional value of diversity from a limited business perspective of increasing performance through creativity and innovation and designing and delivering products and services to a diverse global market. This view fails to regard diversity from the perspective of leadership ethics where the focus is on helping both the individual and organization flourish. For example, one study of Fortune 500 companies found that diversity officers were seen as driving business success and performance by communicating the importance of diversity and creating and maintaining partnerships in diverse markets (Dexter 2010). This perspective has more foundation in creating a better bottom line for shareholders rather than in valuing the differences of the associates employed by these companies.

The increased popularity of diversity management has come from arguments that workforce diversity provides competitive advantage and is good for business (Shen et al. 2009). However, some studies show current practices have yielded contradictory results. In other words, diversity management as practiced does not always lead to increased performance and better outcomes. Focusing solely on a business case for diversity management has overshadowed its original intent of creating an inclusive environment in which individuals are accepted for their unique characteristics and are provided opportunities to fulfill their potential (Mor Barak et al. 2016).

Traditional diversity management practices usually include diversity as an organizational pillar within the corporate context. This is manifested most visibly in the form of organizational mission statements and strategy development that address diversity issues. Practices also include developing a diversity statement. An organization's diversity statement may affirm that the organization embraces diversity and considers it a top ethical and business imperative, providing examples of how the value of diversity is implemented by the organization. The diversity statement must be supported by specific diversity policies. These policies may include requirements for educating the organization's workforce about diversity; ensuring open pathways to promotion and management positions by selecting the best applicant for a job regardless of race, gender, age, or other non-merit factors; requiring that diversity criteria be included in business agreements; and establishing a formal diversity organizational structure that implements, measures, and monitors diversity policy.

Organizations routinely develop diversity and inclusion committees as part of the organizational structure to support diversity management. Diversity and inclusion committee responsibilities may consist of advisement, recommendation, establishment, or oversight of recruitment and retention policies, implementation of diversity training throughout the organization, and methods and programs for incorporating diversity into human resources and communication. The following is a summary of traditional diversity management best practices.

- Top leadership is committed to diversity throughout the organization.
- Diversity is incorporated into the organization's strategic plan.
- Diversity is linked to positive business performance.
- Diversity impact is measured by a set of quantitative and qualitative measures.
- Accountability for diversity into performance assessments and compensation of organizational leaders is incorporated.
- A succession pipeline for diversity is created by identifying and developing a diverse pool of talent for an organization's potential future leaders.
- A supply of qualified, diverse applicants for employment are attracted and recruited.
- Employees are involved in driving diversity throughout an organization.
- Diversity training to inform and educate management and staff is developed and implemented. (GAO 2005)

Companies also attempt to heighten diversity awareness using approaches such as providing diversity awards, broadcasting diversity successes, and appointing diversity managers. While these approaches may provide certain benefits such as raising awareness of biases—unreasoned and unfair opinions about a person or group—and changing norms around the expressions of bias and unjust or prejudicial treatment of others (discrimination), they also create an illusion of fairness of the treatment of underrepresented groups (Kaiser et al. 2013). Those in leadership positions wrongly perceive that the presence of a diversity program automatically makes an organization fairer for underrepresented groups. This thereby decreases leaders' estimation of discrimination in the organization and makes them less sympathetic to those who claim experience with discrimination. In other words, checking the boxes of a diversity management program checklist does not necessarily mean the outcomes of diversity and inclusion are achieved.

The conclusion of one group of researchers is that "although diversity management is big business in the United States, there is surprisingly limited research on the psychological effects of diversity initiatives or their effectiveness with regard to increasing diversity, promoting equity, or reducing bias," (Kaiser et al. 2013). Because of this void, the implications for leaders are that appropriate outcomes of diversity program must be identified and measurements of program effectiveness be developed, implemented, and analyzed.

As a result of this gap, some companies are broadening their view of diversity management and are differentiating between legal compliance and inclusion principles and looking toward more social responsibility in creating a culture of inclusiveness. Organizations are expanding the title of initiatives—from diversity management to diversity and inclusion management—to represent a more equitable, ethical, and inclusionary culture. The new title reflects organizations' awareness that meeting the legal requirements of nondiscriminatory practices or establishing a diversity program does not necessarily meet the criteria for ethical practice or achieve inclusion. The following section discusses principles and criteria that provide a baseline and specific examples for expanding diversity management and becoming more inclusive organizations.

Inclusive Management Principles and Criteria

An inclusive organization is defined much more broadly than a diverse one. It does not measure itself as successful by merely evaluating its track record on the number of recruited, employed, and retained individuals in certain groups based on ethnicity, gender, age, disability, or sexual orientation. Instead, an organization that meets the standard of diversity and inclusiveness is one that cultivates inclusiveness both within organizational boundaries and in its immediate community and beyond. An inclusive organization meets the following criteria.

- **"Values and utilizes individual and intergroup differences within its workforce."** This criterion refers to how an organization relates to its workforce. Meeting the criterion means the organization respects the cultural perspectives of its employees and strives to accommodate and incorporate these within the workplace. For example, a healthcare system may include as part of its values statement that it promotes respectful relationships among all of its employees, and that it delivers on this value through diversity training and by ensuring that there is an open pathway for promotion opportunities for all employees.

- **"Cooperates with and contributes to the surrounding community**." This criterion refers to the degree an organization connects and integrates with the community in which it operates, regardless of whether or not the organization derives profits from that community. Meeting this criterion means the organization acknowledges it has a responsibility beyond its financial stakeholders that extends to the community in which it is located. For example, a healthcare clinic may support a local nonprofit service organization by co-sponsoring a 5K run to raise funds for literacy.
- **"Alleviates the needs of disadvantaged groups in its wider environment**." In meeting this criterion an organization demonstrates that it values its social accountability by recognizing the disenfranchised as a potentially stable and upwardly mobile labor force rather than as disposable labor. This criterion may be exercised by an organization through collaboration with state or national initiatives to help disadvantaged populations such as the long-term unemployed, low-income families, welfare recipients, and domestic violence survivors. For example, a healthcare system may participate in a federal or state initiative such as the Temporary Assistance for Needy Families (TANF) program that helps recipients secure jobs to support themselves and their families.
- **"Collaborates with individuals, groups, and organizations across national and cultural boundaries**." An inclusive organization meets this criterion by demonstrating that it values collaborations across national borders and focuses not only on social responsibility at a local level, but on a global level as well. An example is a mental health practice that collaborates with an international nonprofit organization to provide training for mental healthcare professionals in a developing country. (Mor Barak 2014, 37)

The next section provides an opportunity to assess diversity and management by applying the principles and criteria identified in the two previous sections.

Assess Diversity and Inclusion Practices

Assess the status of diversity and inclusion management at your school or place of employment by doing the following:

- Obtain a copy of the diversity statement of your school or place of employment (usually available on the organization's website) and, if possible, their diversity plan.
- Compare the diversity statement to the diversity management recommendations of the Government Accountability Office (GAO) and the inclusion criteria presented by Mor Barak (2014) cited earlier in this chapter using the checklist provided in table 10.1.
- Given your assessment, would you categorize the statement as having both a diversity and inclusion focus? Explain your answer in the following space provided.

- If you were to rewrite the statement, what key additions would you make? Summarize these in the following space.

Table 10.1. Diversity statement assessment

Does the diversity statement include a reference to:	Yes	No	Comments
Leadership commitment to diversity			
Diversity incorporated into organization's strategic plan			
Diversity linked to positive business performance			
Diversity impact measured by a set of quantitative and qualitative measures			
Accountability for diversity incorporated into performance assessments and compensation of organizational leaders			
Commitment to developing a diverse pool of talent for an organization's potential future leaders			
Attraction and recruitment of a supply of qualified, diverse applicants for employment			
Employee involvement in driving diversity throughout an organization			
Development and implementation of diversity training to inform and educate management and staff			
The value and utilization of individual and intergroup differences within the workforce			
Recognition of social responsibility to the immediate community by cooperating with and contributing to the surrounding community			
Alleviation of the needs of disadvantaged groups in its wider environment			
Collaboration with individuals, groups, and organizations across national and cultural boundaries			

Ethical Frameworks for Diversity Management

Embracing an ethical context for diversity management has remained out of the mainstream for most organizations that have focused on a market-driven and compliance case for diversity. Furthermore, the relationship between diversity management and ethical theory has remained a relatively unexplored area in the management and organizational sciences. For example, organizations have rarely associated their diversity practices using virtue ethics or the ethics of care as guides (Gotsis and Kortezi 2013). However, researchers and ethicists are attempting to fill this gap by framing diversity management in ethical theory so that it is not justified as primarily a business imperative supporting the bottom line, but is a practice fundamental for ethical leadership (Gotsis and Kortezi 2013).

The following sections examine diversity management from the perspective of four ethical theories: utilitarian, Kantian, and virtue theories (discussed in chapter 8), and the ethics of care introduced in this chapter. The ethics of care theory focuses on the creation and maintenance of relationships among people. The chapter makes the case for applying non-utilitarian ethical theories to diversity management and suggests best practices for going beyond diversity and becoming an inclusive organization.

Utilitarian Theory and Diversity Management

The argument that diversity increases creativity, performance, and the organization's bottom line supports the position that diversity management be supported by the utilitarian theory. Utilitarian theory asserts that decisions about right or wrong should be based on whether the consequences of the decision are useful in helping the greatest number of people and maximizing human welfare.

If this perspective is true, what happens when diversity does not increase creativity, performance, and the organization's bottom line? Looking at a diverse workforce from purely tangible consequential benefits may make it ethical for one organization to implement diversity management, but not for another. For example, if the for-profit healthcare system A finds that having a diverse workforce boosts its profits, then diversity management is justified from utilitarian theory. However, if the for-profit healthcare system B finds that it does not achieve the similar benefits from a diverse workforce, then healthcare system B would not be ethically required to implement diversity management practices. Consequently, ethicists argue that utilitarian theory is not sufficient to support workforce diversity and diversity management practices because it does not ensure the rights of disadvantaged groups and individuals are adequately represented (Gotsis and Kortezi 2013). Therefore, from an ethical perspective, the foundation for diversity in the workforce must go beyond utilitarian theory.

Kantian Theory and Diversity Management

Another perspective is to apply Kantian theory as an ethical base for diversity management in the workforce. Using the rule-based principles of this theory, the universal maxim states that all people are equal and should be treated the same, for example, in recruitment, hiring, and evaluation practices. According to Kantian theory, whether or not an organization is practicing ethical behavior depends upon the motivation in following the rule. For instance, "We have a diversity program because we have an obligation to follow a moral rule that all people are equal," shows the organization's intent is to uphold a duty. If the motivation is based on self-interest, such as "We have a diversity program because it improves performance and increases the bottom line" the organization's actions are considered unethical. Strictly speaking, the organization has met criteria for implementation of the rule, but has not met the criteria for motivation for its actions.

The ethics of diversity and the progression of thought to inclusion management exceed the application of Kantian theory. Diversity by its very definition acknowledges differences among people with inclusion providing a valuing perspective of individual differences. Consequently applying a universal rule in recruitment, hiring, and evaluation to increase diversity does not address valuing the "otherness" of people and helping them fulfill their potential. In other words, it is not enough for an organization to implement practices that increase diversity but not address practices that value the uniqueness of individual workforce members and help each reach their potential.

Virtue Ethics and Diversity Management

A third ethical perspective applies virtue ethics as the foundation of diversity. Virtues are admirable characteristics that people ought to strive to achieve. Unlike the application of utilitarian theory, virtue ethics theory advocates that virtues such as humility, forgiveness, compassion, courage, justice, and temperance should be practiced for individual well-being and for the common good of the community and its members. Embracing a virtues-based foundation helps organizations develop practices pertaining to openness that support people in fulfilling their potential and helps workgroups develop positive interactions (Gotsis and Kortizi 2013). Virtue ethics surpasses utilitarian theory of positive consequences defined in terms of efficiencies and Kantian theory of ethical decision making based on a duty or obligation. Virtue ethics expands the scope of the ethical justification for diversity because it suggests that virtues should be practiced for individual well-being as well as for the common good of workgroups, the organization, and the greater community.

Ethics of Care

Ethics of care is a moral development theory that focuses on relationships among people. It is based on a mutual caring relationship that nurtures empathy and responsiveness to one's own needs and the needs of others. This ethical foundation supports practices such as recognizing all people should be given equitable treatment and opportunity. But it also emphasizes caring practices that accept the otherness of people and extends practices to help vulnerable groups and individuals develop higher levels of self-esteem. Applied to diversity management, ethics of care asserts that all workers have the potential for growth and encourages organizational practices that nurture growth so people can advance and flourish (Gotsis and Kortezi 2013). Application is therefore sensitive to all stakeholders (namely, workers, customers, and the greater community) and has a positive effect on the advancement and well-being of all social identity groups in the workplace. For example, the ethics of care supports all four criteria for an inclusive organization cited previously.

Self-Awareness and Implicit Bias

Diversity awareness and training try to help people learn about their own attitudes as a way of motivating positive change. However, diversity and awareness training are only successes to the extent that people are aware of their own biases, assumptions, and judgments about others. When these biases are unconscious, they are referred to as implicit and are thoughts and feelings outside of conscious awareness and control. Implicit biases play a role in how one feels about and acts toward others.

Being an authentic and ethical leader and applying emotional intelligence requires leaders to assess potential areas of blind-sightedness in self-awareness, self-control, social awareness of others, and in managing relationships (chapter 2). Project Implicit, in association with Harvard University, is a nonprofit organization and international collaboration between researchers who are interested in implicit bias. The goal of the organization is to educate the public about hidden biases and to provide a virtual laboratory for collecting data on the Internet. The project has several implicit bias assessments available online at no charge. Among these are assessments about beliefs and feelings about age, gender, sexuality, ethnicity, race, religion, and disability among others.

To raise your self-awareness of implicit biases, take one or more assessments (available at https://implicit.harvard.edu/implicit/) then answer the questions that follow.

- What did you learn from taking the implicit bias assessment? How has taking the assessment raised your awareness of your own implicit biases?

- What measures can you take to reduce your implicit bias? How will you do this?

The following section provides a scenario-based exercise that gives you the opportunity to apply diversity and inclusive management concepts.

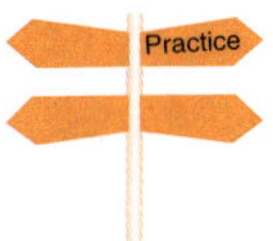

Applying Diversity and Inclusive Management Concepts

You are a manager in a large chiropractic organization that spans five states. You are a member of your organization's newly formed diversity and inclusion committee developed as part of an organization-wide diversity and inclusion management initiative. Part of the initial task of the committee is to develop the committee's mission, description of its purpose, and overview of functions. As a member of the committee you have been assigned to review the mission, goals, and activities of five different organization's diversity and inclusion committees and synthesize the similarities and differences among these. This information will provide your committee a varied perspective on the roles, functions, and responsibilities of an inclusion and diversity committee.

- To begin your task, search the Internet for three diversity and inclusion committee charters and the webpages of diversity and inclusion committees. Use figure 10.1 to help organize the collected information and then provide a brief summary of the similar elements throughout the charters and webpages that you believe your committee should consider when developing its mission, purpose, and functions.

- List the key elements included in the purpose and functions that are common across most of the charters and you think should be included in your committee's charter.

Figure 10.1. Summary of inclusion and diversity committee charters

Organization Name and URL	Committee Purpose
Primary Functions	
Organization Name and URL	Committee Purpose
Primary Functions	
Organization Name and URL	Committee Purpose
Primary Functions	

References

Berns, C., K. Barton, and S. Kerby. 2012 (July). The State of Diversity in Today's Workplace. Center for American Progress. https://cdn.americanprogress.org/wp-content/uploads/issues/2012/07/pdf/diversity_brief.pdf

Dexter, B. 2010. The Diversity Officer Today: Inclusion Gets Down to Business. Heidrick and Struggles. http://triec.ca/uploads/344/inclusion_gets_down_to_business_cdo_summ.pdf

Egaly, A. and J. Chin. 2010. Diversity and leadership in a changing world. *American Psychologist* 65(3):216–224.

Gotsis, G. and A. Kortezi. 2013. Ethical paradigms as potential foundations for diversity management initiatives in business organizations. *Journal of Organizational Change Management* 26(6):948–976.

Government Accountability Office. 2005. Diversity Management Expert Identified Leading Practices and Agency Examples. A Report to the Ranking Minority Member, Committee on Homeland Security and Governmental Affairs, U.S. Senate. January 2005. http://www.gao.gov/new.items/d0590.pdf

Kaiser, C., I. Jurcevic, T. Dover, L. Grady, and J. Shapiro. 2013. Presumed fair: Ironic effects of organizational diversity structures. *Journal of Personality and Social Psychology* 104(3):504–519.

Mor Barak, M., E. Lizano, A. Kim, L. Duan, M. Rhee, H. Hsiao, and K. Brimhall. 2016. The promise of diversity management for climate of inclusion: A state-of-the-art review and meta-analysis. *Human Service Organizations Management* 40(4):305–333.

Mor Barak, M. 2014. *Managing Diversity: Toward a Globally Inclusive Workplace*, 4th ed. Thousand Oaks, CA: Sage.

Rahim, E. 2013 (March 29). The Dilemma of Ethics and Cultural Diversity. http://www.coloradotech.edu/resources/blogs/march-2013/ethics-cultural-diversity

Shen, J., A. Chanda, B. D'Netto, and M. Monga. 2009. Managing diversity through human resource management: An international perspective and conceptual framework. *The International Journal of Human Resource Management* 20(2):235–251.

Part III
The Team Leader

Teams and teamwork are popular subjects in leadership because organizations are relying more and more on team leadership for systems, customer service, and product innovation. Since many organizations are committed to building team-based cultures, a leader's success is often attributed to the effectiveness of the organizational teams they lead. Peter Drucker, an internationally recognized expert, consultant, and author in leadership and management, for example, is attributed to saying that leaders who are most effective are ones that never say "I" because they think in terms of "we" and "team." These leaders take on the responsibility to make teams function, creating trust that enables the team to accomplish its work.

Since teams and teamwork are so critical to leader and ultimately organizational success, what are the practices and behaviors that make teams successful? How should teams be created, organized, coached, and managed? To answer these questions, the chapters in this part of the book examine historical and contemporary thought about teamwork and introduce several key actions and practices for supporting team success. While the traditional structure of teams, headed by a team leader, is the norm in many healthcare institutions, this book views team leadership more broadly as a responsibility of every team member. In other words, each team member has the obligation to actively execute leadership behaviors that ensure team success. Therefore, ethical leadership behaviors discussed in chapters 8, 9, and 10 are highlighted and aligned with the key actions and practices for team success suggested here.

Why Teams and Teamwork Matter

This book uses the definition of a team as "a small number of people with complementary skills who are committed to a common purpose, set of performance goals, and approach for which they hold themselves mutually accountable," (Katzenbach and Smith 1993). Teamwork here means the process where team members use their knowledge and skills in an effective, efficient, collaborative, and interdependent way to achieve a specific goal. Teams and teamwork are important in the workplace for many reasons. For example, for centuries people have known that cohesive workgroups performing interdependent tasks with common goals outproduce and outperform any random collection of individuals (Cooper and Kagel 2004). There is evidence of this every day in community organizations, churches, professional associations, athletic groups, and social institutions.

Another reason is that in today's world, businesses and organizations believe that creating interdisciplinary teams is the most productive approach for making large-scale improvements. Companies have learned that knowledge, experience, and information from a broad base of people who make up interdisciplinary teams are critical for decision making and execution of project work. Research also confirms this thinking. Study results show that companies with successful teamwork increase employee communication and involvement in decision making. This results in a company that is more flexible and can make changes more quickly and easily than companies who do not have cohesive teams (Mohrman et al. 1995).

Another benefit of teams is the learning and knowledge transfer that occurs among team members. Teams work more strategically than any one individual acting alone (Cooper and Kagel 2004). In addition, people who work in teams seem to feel better about decisions they make themselves and are able to implement those decisions more collaboratively as opposed to decisions that are made and promulgated by others (Rico et al. 2011). Businesses that use teams report improved productivity, safety, and worker attitude, and decreased absenteeism (Harris and Beyerlein 2003).

Besides these benefits to the organization, team members can profit individually from engaging in teamwork. For example, students who work in a collaborative learning work environment learn more, remember what they learn longer, and develop better communication, reasoning, and critical thinking skills through cooperative, team-learning experiences (Gokhale 1995). Likewise, workers who belong to well-functioning teams learn from each other and gain individual benefits such as receiving social support and increasing self-confidence.

So teams do matter and can deliver benefits to the organization and its workers, given one caveat: they must be high-functioning teams. Studies show that teams are either very good or very bad and there does not seem to be much in between. Teams either deliver the desired results or they do not (Harvard Management Update 2008).

What we know intuitively and what researchers have verified is that well-functioning teams do not just happen. Team success requires work and depends on two things: good leadership and effective management that includes planning, implementation, monitoring, and evaluation. Leadership and management are distinct from each other. Management focuses on maintaining the status quo, ensuring operational efficiency, and establishing order and consistency within organizations through the processes of planning, organizing, staffing, and controlling. Leadership, however, promotes opportunities for growth, innovation, and improvement, and fundamentally seeks to produce change. The management dimension of teams is addressed in this part of the book with the Key Action items and their associated activities. The leadership dimension of teams is examined by showing the connection of leadership ethics and ethical leader behaviors to the key action items and their activities.

Leading Teams

Creating, leading, and managing successful teams is not rocket science, but it does require that you develop the skills and learn the strategies for success. This part of the book presents the conditions that successful teams share and helps you integrate the skills and essential strategies with leadership behaviors that are necessary for high-performing teams. Each chapter is described briefly as follows.

Chapter 11: Key Actions of Successful Teams

This chapter introduces five conditions necessary for successful teams and provides an overview of how these conditions are met through nine key actions.

Chapter 12: Creating and Organizing Successful Teams

This chapter covers the fundamental organizing principles for successful teams including how to develop team beliefs, set expectations, clarify the team mission, and establish operating norms of behavior.

Chapter 13: Leading the Team to Success

This chapter focuses on what it means to use leadership behaviors that coach and motivate people and to constructively handle conflict to fulfill their potential and be members of successful teams.

Chapter 14: Managing and Leading Teams

Supportive structures must be in place to help teams be successful. These are a combination of processes and tools. But leadership behaviors that help the team leverage their complementary skills to achieve a common goal are essential in effectively supporting these processes. This chapter examines how the integration of management and leadership ensures team success.

References

Cooper, D. and J. Kagel. 2004. Are two heads better than one? Team versus individual in team signaling games. *American Economic Review* 95(3):477–509. http://www.econ.ohio-state.edu/kagel/teamsd.finalAER.pdf

Gokhale, A. 1995. Collaborative learning enhances critical thinking. *Journal of Technology Education* 7(1):22–30.

Harris, C. and M. Beyerlein. 2003. Team-Based Organization Creating an Environment for Team Success. Chapter 10 in *International Handbook of Organizational Teamwork and Cooperative Working*. Edited by West, M., D. Tjosvold, and K. Smith. West Sussex: Wiley.

Harvard Management Update. 2008 (February 28). Why Some Teams Succeed (And So Many Don't). https://hbr.org/2008/02/why-some-teams-succeed-and-so-1

Katzenbach, J. and D. Smith. 1993. The discipline of teams. *Harvard Business Review* March-April 1993:111–119.
Mohrman, S., S. Cohen, and A. Mohrman. 1995. *Designing Team-Based Organizations: New Forms for Knowledge Work*. San Francisco: Jossey-Bass.
Rico, R., R. Alcover, C. Tabernero. 2011. Workteam effectiveness: A review of research from the last decade (1999–2009). *Psychology in Spain* 15(11):57–79.

11 Key Actions of Successful Teams

Successful teams do not happen by chance. In fact, successful teams are the result of practicing good management and leadership behaviors. This chapter provides an overview of specific actions that are evidence of good leadership. Specifically, ethical leadership behaviors such as establishing trust with others, treating others with respect, providing an environment that allows for the input and consideration of everyone, implementing shared decision making, clarifying role expectations, and allowing for open communication are among the leadership behaviors supported by the actions reviewed in this chapter.

While most teams usually have an appointed team leader responsible for the general oversight of team activities and outcomes, successful teams have team members who practice good leadership behaviors as well. In other words, successful teams result from good leadership behaviors of both the team leader and team members. Together the team leader and the team members create the synergy that yields positive relationships, ethical behavior, and productive outcomes.

Previous chapters have discussed good leadership behaviors associated with authenticity and ethical leadership (chapters 1 and 8). While these are essential leadership behaviors to be practiced in all leadership situations, there are several other behaviors considered necessary for leading successful and productive teams. Authorities in team leadership generally agree that there are a number of things that contribute to successful teams. These have been summarized as five essential conditions (figure 11.1) and are described here.

- A team must meet the definition of a team—a group of designated people with complementary skills who are given the authority to perform a specific task and who work collaboratively.

- A team must have a compelling direction. The mission, purpose, and what is to be achieved is clearly communicated and understood by the team.
- A team must have an enabling structure in which to perform their work. This means developing an organizational structure, planning for the right mix and right number of people, and establishing norms of behavior. The organizational structure must facilitate, not impede the work of the team.
- A team must work in a supportive organizational context and receive recognition for their work as well as resources to ensure their work is supported.
- A team must receive coaching on group process and interaction. Teams must be orientated sufficiently, build shared commitment, and be provided feedback on their progress to help them continually strive to improve working together as a cohesive group. (Hackman 2002, 41)

Organizations can meet these five conditions by supporting the success of teams in several ways. The following are nine key actions to help ensure the conditions for successful teams are met (Johns 2007). An overview of each of these actions (figure 11.2) is provided in the next section and is described in more detail in chapters 12 through 14.

Figure 11.1. Five conditions for successful teams

Meets team definition
Compelling direction
Enabling structure
Supportive context
Team coaching
Conditions for successful teams

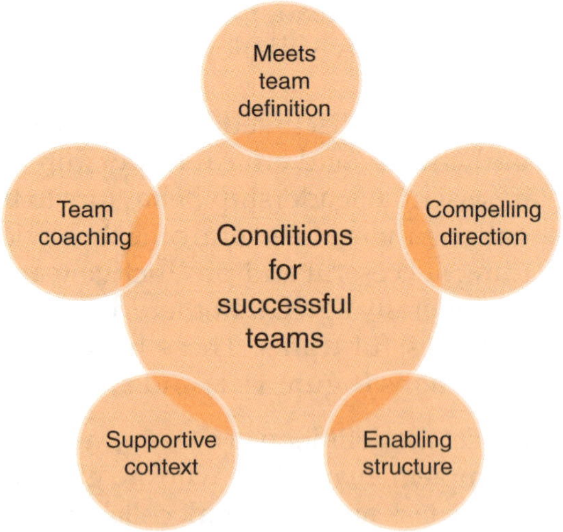

Adapted from Hackman 2002, 41

Figure 11.2. Key actions of successful teams

©Merida L. Johns

Key Action 1: Solidify Team Belief and Trust

A successful team believes that the simultaneous actions of separate team members together have greater total effect than the sum of their individual parts (Johns 2007). Trust and cooperation are the foundation for the success of any team, but in business there has been a tradition from the industrial era work culture of the 1800s that has promoted rewarding individual effort. In this culture, the usual work contract is the exchange of individual labor for individual pay. Theories such as Taylor's scientific management, Skinner's behavioral model, and Maslow's hierarchy of basic human needs view the manager–worker association as a parent–child relationship where workers perform their jobs without deviation and are motivated by adherence to rules and survival needs (Koulikov 2006). Even though the modern work environment requires autonomous teams, accepting a change to a team-based workforce still remains a challenge. The perception "I have my job and I am paid for my own efforts," lingers for some workers. A common feeling in work teams is, "I do not want anyone else to profit from the work I put into a project." Or, "I do not want someone else getting a raise or better evaluation review because of my work." These attitudes must be overcome before a work team can function effectively (Koulikov 2006). To do this, team members must embrace a belief in the value of the team and trust each other. Solidifying team belief means that each team member accepts the following premises.

- A team is a group of individuals but is also a social entity.
- A team works toward a common goal, and the tasks that members perform are interdependent.
- Each member of the team acknowledges and respects the contribution of every other team member.
- Each member of the team contributes information, perspective, experience, and competencies to achieving the common goal.

One way of establishing team belief and trust is through team orientation that includes team building activities (chapter 12). Use of values, personality, and style assessments—such as the Values in Action (VIA) assessment (chapter 1)—can help team members to understand each other and build trust. Establishing trust and respect is a fundamental tenant of leadership (chapter 9), and trust and respect among team members can be fostered through a formal agreement on behavior norms, expectations, and team mission and purpose documented in a team charter (all discussed in chapter 12).

Key Action 2: Align Team Talents and Size to Tasks

A high-powered team matches team members' knowledge, skills, and abilities and the size of the team with the tasks to be accomplished. Many work teams fail because the group composition is inappropriate. For example, the team might be too large or too small, or the team does not have the right mix of skills to complete the project. Work teams must be the correct size, include the right talents to accomplish the tasks, and have members diverse enough to learn from one another (Hackman and Walton 1986).

The following should be considered when creating a team.

- **Team size**. There is no conclusive research that recommends a specific team size; it depends on several variables including the tasks required, time frame for project completion, and available resources. When teams are too large, communication and coordination become more complex. In large teams it is harder to create a culture of trust among members. This may result in cliques developing within the team. When teams are smaller, member performance levels are better (Mueller 2012, 124). Although the number of team members depends upon the work task, a team of five to six is ideal.

- **Right talents**. A highly competent person who is matched with the wrong task can throw a team into a tailspin. Likewise, team members who do not have the required competence can negatively affect how a team functions. Work teams must contain the correct skill sets to perform team tasks.
- **Heterogeneity**. Having a diverse team composed of a mixture of skills and skill levels provides opportunities for team members to learn from each other and distribute work appropriately (Johns 2007, 16).

Chapter 12 provides specific actions for organizing teams so that ethical leadership behaviors are applied that maximize respect for each team member, ensure each member's strengths and values are appreciated, and cultivate an inclusive environment.

Key Action 3: Define Team Mission and Establish Goals

A high-functioning team defines its mission and identifies its goals to achieve purposeful work, coordination of effort, and efficient use of resources. It is difficult to get somewhere if you do not know where you are going. Yet teams often fail because they have no clear mission or have not identified their goals (Hackman 2002).

Effective work teams require a clear direction and stated mission, which are covered in detail in chapter 12. A mission statement defines the team's purpose, identifies whom the team serves, and specifies the team's values about service, quality, and teamwork. Clear, achievable goals are the companion pieces to the mission statement. Goals make teamwork purposeful, enhance coordination, and provide a basis for follow-up and reward. Goal statements usually specify a level of performance, a deadline, or an objective. For example, for an information systems project that requires the team to develop a database that tracks release of patient information, the following are possible goals:

- Within four weeks, deliver a relational database that tracks release of patient information in compliance with HIPAA (Health Insurance Portability and Accountability Act) standards.

- Within six weeks, develop an end-user interface that permits data items to be entered, deleted, or modified in the database.
- Within eight weeks, develop a user manual that trains users to enter, delete, or modify data items in the database.

Generally, there are several benefits to setting a clear direction and establishing team goals (Seijts and Latham 2006). First, goals keep the team focused on what is relevant to the mission and purpose of the team. Goals like those mentioned help prevent the team from digressing, doing unnecessary work, and wasting time. Goals also help the team allocate the appropriate amount of effort to the project. In the example given, the team knows that members must complete three different tasks and that each of these has a specific deadline. Another advantage is that goals keep the team motivated by laying out a roadmap of what needs to be done. Knowing and meeting these goals helps to keep team morale high. All of these benefits support participative leadership behaviors and communication necessary to maintain trust and respect (chapter 9).

Key Action 4: Value Personal Style and Diversity

A high-powered team is composed of and values members with different work experience, personalities, and decision-making and social styles. Teams of people with a variety of perspectives, experiences, areas of expertise, personal styles, and strengths can be more successful than those without member diversity, provided the diversity is appropriately aligned and managed effectively (Joshi and Jackson 2003).

However, team diversity is not enough for a work team to succeed. For example, a team may consist of people of different ages, gender, and experiential, educational, and cultural backgrounds, but if the team does not respect the strength that diversity provides, the team is unlikely to become a cohesive, productive, and successful workgroup. When team members do not understand that people receive information, form opinions, and communicate with others in different ways, conflict can easily surface and lead to poor performance. For example, some people are excellent information gatherers but poor innovators. Others may be great at generating new ideas but are weak with implementation. When teams understand the various work and decision-making styles of their team members, the teams will do their best work (chapter 12).

One way for team members to value and respect diversity and individuality is to identify their individual strengths, social style, and emotional intelligence using assessment tools. Some of these (such as the VIA) have been discussed in part 1 of this book. When team members use the results of these tools they can form a team that performs more smoothly (Varvel et al. 2003).

Key Action 5: Establish Team Norms

A successful team establishes team norms and a means for holding each team member accountable to those norms. For example, the team member who arrives late for or skips meetings, does not complete work on time, or completes work at the last possible minute frustrates other team members and disrupts teamwork. This type of behavior leads to low team morale and poor work performance, and results in interpersonal conflict. To counteract these types of behaviors, teams should establish requirements for behavior called team norms. Chapter 12 addresses different types of norms and how to develop them.

Team norms are patterns of behavior and activities that create ground rules for how team members will interact. A norm is a system of shared values, beliefs, and control systems to produce patterns of behavior. Norms have several benefits for work teams:

- They communicate what behavior is expected.
- They help maintain order.
- They eliminate having to rethink every action.
- They provide a sense of security. (Buchholz and Roth 1987)

It is difficult to hold individuals accountable for their behavior without written norms that team members have agreed to follow. Team norms should be developed when the team is organized. If the team does not identify expected behaviors from the start, it is harder to return to a cohesive working group when behaviors become disruptive.

Team norms can be divided into the following categories:

- **Meeting norms** address when, where, and how often to meet, as well as expectations of attendance, timeliness, and preparation.
- **Relationship norms** set expectations for how team members treat each other.
- **Communication norms** explain how information is exchanged during meetings and outside of meetings, and what listening, information sharing, and communication behaviors are expected.

- **Leadership norms** define the accountability of each team member for ensuring balanced participation and input from all members, and guide the team in making consensus decisions, resolving conflict, and keeping the team focused and on-task.
- **Decision-making norms** establish the expectations and ground rules for making team decisions.
- **Conflict-management norms** are the ground rules for avoiding unhealthy disagreements and arguments.
- **Task-related norms** outline expectations for quality of work, timeliness, and workload distribution standards.

Establishing team norms is an example of practicing ethical leadership behaviors such as promoting open communication, establishing role clarification, and encouraging mutual respect and shared decision making.

Key Action 6: Conduct Productive Meetings

Successful teams conduct productive meetings by identifying meeting purpose and desired meeting outcomes and by using process controls to conduct meetings. About half of all meeting time is wasted (Williams 2012). While meetings play an important role in team communication, planning, and control, meeting mismanagement can result in wasted time, frustration, deflated energy, conflict, and lowered team morale.

Inefficient meetings share several characteristics. Among these are poor preparation, inadequate agendas, insufficient facilitation, ineffective decision making, rambling discussions, and domination by a few members. Unproductive meetings are primarily due to deficient process in planning and managing meetings, and this is correctable. Process measures that can help in making meetings more efficient and effective include well-developed agendas, documented meeting results in well-prepared minutes and other meeting documentation pertinent to the meeting agenda, and use of meeting and behavioral norms developed by the team.

Well planned and managed meetings demonstrate leadership behaviors that create trust and respect among people, create an environment that allows for the input and consideration of opinions of others, and provide opportunity for shared decision making. Techniques for leading successful meetings are covered in chapter 14.

Key Action 7: Promote Communication and Cooperation

Successful teams use behaviors to promote and encourage open communication and cooperation. Successful teams work well together because they use constructive communication techniques, such as exercising personal and social awareness, respecting others, listening to others, and having empathy for others (chapter 2). Ineffective teams allow communication problems to produce stress and tension among team members, which lowers productivity (Montebello 1994). For example, when there is poor communication there are information gaps. Without information, people sometimes make assumptions and try to figure out things based on their own experience and knowledge. They create explanations for why an individual may have acted in a particular manner and misunderstandings occur when people act on these unsupported assumptions. The most threatening assumptions to teamwork involve the motives of others—why a team member did or did not do something.

To function at a high level, teams must have open communication with no hidden agendas and team members need to share information with each other (chapter 13). Team communication and collaboration can be established by refraining from using impeding behaviors such as judging, manipulating, and controlling.

Teams can build communication by using constructive communication behaviors that demonstrate emotional intelligence (chapter 2) and ethical leadership (chapter 8) such as these:

- Speaking candidly
- Listening
- Acknowledging others' views
- Discussing similarities and differences in views
- Explaining perceptions
- Negotiating agreement

Key Action 8: Manage Conflict

Successful teams manage conflict through mutual respect, willingness to resolve disputes, and effective communication. Conflict such as disagreements about decisions and differences in opinions and perceptions frequently occur in work teams. Conflict in a work team can have a disruptive effect if it is not managed correctly (McDaniel et al. 1998). Unmanaged conflict can severely damage team energy and relationships, as well as task accomplishments.

It may be surprising, however, to learn that several benefits can result from conflict, which is a driving force of change. In fact, the work of a team depends on conflict in order to thrive and prosper (Lencioni 2002,99). The key is to manage conflict. When teams manage conflict, many positive results occur. New ideas and creative problem solving can result from managed conflict.

How is conflict best managed in work teams? Teams should not necessarily reduce conflict since it is fundamental for change and innovation, but should learn how to handle it constructively (Rayeski and Bryant 1994). To do this, team members must respect one another and be willing to resolve disputes. In addition to other key actions items mentioned, an effective way of handling conflict in teams is using communication techniques such as learning to confront others constructively, listening to others' concerns, acknowledging opposing perspectives, and responding appropriately. Chapter 13 provides ways of managing conflict using a variety of communication and other techniques.

Key Action 9: Manage the Project

High-powered teams use effective techniques to organize, define, plan, and manage the project.

Simply mastering the eight actions already discussed will not create a winning team. To be effective, the eight key actions must be integrated within a comprehensive plan that manages the total team project. This means the team leader, working with all team members, needs to put into practice the eight action items along with techniques to identify what work needs to be done, when it will be done and how to keep it on schedule, and who will do it. Techniques are examined further in chapter 14.

Work teams are successful when they use the following steps to organize and manage their teams and ensure success. The following descriptions of each of the steps show how many of the key action items are incorporated as well as additional techniques to help plan project work and keep it on schedule. Figure 11.3 provides one of many ways the relationship among the nine key action items and the steps for team organization and management may be viewed.

Figure 11.3. Relationship between key actions and key steps for successful teams

Create the team	Organize the team	Conduct productive meetings	Define the project	Plan the project	Manage the project	Finish and evaluate the project
Align team talents and size to task	Solidify team belief and trust	Value personal style and diversity	Define team mission and establish goals	Define team mission and establish goals	Define team mission and establish goals	Define team mission and establish goals
Define team mission	Define team mission and establish goals	Establish team norms	Establish team norms	Establish team norms	Establish team norms	Establish team norms
Value personal style and diversity	Value personal style and diversity	Promote communication and cooperation	Promote communication and cooperation	Promote communication and cooperation	Promote communication and cooperation	Promote communication and cooperation
	Establish team norms	Manage conflict	Manage conflict	Manage conflict	Manage conflict	
	Promote communication and cooperation					

Step 1: Organize the Team

Team organization involves several key actions such as solidifying the team belief and aligning team size and talents to the project. Team-building activities and various assessments are used to construct team belief and identify the competencies and work and personal styles of each team member. Team organization consists of selecting the team leader, identifying team member responsibilities, and developing written team norms.

Step 2: Develop Team Charter

Once the team is organized and ground rules for operation are established, a team charter should be developed. The team charter usually serves as a contract among team members, the project sponsor, or the project client. Policy on who creates the document and how it is prepared varies among organizations. Many elements compose a team charter; some of these have already been described—such as developing the team mission, goals, and norms—and others will be described in chapter 12.

Step 3: Conduct Productive Meetings

Team meetings are an essential part of making decisions and getting work done. However, a lot of wasted time and effort can result from poorly managed meetings. An effective team is one that makes sure it has effective meeting processes that yield positive outcomes. Chapter 12 provides details on how work teams can use simple techniques that result in highly productive meetings.

Step 4: Define the Project

One of the most common stumbling blocks preventing teams from succeeding is not clearly defining what work needs to be accomplished at the beginning of the project. Defining a project provides a common understanding among all team members of the extent and nature of the project.

Step 5: Plan the Project

Once the team is organized and has developed its charter and defined the project, it is time to details how the project will be carried out. Time and again, teams fail because they have not taken time at the very beginning of the project to identify the tasks to be completed, timeframe, resources, and communication mechanisms needed. To be successful, the team must attend to the details.

Step 6: Manage the Project

Managing project work involves tracking the team's progress in meeting its goals. The team should hold interim meetings to assess task status and completion, scheduling, and resources needs. In team meetings, identify problems and determine if task schedules and assignments need readjustment. Interim team reports that document the continuing status of the project function as internal communication for the team. Project status reports are usually used as a means of communication to stakeholders outside of the project team and document progress to date compared with the original project plan.

Step 7: Finish and Evaluate the Project

Once the project is completed, the team performs a number of wrap-up activities such as preparing a final project report and conducting a post-project evaluation review.

Assess Key Actions

Chapters 12, 13, and 14 provide additional details and activities for assessing and implementing each of the nine key actions for team success. The following activity gives you an opportunity to assess the success of past team experiences and identify where the team could have improved. This assessment and diagnosis of past team challenges prepares you for the following chapters in understanding how implementing the key actions contributes to team success.

1. Think about two team experiences you have had in the past—one that you consider successful and one that you consider unsuccessful. Write a brief synopsis of each of these in the space that follows.

Successful Team Experience: Describe what made this team successful. How were the positive outcomes achieved and how did the team work together?

Unsuccessful Team Experience: Describe why this team was not successful. Were goals not achieved? What challenges in working together did the team face?

2. Use table 11.1 to evaluate and contrast the successful and unsuccessful team experiences as detailed in the previous question. On a scale of one to five, with five being the best, rate each team on how they applied each of the key action items for a successful team. Then answer the questions that follow.

Table 11.1. Evaluation of team experience

Key Action Item	Successful Team	Unsuccessful Team
Solidify team belief and trust	1 2 3 4 5	1 2 3 4 5
Align team talents to size and task	1 2 3 4 5	1 2 3 4 5
Define team mission and establish goals	1 2 3 4 5	1 2 3 4 5
Value personal style and diversity	1 2 3 4 5	1 2 3 4 5
Establish team norms	1 2 3 4 5	1 2 3 4 5
Conduct productive meetings	1 2 3 4 5	1 2 3 4 5
Promote communication and cooperation	1 2 3 4 5	1 2 3 4 5
Manage conflict	1 2 3 4 5	1 2 3 4 5
Manage the project	1 2 3 4 5	1 2 3 4 5

1. How do the assessments between the two teams compare? In which areas were there major differences?

2. Which action items do you believe contributed the most to the successful team? Why do you think these had the most impact?

3. For the unsuccessful team, what contributed most to its failure? Performing which action items would have prevented a catastrophic failure?

4. For the successful team, in which areas could the successful team have improved? If you were the team's leader, where would you focus your efforts to help the team be even more successful?

Implement Key Actions

Use table 11.2 to identify opportunities for implementing key actions for team success.

Table 11.2. Opportunities for implementing key actions

Team	Key Action	Positive Impact	Implementation

- Make a list of three of your current teams.
- For each team, identify one key action that would make the team operate more smoothly and be more successful.
- Explain why this key action would create a positive impact.
- For each key action, how would you plan to implement that action for the team?

References

Buchholz, S. and T. Roth. 1987. *Creating the High-Performance Team*. New York: John Wiley and Sons.

Hackman, J. 2002. *Leading Teams*. Boston: Harvard Business Review Press.

Hackman, J. R. and R. E. Walton. 1986. Leading Groups in Organizations. In *Designing Effective Work Groups.* Edited by Goodman, P.S. San Francisco, CA: Jossey-Bass.

Johns, M. 2007. *Creating, Coaching, and Managing High-Powered Teams.* Raleigh: Lulu Press.

Joshi, A. and S. Jackson. 2003. Managing Workforce Diversity to Enhance Cooperation in Organizations. Chapter 14 in *International Handbook of Organizational Teamwork and Cooperative Working.* Edited by West, M., D. Tjosvold, and K. Smith. West Sussex: Wiley.

Koulikov, M. 2006. Facilitation of Teams in the Context of Modern Industrial Development. http://www.themedfomscu.org/media/team_building_articles.pdf

Lencioni, P. 2002. *The Five Dysfunctions of a Team A leadership Fable.* San Francisco: Josey-Bass.

McDaniel, G., S. Littlejohn, and K. Domenici. 1998. A Team Conflict Mediation Process that Really Works! In *The International Conference on Work Teams Proceedings: 1998.* Edited by Bullock, M., C. Friday, K. Belcher, B. Bisset, S. Hurley, C. Fotte, and D. Thai. Denton, TX: University of North Texas, Center for the Study of Work Teams.

Montebello, A.R. 1994. *Work Teams that Work Skills for Managing Across the Organization.* Minneapolis: Best Sellers Publishing.

Mueller, J. 2012. Why individuals in larger teams perform worse. *Organizational and Human Decision Processes* 117(1):111–124.

Rayeski, E. and J. Bryant. 1994. Team Resolution Process: A Guideline for Teams to Manage Conflict, Performance, and Discipline. In *The International Conference on Work Teams Proceedings: Anniversary Collection. The Best of 1990–1994.* Edited by Beyerlein, M. and M. Bullock. Denton, TX: University of North Texas, Center for the Study of Work Teams.

Seijts, G.H., and G.P. Latham. 2006. Learning goals or performance goals: Is it the journey or the destination? *The Ivey Business Journal* 7(5). http://iveybusinessjournal.com/publication/learning-goals-or-performance-goals-is-it-the-journey-or-the-destination/

Varvel, T., S. Adams, and S. Pirdie. 2003. A Study of the Effect of the Myers-Briggs Type Indicator on Team Effectiveness. https://www.researchgate.net/publication/266881677_A_Study_of_the_Effect_of_the_Myers-Briggs_Type_Indicator_on_Team_Effectiveness

Williams, R. 2012. Why Meetings Kill Productivity. https://www.psychologytoday.com/blog/wired-success/201204/why-meetings-kill-productivity

12 Creating and Organizing Successful Teams

When assembling a group of people to work on a specific task, one should first ask the question, "Does this group meet the definition of a team?" This book defines a work team as a group of designated people with complementary skills who are given the authority to perform a specific task and who work collaboratively (chapter 11). These characteristics make a team different from a group of people who come together for an event, a meeting, or are part of a task force (Grigsby 2008). For example, a group of people who assemble for a meeting or event may not have complementary skills, performance standards, or hold each other mutually accountable for outcomes. The same is true of a task force, which is a group of individuals usually with the same expertise that convene to provide advice or recommendations, but who do not necessarily have performance standards or hold each other mutually accountable for work products or outcomes. Thus, in designating a group of people as a team the leader must ensure that specific standards and the definition of a team are met.

Once a team is created, it needs to be organized. From a management perspective, organizing a team involves designing the team structure, identifying the team operational processes, and providing the resources required for the team to reach the desired goals (Swensen 2016). All of these activities must be supported by ethical leadership behaviors such as honesty, trustworthiness, fairness, principled decision making, open communication, and role clarification (chapter 8). This chapter provides an overview of the activities and key actions for creating and organizing successful teams and determining team readiness. Operational processes and team resourcing are covered in subsequent chapters.

Creating the Team

Three of the key action items discussed in chapter 11 directly apply when a team is created. These include:

- Key Action 2: Align team talents to size and tasks
- Key Action 3: Define team mission and establish goals
- Key Action 4: Value personal style and diversity

Usually teams are created by a manager, referred to as the team sponsor. For example, a chief information officer may create a team to develop computer safeguards for a specific information system. Or a corporate director of health information management (HIM) may create a team to develop coding audit policies and protocols and monitor their implementation. When a team is created, the sponsor should apply a specific standard that defines the characteristics a team should meet. The foundation for successful teams includes the following:

- Consist of two or more individuals
- Perform tasks relevant to organizational strategy
- Establish common goals
- Interact socially through norms, roles, and expectations
- Have interdependent tasks among its members
- Maintain and manage boundaries in regard to project scope
- Include boundaries and constraints set by the organization
- Engage in exchanges with other units in the organization (Kozlowski and Bell 2001, 6)

When the team is created, characteristics such as these are used as a template by the team sponsor or by the team itself to measure if there is a foundation for success. For example, are the team mission and purpose clear so that the constraints and boundaries the team operates within are well-defined? Are the team's authority and responsibilities spelled out? Has the team sponsor assigned the appropriate number of people to the team who have the right mix of complementary abilities and skills to achieve the team's mission and goals? And, finally, is there an allocation of sufficient resources to support the team's work? This includes, for example, an adequate budget and supporting personnel and infrastructure. The following sections describe activities supporting key actions 2 and 3.

Align Team Talents to Size and Task

Having team members with the right abilities and skills to achieve the team's mission is essential to team success. This seems to be a common sense statement, but many teams fail because of the wrong skill mix. Skills can be defined as specific talents such as programming, coding, or statistical expertise; and specific knowledge and abilities can be defined as constructs such as personal style, personality, and strengths. For instance, it would be expected that the members of a team whose mission is to identify gaps in the security protections of an enterprise computer network would have a mixture of network and computer security skills, knowledge of HIPAA (Health Insurance Portability and Accountability Act) security provisions, and project management skills. A mix of personal styles and strengths (chapter 1) would also help balance the team and ensure team success. For example, having some individuals on the team who are detail oriented and including others who are strategic thinkers would provide a diversity of perspectives, insights, and ideas for accomplishing the team mission.

Define Team Mission

Successful teams have a compelling direction and know their mission. A mission statement is created by high-level organizational management or the team's sponsor and is a brief summary that describes why the team is formed and its purpose. The following are examples of clearly written mission statements developed by teams.

- The mission of the MERIT team is to develop prototypes of computer applications that meet the quality and functionality specifications of our organizational clients and to manage these so that they are delivered on time and within budget.
- The New Learning Team effectively uses its team's capabilities for designing and implementing continuing education programs that are commissioned by our organizational clients and that

meet educational development standards and the quality and delivery expectations of our clients. (Johns 2007)

Notice how a compelling direction, team boundaries, and shared goals are contained in each of the mission statements. In the case of the MERIT team, the team's purpose is limited to developing prototypes of systems for organizational clients. This means the MERIT team does not develop operational systems and does not develop prototypes for anyone except the organization's clients. In addition, the MERIT team's prototypes must meet quality and functional specifications of its organizational clients and the team must deliver the prototypes on time and within budget.

There are several benefits of a clear mission. First, it energizes and motivates the team because members know what they are working toward. When a team knows their end goal, they stay more committed and will likely continue working toward the goal. Second, a compelling mission establishes direction and focuses the team's attention and action, keeping them on track and doing what is important to achieve outcomes. When everyone on the team has a collective focus, it is less likely that the team will get sidetracked in the wrong direction. Finally, clarity of direction and mission helps ensure the team's talents are used appropriately. This is because the members' complementary skills are aligned with the appropriate work to achieve the team's goals (Hackman 2002).

Usually the team direction and mission are set by the team sponsor. However, this is not always the case. Sometimes the mission may be set by the team leader or the team itself. Whoever sets the direction and mission, however, must have the legitimate organizational authority to do so (Hackman 2002). A team develops goals in order to carry out its mission. Goal setting is part of key action 3. How goals are identified and developed is part of organizing the team and is described in the next section.

Organizing the Team

Before any other work is done, the team must organize itself into a unified group, and establish trust and team belief. Four of the key actions described in chapter 11 directly apply to team organization:

- Key Action 1: Solidify team belief and trust
- Key Action 3: Define team mission and establish goals

- Key Action 4: Value personal style and diversity
- Key Action 5: Establish team norms

The following section describes team organization challenges and is followed by examining ways these are commonly addressed in organizing a team into a unified working group.

Challenges to Team Organization

Several challenges often present themselves in the team's organizing phase. These include previous experiences with teams, bias against teamwork, and uncertainty (Johns 2007).

Previous Team Experience

Previous team experience plays an important role in how individual team members react to being part of a team. Team experiences have been poor for many workers. One study, for example, found that 75 percent of cross-functional teams are dysfunctional (Tabrizi 2015). Workers usually report that the common problems causing team dysfunction include such things as

- High degree of conflict
- Lack of communication
- Social loafing (lack of accountability)
- Dissatisfaction
- Lack of clear goals

These experiences create a preconceived notion that teams cannot work well and present a significant challenge in creating a unified and cohesive team.

Bias Against Teamwork

Even without prior poor teamwork experience, it is very possible that some team members have a bias against working on a team. They may object to working in teams because most of their work experience is based on individual effort. They feel uncomfortable helping others or seeking help themselves. Some team members may hold views such as

- I do not want my co-workers evaluating me
- I want to keep my knowledge, skills, or information to myself
- I do not want to make mistakes in front of other people

Other times previous team experience forms the bias against teamwork, because some team members may have worked together and have formed opinions such as

- I do not get along with these people
- These people do not understand me
- These people are not organized
- I would get the job done better by myself than working with these people
- Jane (or John) is obnoxious
- Jane (or John) always thinks she (he) is right

These kinds of attitudes produce reluctant team members and are more reflective of an individual's view of the world rather than his or her skills or abilities. In these cases, team building and establishing team norms (discussed later in this chapter) and coaching (discussed in chapter 13) by the team leader is essential in reframing the individual's views.

Uncertainty

When a team is formed there is usually uncertainty. Even when there is an attempt to select team members based on a specific set of skills, it is unlikely that everyone knows each other's personality and work styles, work background, or personal interests. Uncertainty is frequently expressed by team members asking themselves questions such as

- Will I fit in with this team?
- Who are these other people?
- Can we work well together?
- What will I be responsible for?

Solidifying team belief through team-building exercises, establishing team norms, defining roles and responsibilities, and practicing effective communication helps to overcome many of these challenges.

Meeting Team Organization Challenges

To counter the biases and uncertainty concerning teamwork discussed previously and to establish a trust relationship, the following activities should be key agenda items for completion during the team's first few meetings.

- Solidify team belief
- Establish team goals
- Understand the personal styles of team members
- Develop team charter

Solidify Team Belief

For centuries, cohesive workgroups with interdependent tasks and common goals have proven that they can outproduce and outperform any individual or any random collection of individuals. For team success, team members must embrace the belief that the team has value. This is called *team belief*. Elements of team belief include:

- Seeing the team as a social entity where team members experience a sense of belonging, have interdependencies among each other, and interact with each other through agreed upon norms
- Committing to achieving a common goal
- Acknowledging that each member of the team adds information, perspective, experiences, and competencies to achieve a common goal
- Accepting the interdependency of the tasks and each member's dependence on others on the team
- Respecting the contribution of every team member (Johns 2007)

Team-building exercises are used to build team belief by demonstrating how a wide level of support helps to achieve a common goal, how tasks are interdependent, and how trust among team members is essential for team success.

Establish Team Goals

Goals are the companion pieces to the team mission statement. To accomplish the team's mission, goals are usually developed by the team. A goal specifies action and includes a specified level of performance and time frame for achievement. Goals must be attainable (not impossible) and relevant to the team mission. Goals help keep the team focused. For example, look at the following goals developed by one work team whose mission was to create a relational database application for an in-house organizational client. Notice how the goals are specific and attainable and support the team's mission.

- Deliver a relational database solution on time and within budget that meets 100 percent of client functional and usability needs.

- Follow department standards for design and development of relational databases 100 percent of the time.
- Provide an excellent customer experience, responding to phone calls, e-mails, and other requests within 15 minutes, 98 percent of the time.
- Work together efficiently as a team of professionals, following team norms and ethical practices 100 percent of the time.

In establishing specific goals team members are practicing ethical leadership behaviors by providing clear communication of expectations and role clarification that consequently results in a higher level of trust within the team.

Value Personal Style and Diversity

Another critical activity in organizing a team is to provide ways for each team member to understand the personal styles and strengths of every other team member. This understanding helps strengthen the team, match style and strengths to team tasks, and helps reduce conflict. Teams consist of people with different experiences, areas of expertise, and personal styles. Some team members may be idea generators, others may be implementers, and still others may be detail oriented. While diversity makes teams strong, it can also cause conflict that leads to poor performance when team members do not understand that differences exist in the way people receive information, form opinions, and communicate.

Everyone on a team needs to value and respect the strength that diversity brings to the team. Equally important, teams must recognize that if they lack certain traits, it will be difficult for them to complete, or in some cases to begin, tasks. For example, if a team is composed of members who are strong as idea generators but has no members who excel as implementers, then likely the team will have difficulty in translating ideas into action. Several types of tools are used to determine how people view their world and how they make decisions. Three of these include:

- Strengths assessments: Assess an individual's unique combination of strengths. The Values in Action (VIA) survey examined in chapter 1 and the Clifton Strengthsfinder® are two examples.
- Behavioral style assessments: Assess an individual's preferred behavioral style and usually categorizes it into one of several

styles. Each style demonstrates a preferred way of acting, thinking, and making decisions. Examples of assessment instruments that measure behavioral style preferences include Social Style®, and DISC®, among others.

- Personality inventories: Assess an individual's unique characteristics such as sociability, competitiveness, conscientiousness, adaptability, and stableness. Examples of these type of assessments include Myers-Briggs Type Indicator® and the Big Five Inventory (BFI).

Many of the popular personality assessments are based on the work of Carl Jung, Isabel Briggs Myers, and Katherine Briggs and describe four psychological types. Each psychological type has two styles, and each style has a descriptive tag. The four psychological types and styles of each include the following.

- *What environment (world) do you prefer?* Do you prefer being out in the world and being with people (extrovert)? Or are you more comfortable being alone and doing things on your own (introvert)?
- *How do you prefer to handle information?* Do you prefer to have all the facts, look at details, and then form a big picture (sensor)? Or do you like to see the big picture first and then find out the facts (intuitive)?
- *How do you like to make decisions?* Do you like to make decisions with your head, analyze the pros and cons, and be logical in decision making (thinker)? Or do you like to make decisions with your heart and are most concerned with maintaining harmony (feeler)?
- *Do you like things structured or unstructured*? Are you task oriented, like to get things done, and prefer to avoid rushing before a deadline (judger)? Or do you like to be unstructured and casual and are stimulated by an approaching deadline (perceiver)?

It is not difficult to understand that conflict can occur among team members who have opposite psychological types. For example, a sensor who likes to look at details before forming the big picture would likely conflict with an intuitive who likes to see the big picture first before dealing with details. It is also clear that if all team members have the same style, completing tasks might be difficult. For example, if everyone on your team is a perceiver deadlines may not be met.

Develop the Team Charter

A team charter is a written agreement among team members about the team's mission and goals, and the ground rules for operating as a team. The charter is a powerful document because it gives purpose and direction to the team and delineates boundaries and expected behaviors. Specifically team charters prompt teams to

- Ensure they have a team mission and objectives
- Identify individuals or groups who have a stake in the project, outcome, or functions of the team
- Ensure that team members' strengths, weaknesses, and work styles are identified
- Clarify team member roles and responsibilities
- Determine how the team will function; for example, identify practices for decision making, communication, and accountability
- Stipulate how the work of the team is done; for example, develop norms of behavior and policies
- Determine how to handle communication within the team and to stakeholders
- Establish how performance will be evaluated (Mathieu and Rapp 2009, 92)

Figure 12.1 is an example of a team charter that includes these noted elements. Notice how the team's name reflects the team's mission. Team goals are clearly and concisely stated and are associated with specific outcomes. Norms and behaviors have been identified so that all team members are aware of the expectations for performance.

Since the charter includes the purpose and direction of the team, it should be the first activity the team completes after solidifying team belief, establishing goals, and understanding personal styles. The team charter must be specific to the team, not a boilerplate, and reflect the team's purpose and values of team members. The charter's power comes from discussions and agreement on the team's ground rules. Similar to other team creation and organizing activities, development of a team charter demonstrates the use of ethical leadership behaviors for establishing trust and respect, role clarification, and open communication.

Figure 12.1. Sample team charter

Team Charter
Our team charter is an agreement among our team members about our team mission and goals, and the ground rules for behavior, operation, and management of the team.
Date Approved: 12/01/2017
Team Members: S. Davis, M. Caldwell, H. Baxter, J. Preston, W. Holden, E. Monroe

Team Name
Revenue Cycle Efficiency Team

Team Mission
Develop a relational database application that tracks claims at every checkpoint and provides a dashboard and metrics for assessing revenue cycle efficiency and management.

Team Goals (specific actions with performance levels and time frames)

- Deliver a relational database solution on time and within budget that meets 100 percent of client functional and usability needs
- Follow department standards for design and development of relational databases solution 100% of the time
- Provide an excellent customer experience, responding to phone calls, e-mails, and other requests within 15 minutes, 98 percent of the time
- Work together efficiently as a team of professionals, following team norms and ethical practices 100 percent of the time

Norms (behaviors and ground rules for team interactions)

Meeting norms (ground rules for team meetings)

- Meets every Tuesday from 8:00 to 9:00 a.m. and meetings start and end on time
- Minutes are taken for each meeting and archived in the electronic team notebook
- Agendas are prepared by team leader and distributed 48 hours in advance of meeting
- Meetings follow agenda
- All members will be on time and no interruptions (namely, cell phones)
- No one member will dominate discussions; The "pass the pencil" technique will be used
- Topics outside the agenda will be noted in the "Parking Lot" and scheduled for a later time

Relationship norms (expectations for how team members treat each other)

- We will treat each other with respect
- We will ask questions when in doubt
- We will acknowledge and respect the value of each team member
- We will leverage the strengths of each team member
- We will listen to and consider the opinions of others

Communication norms (ground rules for regular contact with each other for information and idea exchange)

- Communication outside of meetings is on designated team intranet group site
- Respond to e-mails or phone calls within 2 hours

Leadership norms (behaviors for promoting fairness, team work balance, and cooperation)

- Work is distributed evenly among members
- Tasks are assigned to leverage skills, abilities, and strengths of members
- Be flexible in meeting unplanned challenges and accept workload changes
- Perform weekly evaluation of team progress and member contribution

Figure 12.1. Sample team charter (continued)

Decision-making norms (ground rules for making decisions) • Strive for consensus decisions • Prioritize options • If consensus cannot be achieved then decisions are made by majority vote
Conflict-management norms (guidelines for handling and avoiding dysfunctional arguments and conflict) • Be transparent; no hidden agendas • Share and do not withhold information • Address issues, not persons or personality • Ensure each member's voice is heard
Task-related norms (responsibility for assignments) • Tasks are completed on time and with acceptable quality • Come prepared to meetings • Ask for input or help if task is unclear or if assistance with completing it is needed • Alert team if there is time slippage with a task • Assist other members in meeting deadlines due to unplanned challenges
Team roles (list responsibilities of team leader, secretary, historian, and other roles and name individuals assigned to each role) • Team Leader: Responsible for facilitating each meeting; preparing agendas; communicating with project sponsor and administrative lead; preparing and submitting interim reports; developing project timeline; monitoring project status; overseeing budget; adjusting project milestones and assignments due to unplanned circumstances; archives all project materials in group site team notebook • Secretary: Responsible for taking meeting minutes and distribution of same within 48 hours of each meeting; archives meeting minutes in group site project notebook • Members: Responsible for self-evaluation; completing assigned project tasks; meeting deadlines, and preparing documentation, such as DFD, ERDs, Use Cases that meet organization standards; complying with all team norms
Signatures of team members

Team Name

Naming and identity go hand-in-hand. The team name reflects the attributes that are important to the team's mission and goal. Research shows that project branding puts teams in a better position to achieve their goals (Brown et al. 2011). Project branding is creating a name or symbol that differentiates a project from others and identifies what the project is, what it does, and what it intends to accomplish. While branding consists of more than a name, the first step in identifying the brand of a team is its name. The team or project name should express what the team is to accomplish and why this is important. Take the following scenario as an example.

A corporate HIM director was the lead for a master patient index (MPI) clean-up. The project name was "The MPI Clean-Up Project." When asked by the healthcare chief executive officer (CEO) what the business case for the project was, the director responded: "When duplicate records in the MPI are reduced, the revenue cycle efficiency increases." When asked about the project's impact on patient care was, the director responded: "When duplicate records in the MPI are decreased, patient safety increases." Given this scenario, the CEO suggested a better name for the project might be "Patient Safety and Identity Management Project" or "Revenue Cycle Efficiency Project."

Descriptive names based on business cases, quality, or other outcomes provide better brand identity for the project while demonstrating how the project supports key organizational initiatives. Clarification of how the team and its project support the organization is evidence of ethical leadership behaviors of clarifying roles and engaging in open explanation. Ethical leadership of working toward a higher purpose and common good beyond the team is clearly communicated in a descriptive name that reflects how the team's work supports larger organizational goals. Furthermore, this type of naming strategy demonstrates ethical leadership behavior for motivating people. Most would prefer being assigned to the "Patient Safety and Identify Management Project," instead of the "MPI Clean-up Project."

Team Mission and Goals

The team mission and goals established earlier in the team creation and organizing phases are incorporated into the team charter. Including these into the charter codifies and clarifies the team's purpose and what it is expected to achieve.

Establish Team Norms

Team norms are patterns of behavior and activities that form the ground rules for how team members will interact and work together. Norms publicize a system of shared values, beliefs, and controls that moderate team behaviors. Norms are the way a team manages member behavior.

Norms are also an important strategy for minimizing situations where team members do not carry their fair share of the work.

Besides these important elements, norms provide a benchmark for evaluating how well each team member works on the team and how well the individual contributes to the project. Throughout the life span of the team, teams can evaluate how well the team and each of the team members does in meeting each team norm. Norms are usually included as a section within the team charter (figure 12.1). Various types of norms are discussed as follows.

Meeting Norms. Meeting norms address when, where, and how often to meet, and expectations of attendance, timeliness, and preparation. The following are some examples of meeting norms developed by teams.

- Team meetings will be held every Tuesday morning from 7 a.m. to 8 a.m.
- The team leader will facilitate team meetings.
- Team members are expected to:
    - Attend all meetings
    - Be on time to meetings
    - Come prepared to participate in meetings by completing meeting preparatory work
- A meeting will have an agenda developed by the team leader. The meeting agenda will be distributed by e-mail to all team members at least two days in advance of each team meeting.
- Minutes will be kept of all team and sub-team meetings and distributed to all team members within three days after the meeting.

Relationship Norms. Relationship norms set expectations for how team members treat each other. The team develops relationship norms to ensure that all members are treated equitability and with respect. The following are examples of relationship norms developed by teams.

All team members will:

- Maintain a superior level of professionalism by not bringing personal issues into a team meeting, listening to and acknowledging the ideas and opinions of others, and being honest and trustworthy
- Contribute ideas and solutions
- Recognize and respect the differences in personal style of others

Be flexible and respect the partnership created by the team and strive to achieve a win-win situation where action considers both group and individual interests

Communication Norms. Communication norms are behaviors and activities related to how team members exchange ideas and information and maintain contact with each other. Contact information, including phone numbers, e-mail, and addresses (that is, work or home address if it is a virtual team), for all team members should be gathered and placed in the team charter.

Frequent problems arising in work teams are the result of poor communication among team members. To reduce potential conflict, communication norms are developed. The following are examples of communication norms developed by work teams.

- The primary form of communication among team members is a dedicated Web bulletin board that is accessible to all team members at all times. Every team member is expected to check the bulletin board each weekday, read and make appropriate posts, and attach project files.
- The secondary means of communication includes e-mail and telephone. The project leader will be copied on all project-specific e-mails. The initiator of a phone call must log a summary of the call on the Web bulletin board.

Leadership Norms. Leadership norms include team member and team leader responsibilities for promoting fairness, balance, and an environment conducive for collaboration. Teams that have leadership norms are less likely to engage in unhealthy conflict. The following are examples of leadership norms developed by teams.

Every team member is expected to:

- Ensure that the team is striving for excellence in all facets of the project
- Guide the team in making consensus decisions, resolving conflict, and keeping the team focused on its task
- Create an environment that is conducive to open participation

Decision-Making Norms. These norms are expectations and ground rules for making team decisions. It is important that the team decide ahead of time how decisions are going to be made.

Knowing the basis for decision making reduces misunderstandings and conflict. The following two examples illustrate decision-making norms from two different teams.

- The team leader will seek consensus from team members on decisions affecting the outcome of the project or management of the project. When agreement cannot be reached by consensus, the decision will be determined by majority vote of those present at the meeting.
- Decisions made at team meetings: All decisions affecting the outcome or management of the project will be determined by majority vote of team members. All votes must take place during regularly scheduled team meetings with at least three of the five team members present.

Conflict-Management Norms. Ground rules for avoiding disagreements and arguments are called conflict-management norms. Teams that use conflict-management norms are more likely to engage in healthy debate rather than arguments. The following are examples of conflict-management norms.

- Do not interrupt another member.
- Acknowledge valid points made by team members.
- Accept all ideas as valid when presented.
- Build on each other's ideas.
- Do not dismiss any idea without exploring it.
- Do not engage in personal attacks with another member.
- Call for a break in the meeting if discussions are heated or going in circles.

Task-Related Norms. These norms include behaviors related to team member responsibilities for task completion. Specific task-related norms may be assigned to the team leader and to team members. The following are examples of task-related norms.

- The team leader is responsible for:
  - Developing and distributing meeting agendas
  - Facilitating team meetings
  - Coordinating team tasks
  - Maintaining the team notebook containing all project documentation
  - Submitting weekly written reports to the project sponsor

- All team members are responsible for:
    - Completing tasks on time at a high-quality level
    - Coming prepared to all meetings
    - Participating in all meetings, sharing information, and providing input
    - Ensuring a balanced workload among team members

Assign Team Roles

Teams assign specific tasks for organizing, monitoring, and evaluating work to ensure the team runs smoothly. This is accomplished by developing an organizational structure to delegate these responsibilities to people on the team. The type of project determines what key roles are needed. For example, in a complex project where the team might consist of seven or more members, there may be a team leader and several sub-project leaders. In smaller teams, there may be a team leader and a team secretary. At the minimum, every team should have a team leader and a team secretary.

The leader of a team should be a collaborative leader. This is different from leaders in a hierarchical structure. The collaborative team leader guides rather than controls and motivates rather than directs. Collaborative leaders safeguard the process (the norms established by the team) and facilitate interaction (Carter 2006). Team leaders are usually responsible for the following activities:

- Preparing and distributing meeting agendas
- Facilitating team meetings
- Guiding activities of the team
- Making team assignments
- Coordinating team activities
- Tracking team progress

Documentation is an important part of team function. Documents such as agendas, meeting minutes, progress reports, timelines, and evaluations must be maintained in a team notebook. The team historian or secretary can be responsible for collecting and keeping all of these materials together. The team notebook is usually maintained for a designated period of time, serving as the official document of how team work was conducted. Each organization should have standards for maintenance and retention of the team notebook, which can be in paper or electronic form. Organizational standards will dictate what electronic platform is used and how team members can edit, update, and store and retain electronic documents, images, or other digital materials.

Meeting minutes must be taken for every team meeting by a team secretary. Some teams rotate the secretary task among all team members, with the exception of the team leader. This gives all members experience in the task and balances the workload. At the beginning of the project, the team makes the decision to rotate the function or give it to a specific team member for the entire project.

Assessing Team Readiness

Use the checklist in table 12.1 to assess a student team, work team, volunteer group team, or other team you have been part of. Answer the questions in the checklist to determine the degree of the team's readiness for success based on how well the team was created and organized. After completion of the checklist answer the questions that follow.

- On a scale of 1 to 10, with 10 being the highest state of readiness and 1 being the lowest state of readiness, how ready do you believe your team was for success? Explain your evaluation.

- Use table 12.2 and list two or three problem situations your team encountered. Assess these situations against the checklist. Were there specific actions from the checklist your team could have performed that would have mitigated or avoided the problem situation? If so, explain. If not, explain what other actions the team should have taken to avoid the problems that occurred.

Table 12.1. Team readiness checklist

Team Readiness Characteristics	Yes	No	Uncertain
Does the team meet all the characteristics required for success such as: • Consists of two or more individuals • Performs organizationally relevant tasks • Shares common goals • Interacts socially through norms, roles, and expectations • Has interdependent tasks • Maintains and manages boundaries • Has boundaries and constraints set by the organization • Engages in exchanges with other units in the organization			
Is there a clearly written team mission?			
Are there specific written goals that focus on achieving the team mission?			
Is there an appropriate mix of team skills to perform team tasks?			
Is team size appropriate to achieve the team mission?			
Is team belief and trust established?			
Have team member strengths and styles been assessed?			
Have team norms been developed?			
Has a team charter been developed and signed by team members?			

Table 12.2. Team readiness evaluation

Problem statement	Actions that could have mitigated or avoided the problem	Explanation of how actions could have mitigated or avoided problem

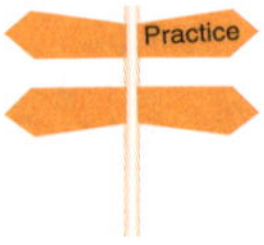

Create and Organize a Team

Creating and organizing a team includes developing member socialization so that members have a sense of identity and belonging and develop trust among one another. Team-building exercises and development of the team charter are ways socialization is accomplished. The following exercises provide an opportunity to engage in team-building exercises and development of a team charter.

Team-Building Exercises

There are many team-building exercises that are available free of charge. Two of these are from the National Aeronautics and Space Administration (NASA). Use the team exercises from NASA to build team belief with a current team or in the future for a student, work, volunteer, or other team you may join. See http://www.nasa.gov/pdf/166504main_Survival.pdf.

Team Charter Development

The team charter is a consolidation of all the activities for creating and organizing a team. The following exercise gives you the opportunity to apply the information and techniques described in this chapter to create and organize a team. Use the template in figure 12.2 to create a team charter with your team members for an upcoming or current student, work, volunteer, or other team.

Figure 12.2. Team charter template

Team Charter Our team charter is an agreement among our team members about our team mission and goals, and the ground rules for behavior, operation, and management of the team. **Date Approved:** **Team Members:**
Team Name

Figure 12.2. Team charter template (continued)

Team Mission
Team Goals (specific actions with performance levels and time frames)
Norms (behaviors and ground rules for team interactions)
Meeting norms (ground rules for team meetings)
Relationship norms (expectations for how team members treat each other)
Communication norms (ground rules for regular contact with each other for information and ideas)
Leadership norms (behaviors for promoting fairness, team work balance, and cooperation)
Decision-making norms (ground rules for making decisions)
Conflict-management norms (guidelines for handling and avoiding dysfunctional arguments and conflict)
Task-related norms (responsibility for assignments)
Team roles (List responsibilities of team leader, secretary, historian, and other roles and name individuals assigned to each role)
Signatures of team members

References

Brown, K., R. Ettenson, and N. Hyer. 2011 (June 22). Why Every Project Needs a Brand (And How to Create One). *MIT Sloan Management Review*. http://sloanreview.mit.edu/article/why-every-project-needs-a-brand-and-how-to-create-one/

Carter, M. 2006. The Importance of Collaborative Leadership in Achieving Effective Criminal Justice Outcomes. Center for Effective Public Policy. Department of Justice National Institute of Corrections.

Grigsby, K. 2008 (January). Committee, Task Force, Team: What's the Difference? Why Does It Matter? *American Physician and Scientist*. https://www.aamc.org/download/164730/data/grigsby_committee_task_force_team.pdf

Hackman, J. 2002. *Leading Teams*. Boston: Harvard Business Review Press.

Kozlowski, S.W.J. and B.F. Bell. 2001. Work groups and teams in organizations. In *Handbook of Psychology*. 12:333–375. New York: Wiley-Blackwell. http://digitalcommons.ilr.cornell.edu/articles/389/

Johns, M. 2007. *Creating, Coaching and Managing High-Powered Work Teams*. Raleigh: Lulu Press.

Mathieu, J. and T. Rapp. 2009. Laying the Foundation for Successful Team Performance Trajectories: The roles of team charters and performance strategies. *Journal of Applied Psychology* 94(1):90–103.

Swensen, D. 2016. Managing and Leading During Organizational Change. In *Health Information Management: Concepts, Principles, and Practices*, 5th ed. Edited by Oaches, P. and A. Watters. Chicago: AHIMA.

Tabrizi, B. 2015 (June 23). 75% of Cross Functional Teams Are Dysfunctional. *Harvard Business Review*. https://hbr.org/2015/06/75-of-cross-functional-teams-are-dysfunctional

13 Leading the Team to Success

Thorough preparation in creating and organizing a team lays the foundation for team success, but it is not enough to guarantee success. Other elements that support the team members and team work must be put in place. These elements include executing an enabling structure and processes that help move the team from point A to point B such as planning, tracking and decision-making processes, communication plans and processes, and adequate resources to support achieving the team's mission.

In addition to these managerial activities, exercising good leadership behaviors that encompass both moral and technical excellence (chapter 8) is fundamental to team success. The leadership role of cultivating a shared vision and inspiring and motivating others frames the leader as a coach, and one who exercises these behaviors is referred to as a leader-coach. This chapter focuses on what it means to use leadership behaviors that coach and motivate people to fulfill their potential and covers ways of handling team conflict. Many of the strategies used for coaching can be applied to managing team conflict. Both coaching and conflict management ultimately support team success and their related leadership behaviors apply not only to the formal team leader, but to all members of the team.

The Leader-Coach

When thinking about a sports team, not only do people know the team member names, but they also know the coach's name. In fact, the coach's identity may even transcend and live longer in one's memories than any one player on the team. The coach not only has an impact on team strategy and technique, but also on the team's performance and earning (Zetou et al. 2016). The role of the leader, like the coach, is to direct strategy and ensure the appropriate structures (techniques) are in place to support achieving the strategy. And like the coach, the leader has an important role in supporting the team so that they deliver the highest performance. "Coaching is a key resource for optimizing potential for both individual achievement and for high-performing, sustainable team excellence" (Kimsey-House et al. 2011, xi). In other words, the leader who exercises coaching behaviors helps team members develop personally and positively contribute to the team and, ultimately, to the organization. These leader-coaching behaviors support the following key actions for successful teams (chapter 11):

- Key Action 7: Promote communication and cooperation
- Key Action 8: Manage conflict

The next sections provide an overview of coaching principles and skills that support leadership behaviors of respecting and valuing others, listening to their input and concerns, and motivating them to be the best they can be.

Coaching Principles

Coaching uses a set of professional tools and a unique way of communicating (Kimsey-House et al. 2011). Coaching achieves its goal of helping people personally develop not by solving their problems or reaching their goals directly. Rather, coaching is an approach that is based on the belief that people are creative, resourceful, and resilient. Through the use of core competencies such as listening, challenging, and questioning, the coach empowers people through development of personal awareness and discovery, and provides support in understanding themselves, developing their skills, finding the right answers to challenges and problems, and making the best choices. Essentially the coach's role is not to direct, but to guide; not to impose, but to enable.

The leader-coach can be viewed from two perspectives. One perspective is using expertise to help team members develop and improve their skills. Another perspective is that the leader-coach's role is to help team members become more self and socially aware. Consider Jack, for example, a member of the quality assessment team. Jack has terrific skills in project management. He can develop plans and use tracking tools to assess a project's status in relation to time, budget, and resources. He is a whiz at statistical analysis and preparing useful reports for the team. In short, Jack has great technical skills, but Jack fails as a team member. He expresses his frustration over project lag times and having to redo plans and project tracking by being cynical and bad-tempered. He wants to make quick decisions and jumps to unfounded conclusions about the delays. He embraces a pessimistic attitude that tasks will not get done, and he discounts opinions of other team members. Jack is unable to engage in critical thinking and use curiosity in helping his team solve critical problems. In Jack's case, the leader-coach's role is to challenge Jack's thinking and help him increase his mindfulness, awareness, and emotional intelligence (chapters 2 and 6). Increasing his mindfulness and self and social awareness, Jack can moderate his temper and cynical behavior, be less judgmental, refrain from drawing unfounded conclusions, and be socially aware and respectful of his colleagues.

Four coaching strategies are the foundation for exercising good leadership coaching skills. These include building relationships with team members and supporting, assessing, and challenging team members in helping them develop their own self-awareness.

Relationship Building

Leadership and coaching are based fundamentally on relationships between people built on trust. Thus, the leader-coach must have the trust of the team members to be effective. Team members develop and transform their behaviors through a sound, constructive, and trustful relationship with their leader (Naude and Plessier 2014). To build trust, leaders must be authentic—practicing the authentic behaviors of self-awareness, emotional intelligence, and mindfulness (chapters 2 and 6)—and demonstrate ethical leadership practices of dependability, truthfulness, respect, fairness, compassion, and doing the right thing (chapter 8).

Support, Assessment, and Challenge

To help team members achieve self-awareness and develop to their full potential, coaches engage team members using three strategies: support, assessment, and challenge (Naude and Plessier 2014).

In addition to establishing trust, the leader supports team members by demonstrating his or her commitment to their success. The leader uses assessment, such as feedback, and encourages personal self-discovery and insight that develops awareness about strengths, social style, and emotional intelligence. The leader-coach challenges team members' thinking and assumptions and helps them see and explore new possibilities. In looking at Jack's story cited earlier, the leader-coach might use these strategies in the following ways.

- **Support:** The leader-coach exercises social awareness by observing and listening to Jack in a non-judgmental manner to sense what he is thinking and feeling. She would acknowledge Jack's emotions of frustration and query him about the causes. She might ask him how he has successfully handled his frustration in the past and if that would work in this situation. Or she might ask Jack, "How do team lag times get in your way?" or "What resources do you need to lessen your frustration?"
- **Assessment:** The leader-coach provides Jack feedback to heighten his awareness of how his frustration and pessimism are hurting the team efforts. For example, she might say, "Jack, at yesterday's team meeting when Larry and Margaret presented solutions to increase throughput, you rolled your eyes and said they were stupid to expect the solution to work. After seeing and hearing this I did not feel that respected our team norms."
- **Challenge:** The leader-coach challenges Jack's thinking and assumptions by asking questions like "How is your frustration serving you and the team?" or "What can you do to follow team norms?"

Studies show the use of coaching strategies such as these for increased personal performance are associated with increased organizational performance. From the organizational perspective, increasing personal awareness and development of workers also contributes to better revenue growth, market share, profitability, and customer satisfaction (AMA 2008).

Coaching Skills

Several skills are associated with effective coaching practice. These include listening, using intuition, curiosity, and forwarding action on the team member's part (Kimsey-House et al. 2011). These skills are used to support the strategies of relationship building, support, assessment, and challenge described in the previous section. Each of these skills is explained as follows.

Listening

As a coaching skill, listening is part of mindful practice (chapter 6). In mindful listening the leader-coach approaches the conversation nonjudgmentally. She is focused and is open to discovering new things. The leader-coach does not consider in advance what she is going to say. She is in the present moment, not on autopilot, or thinking about her to-do list, unanswered e-mails, or other distractions. Through mindful listening, the leader-coach is using her curiosity and looking for the meaning behind the story or conversation. For example, when Jack says "I am frustrated," the leader-coach does not judge Jack, but looks for the meaning behind the frustration by asking him, "What is causing your frustration?" Or when Betty says, "Everyone is piling work on me and no one gives me credit for my work," the leader-coach follows up with curiosity and without judgment and asks "What do you want?" to get to the bottom line.

Intuition

In coaching, intuition is a kind of often unspoken knowledge that resides in the background, but is one of the most powerful skills a leader-coach can use. Intuition is "a sensitivity that goes beyond the physical world," (Kimsey-House et al. 2011, 49). Sometimes it may be referred to as a hunch and is based on the gathering of nonempirical information, picking up on cues that may come from tone of voice, posture, or from an explained shift in a person's emotion or energy. For example, during a team meeting Carla notices that Bob is not offering any comments on a new approach to solving a current problem. This is unusual for Bob. Carla's intuition tells her Bob is uneasy about this solution, but he is not speaking up. Carla, as leader-coach, says to him "Bob, I sense you are anxious about this solution. What are your concerns about this?" Here, Carla uses her listening and intuition together to gather important information for the team.

Curiosity

Curiosity allows the leader-coach to ask questions. Approached nonjudgmentally, the process of asking questions gets to the heart of matters, uncovers answers that may not have been discovered, and helps to develop insight. For instance, Russ's team is trying to make the data entry process in the electronic health record application easier for emergency department physicians. As leader-coach, Russ asks his team a series of questions like: "What is the obvious thing we can do?" and "What is the boldest thing we can do?" and "What does success look like?" These questions challenge the team to look for new possibilities and create new discoveries.

Forward the Action

Action for its own sake rarely produces any appreciable or lasting benefit. Action coupled with learning and change, however, is how successful teams get work done. In the example about Russ's team, the team opens itself to new learning using curiosity. For instance, when the team identifies the boldest thing it could do and describes what success look likes, this increases their learning. The next step is generating the desired change by identifying specific goals, outcomes, and metrics that will support a better end user interface for the emergency department physicians. This is accomplished by using planning and management tools and techniques described in chapter 14.

Leader as Conflict Manager

In the business world, conflict is often thought to have a negative effect on job performance and increasing anxiety (Hayes 2008). However, conflict is not necessarily a bad thing. In fact, teams depend on conflict from differing opinions and perspectives to thrive and prosper (Johns 2007). If everyone agreed on everything, progress likely would not happen. Conflict is a driving force of change. For instance, progress in treating some of the most threatening diseases in history has been the product of a conflict between differing opinions and perspectives. The vaccine for polio, for example, was the product of differing perspectives on whether the use of a live-virus vaccine was better than a killed-virus vaccine.

Nevertheless, conflict can have a disruptive effect if it is not managed properly. Team energy, relationships, and task accomplishment can be severely damaged because of unmanaged conflict. Conflict can occur in meetings, discussions, and e-mails and it must be well managed for the team to be productive. Positive results occur when teams manage conflict by using meeting norms, weighing facts, being mindful and nonjudgmental, and striving for win-win outcomes. The following sections describe how conflict can be managed through these various approaches so that new ideas and creative problem solving can result. Ensuring that these approaches are successful requires the team leader to be an example for team members in exercising ethical leadership behaviors and to remind them, if necessary, to use behaviors such as treating others with respect, being self-aware and socially aware of others, allowing for and listening to the input of others, being fair and trustworthy, and making principled decisions.

Using Meeting Norms to Manage Conflict

Meetings are one of the primary ways that team members formally communicate and frequently this is where conflict arises. Meeting norms should be part of a team's charter. If the team does not use meeting norms, it will likely waste time, be unproductive, become negative, and have poor outcomes, as discussed in chapter 12.

Differing opinions are not conflicts unless the disagreements are allowed to escalate into disrespectful behaviors such as raising the tone of voice, use of inappropriate language, holding a grudge, or passive aggressive behaviors. The following rules used during meetings and in other discussions can help turn conflicting opinions into positive actions.

Listen to Other People's Opinions and Concerns

Each team member assumes responsibility for listening to the opinions of other team members. Often people jump to conclusions without listening to what another person has to say. Listening also means understanding what the other person is trying to communicate. If the message is unclear, it is the team member's responsibility to ask questions in order to understand the other person's point of view.

Address One Subject at a Time

When differences of opinion are limited to one subject or topic at a time, conflict is easier to manage. Team members are forced to focus on a particular subject, and emotion-packed issues and hidden agendas are minimized. Only discussing one item at a time focuses team members on the immediate problem. The following example illustrates this point.

Two team members, Steve and Brian, are discussing the structure of a data model for an electronic record application. Steve does not agree with Brian's concept of the data model and points out where he believes deficiencies exist. Brian counters Steve's assessment by saying, "On the last data modeling project your suggestions did not pan out and caused some major project delays."

In this example, Brian is introducing conflict by rehashing an old event that does not have any bearing on the current discussion. Steve may have made a mistake on the last project, but this does not mean his current suggestions are wrong. If Brian believes Steve's assessment is wrong, then he should stick to the current topic, outlining the reasons why he believes Steve's suggestions will not work.

Using Facts to Manage Conflict

The team leader and other team members should insist that only facts and opinions about the subject at hand be addressed. Team members should not make personal remarks about other members. For example, when Jack said his team members were stupid he made a personal attack against his team members. The appropriate behavior for Jack in that situation would be to discuss the reasons why he believed the solution his team members suggested would not work.

Using a Win-Win Approach to Manage Conflict

Working toward a win-win result in meetings or discussions should be the goal of each team member. A win-win result is when all team members feel that they have gained or benefited from a decision or solution to a problem. Reaching a win-win situation requires that the team leader and team members do the following:

- ***Respect balance in the meeting or discussion.*** Do not dominate the meeting or discussion. This means being ready to engage in mindful listening to another's ideas, observations, and suggestions. At the same time, a discussion or meeting requires active participation. Do not be a silent team member during a meeting or discussion. Be curious and ask questions; be creative and offer solutions.

- ***Come prepared with ideas.*** Be ready to sell your ideas to the team. This means coming prepared with information and defending your view with facts, not emotion, in team meetings and discussions.
- ***Relinquish an idea if it fails to receive the support of the team.*** If your team gives valid reasons for not supporting an idea, relinquish the idea. Many times conflict arises because a team member cannot stop "beating a dead horse," and allows former disagreements to fester.
- ***Evaluate the work of the team.*** Provide evaluation and constructive criticism about the work of the team. It is imperative that honest dialog is maintained within the team. Every team member has the personal and ethical responsibility to speak up if they see that something can be done better or if there is cause for concern that team decision may lead to an adverse event (part 2). For example, in nearly 90 percent of medical mishaps a team member is aware that a medical error is happening or may occur, yet they do not speak up (Muha 2014).
- ***Maintain positive relationships.*** Maintain a supporting, respectful, and healthy relationship with all team members. The old saying "do not burn your bridges behind you" has significant meaning. Once a trust relationship is broken, it is very difficult to repair and the opportunities and advantages of that relationship are lost.
- ***Complete assignments.*** Complete all tasks and assignments on time and at a high-quality level. This is part of being an authentic and ethical leader as well as a leader on a team.

Assessing Conflict Management

Review the checklist in table 13.1. Think about the team meetings you have attended the past two months and evaluate your conflict management behaviors. Determine which areas you need to work on to improve your conflict management style by answering the questions that follow the checklist. Periodically use the checklist to reevaluate how you are doing in managing conflict on your team.

Table 13.1. Individual conflict-management assessment

Use the list below and rate how well you manage conflict.			
	Always	**Sometimes**	**Never**
Do I listen to others' opinions without interrupting?			
Do I allow others to speak without interrupting?			
Do I ask questions during meetings and discussions to clarify what I think I have heard?			
Do I come prepared to meetings and discussions with ideas?			
Do I relinquish ideas that do not have team support?			
Do I provide constructive criticism?			
Do I refrain from verbal personal attacks?			
Do I stick to one topic at a time, rather than deflecting an issue with another topic?			
Do I maintain positive relationships?			
Do I complete assignments on time and at a high-quality level?			

- Review the checklist and identify the actions you most want to improve. List these actions in the space that follows.

- Select two items you have listed and consider how you can improve these actions. For example, if you want to improve completing assignments on time, you might devote a specific time each day to work on the assignment by using the if-then strategy discussed in chapter 7. For instance, "if it is 8 p.m. on a weeknight, then I will work on my student team assignment for one hour."

Methods for Ensuring Conformance to Norms and Expected Behaviors

The previous section provides guidance for establishing norms of behavior and handling conflict. But what happens if a team member does not follow the norms or does not adopt behaviors that prevent conflict? The following sections discuss some methods for handling noncompliance and the reluctant team member. The team leader and all team members are responsible for the execution of leadership behaviors.

Techniques for Guiding Behaviors

One of the best ways to handle members who are not respecting team behavior or other norms is for the team to have techniques in place that check behaviors and guide them back to the desired place. The following examples illustrate this point.

> A radiology department quality team used a pencil as a technique to check monopolizing behaviors during team meetings. At the beginning of every team meeting, the team agreed that a pencil would be placed in the middle of the table and when a member wanted to speak during the meeting, he or she would pick up the pencil. It was also agreed that if the team member who was speaking began to monopolize the discussion or was off the agenda, any team member could say, "It is time to pass the pencil." All team members agreed ahead of time that if they were asked to pass the pencil they had to give up the floor of discussion to another member.

Two things contribute to making this technique work. First, the approach is direct but not confrontational. No personal attacks are made; only an action is requested. Second, peer pressure is a powerful tool that guides people into compliance. In this case, the entire team is exerting the power of peer pressure and expects that the pencil will be passed. The next example illustrates another technique for guiding behaviors.

> A coding audit team used a stuffed toy moose to address potential team conflict. The idea came from the saying, "No one wants to talk about the dead moose lying in the middle of the table." What this means is that people often try to avoid a situation that everyone knows is a problem rather than to confront it directly. Problems usually do not go away by themselves. Avoidance behavior more often than not results in extreme tension among team members and increases rather than reduces conflict.

> The auditing team decided to bring the toy moose, Truman, to every team meeting. When any team member had a potentially confrontational issue to bring up at a team meeting, he or she would say, "I have a Truman." The team member would then put Truman on the table and explain the issue. For example, the team leader might say, "I have a Truman. This Truman involves team members being late to meetings. I want to revisit our meeting norms to determine if our meeting time is still reasonable for all team members. If it is not reasonable, we need to change the meeting time. If it is reasonable, we need to reconfirm our expectations that all members will be on time to meetings."

Like the previous example, the approach is direct but not confrontational. Notice how the team leader phrases the issue: "This Truman involves team members being late to meetings." This is not a personal attack; rather, it is a statement of fact. Making statements of fact and avoiding personal attacks form the basis for resolution of problems. Note that the toy moose is a symbol for addressing a potential confrontational issue. It serves as surrogate or mediator for saying, "I have something that is really bothering me" or "I have a complaint." Presenting the toy moose as the mediator lessens tensions and distances the complaint as a personal attack.

Observe in this example how the team leader returns to the agreed-upon ground rule. The team leader allows for an option if a change in meeting time is warranted. However, the ground rule is still the impartial standard by which everyone is evaluated.

Using Strengths and Personal Style to Guide Behaviors

A third example for guiding behaviors to ensure conformance with behavior norms is recognizing and leveraging individual team members' strength and personal style (chapter 1). A good way to remember each member's dominant strength during team meetings is to make up a name card for each member that includes the strength(s) name. The name card is displayed for each team member during every team meeting. Knowing team members' styles can help reduce conflict. The following example illustrates how this technique is used.

> The systems analysis team is trying to solve a challenging problem in developing a data dictionary. Larry, whose top strength is creativity, keeps fluctuating between different ideas and possibilities. Lori, another team member whose top strength is prudence, wants to work with facts, not ideas, to solve the problem. Lori becomes

> extremely frustrated with Larry's problem-solving approach. Rather than get in an argument with Larry, Lori can point out to Larry that he may be overusing his creativity strength and say, "Your creativity right now is showing a little too much. We should bring the discussion around and look at some facts to approach the problem."

Instead of attacking the individual, this approach acknowledges the characteristics of team members and lets them know that their personal strength now may be inhibiting progress. This strategy has been used successfully in many teams to reduce potential conflict (Johns 2007).

Using a Direct Approach to Guide Behaviors

Teams using a direct approach to a situation have success in guiding behaviors and ensuring conformance to norms. A direct approach is different than a confrontational approach. A direct approach addresses the facts of a situation, uses a problem-solving technique, and looks at a situation objectively. The following example illustrates a direct approach to a potentially confrontational situation.

> A requirements analysis team for an HIM release of information vendor was doing an analysis of its products. One of the tasks was to interview eight HIM directors of critical access hospitals in rural areas. One team member, Marco, was assigned the interviewing task. At the weekly team meetings it was evident that interviews were not being conducted on a timely basis and were off schedule. Not having these results on schedule would put the whole team in jeopardy of not completing the project on time. The team leader addressed the situation in a direct manner during a team meeting with the following statement: "Our team is not meeting its scheduled timeline in completing the analysis interviews. We need to find out why this is happening and how we can rectify it if we are to complete the project on time. Marco, please tell us your perspective on why this task is off schedule."

Notice that the team leader keeps the conversation direct but not personal. The language the leader uses states the fact that the interviews are off schedule and lets everyone know what the ramifications are for the team. The team leader does not accuse Marco of not doing his job; rather, the team leader gives Marco an opportunity to explain what has happened.

In examining the situation, the team found that the interview for each business was taking double the time that had been originally anticipated. Therefore, Marco was behind in his interviews. To rectify this problem, the remaining businesses to be interviewed were divided between Marco and two other team members. This put the team back on schedule for completing the project. A negative rather than the positive outcome may have resulted had the team members jumped to the conclusion that Marco was a "social loafer," who was not exerting sufficient personal effort in the project.

Using these examples as guides, teams should always opt to solve problems directly in a problem-solving rather than a confrontational manner. However, there still may be times when someone on the team just does not want to conform to the team behavior norms. Specific documentation strategies such as maintenance of a team notebook, team meeting minutes, and interim reports to handle this situation are discussed as follows.

Documenting Conformance to Norms and Expected Behaviors

The power of the team in ensuring equitable team member evaluation is in its documentation and evaluation materials. A team notebook (chapters 12 and 14) contains documentation about how the project is being carried out. It should be clear to all team member that the team notebook is a device for the project sponsor or manager and team leader to track and monitor individual member contributions to the final product and ultimately to the individual's evaluation and degree of contribution to the project outcome (chapter 14).

For example, when team members are on time or late to meetings, the team should document this in the team minutes. In reviewing the team minutes, the team sponsor or manager and team leader can see who came on time or late to meetings and how often this occurred. When team members turn in assignments on time this should be documented. Likewise, if a team member does not complete assignments on time, document this in the team minutes as well as the weekly interim team reports. If a team member submits sub-quality work, document this in the weekly interim team reports. In reviewing these reports, the team leader and project sponsor will see who has and who has not completed work on time or at expected quality levels.

In addition to the regular team reports such as minutes and interim reports, the team should complete individual evaluations at the end of the project. This gives each team member an opportunity to evaluate every other team member on several objective measures. Individual team evaluations are turned into the manager at the end of the project and can be used to evaluate how team members contributed to the project outcome.

Practicing Conflict Management

Using table 13.1 you assessed your conflict management behaviors and identified ways for improving these leadership behaviors. Given the methods for guiding conformance to team norms discussed, how might you use these in improving your conflict management behaviors? For example, if you find you interrupt others, you might realize you are overusing a personal strength, such as curiosity. Or if you jump to conclusions and find you confront others, you may want to increase your use of a direct approach or facts to help solve problems. In the space that follows, write three ways you can use these techniques to improve your leadership behaviors.

References

American Management Association. 2008. Coaching: A Global Study of Successful Practices. https://www.opm.gov/WIKI/uploads/docs/Wiki/OPM/training/i4cp-coaching.pdf

Hayes, J. 2008. Workplace Conflict and How Business Can Harness It to Survive. CPP, Inc. https://www.cpp.com/pdfs/CPP_Global_Human_Capital_Report_Workplace_Conflict.pdf

Johns, M. 2007. *Creating, Coaching and Managing High-Powered Work Teams*. Raleigh: Lulu Press.

Kimsey-House, H., K. Kimsey-House, and P. Sandahl. 2011. *Co-Active Coaching: Changing Business Transforming Lives*. Boston: Nicholas Brealey Publishing.

Muha, T. 2014. Medical Errors: Why Nurses Don't Speak Up. http://www.nursetogether.com/medical-errors-why-dont-nurses-speak

Naude, J. and F. Plessier. 2014. *Becoming a Leader-Coach: A Step-by-Step Guide to Developing Your People*. Greensboro: The Center for Creative Leadership.

Zetou, E., A. Fillipou, F. Fillipou, and N. Vernadakis. 2016. Validity and reliability of coaching competency in team sports. *Journal of Physical Education and Sport* 16(2):493–499.

14 Managing and Leading Teams

Thorough preparation in creating and organizing a team and being a leader-coach are two critical aspects of team success. However, if the team leader and team do not manage their activities, team goals will not be achieved. Teams are usually formed to focus on the completion of a specific task. In this chapter, the term *project* is used to describe a project, task, or assignment a team is formed to complete. To accomplish their project, teams put in place an enabling structure and processes that help move the project from start to finish. These include defining and clarifying the project, identifying required tasks and time frames, assigning task responsibilities, and establishing tracking processes. Successful teams also document their activities and maintain up-to-date documentation in a team notebook.

Successful teams are ones that use ethical leadership behaviors in performing these activities. These include behaviors such as honesty and trustworthiness, open communication, respect and valuing of all team members, fair decision-making practices, and exercising self-awareness and social awareness. This chapter reviews the fundamentals of how the team leader and team members manage and coordinate planning and other processes that help teams stay on track for success and apply leadership behaviors.

The activities presented in this chapter are supported by several key actions of successful teams discussed in chapter 11 and include:

- Key Action 4: Value personal style and diversity
- Key Action 6: Conduct productive meetings
- Key Action 7: Promote communication and cooperation
- Key Action 8: Manage conflict
- Key Action 9: Manage the project

Leading Productive Meetings

Meetings are an important communication mechanism for successful teams. Planning how to perform a work project and making decisions relating to the project are all handled through team meetings. Poorly managed meetings, however, can result in wasted time, frustration, deflated energy, team conflict, and inability to meet the team goals. Inefficient meetings are usually the result of inadequate or nonexistent processes for planning and managing meetings. To ensure positive outcomes, the team should use the following three processes.

- Prepare for the meeting
- Manage the meeting
- Complete follow-up action (Johns 2007)

The following sections discuss meeting preparation and management and provide insights to how each of these demonstrate behaviors of the ethical leader. Follow-up action is explored at the end of the chapter.

Prepare for the Meeting

The team charter (chapter 11) identifies the time, place, and frequency of regular team meetings. Additional meetings may also be required depending on project circumstances. Regardless of the type of meeting, preparing for any meeting involves

- Determining meeting type
- Sending out a meeting notification to members
- Developing a meeting agenda
- Distributing resource materials
- Preparing materials and supplies

Determine Meeting Type

The purpose of team meetings is to share information and make decisions. Usually team meetings are held in-person. However, meetings can be conducted via conference call or webinar.

Conference calls and online meetings are useful to exchange information, answer questions about reports, or update members on the team's progress in achieving milestones. Face-to-face meetings are more useful when the team needs to share ideas and opinions, brainstorm and problem solve, and make decisions. The team should determine which method is best for conducting team business.

Send Out Meeting Notification

The team leader is responsible for coordinating team meetings. Meeting participants must be notified in advance of the meeting, regardless of whether the meeting is face-to-face, a conference call, or online. The time required for advance notification should be specified in the team's meeting norms. The time frame for notification will depend upon the type of meeting, reason for meeting, and the attendees. For example, the dates and times of regular team meetings is determined upon team formation and included in team meeting norms. "The Revenue Cycle Improvement team will meet every Thursday from 8 a.m. to 9 a.m. in conference room B," is an example of a regular meeting norm. The team may determine that the team leader should send a broadcast e-mail 24 hours in advance of every regularly scheduled team meeting as a reminder to all team members.

For regular team meetings, the meeting date, time, and place for the next meeting should be reconfirmed at the conclusion of each meeting. Notification for ad hoc or special meetings must be made well in advance to give meeting participants time to make arrangements to attend and prepare. Typically this notice would be 48 hours or more before the meeting, depending upon meeting purpose and urgency. The team leader, or other designated person, is responsible for notification for unplanned meetings. Meeting norms in the team charter should specify how far in advance regular and impromptu meeting notification should be made.

Advanced notification of team meetings demonstrates several ethical leadership behaviors. First, it respects and values team members. Asking people to drop what they are doing to attend a meeting shows a lack of regard for team members and signals that their work is unimportant. Second, advanced notification allows for the participation of the most number of people. Advanced planning that attempts to include everyone indicates that each team member's input is important. Third, it shows effective leadership through appropriate organization.

Develop Meeting Agenda

Because the agenda is the roadmap for the meeting, every meeting must have a pre-published agenda. A well-prepared agenda informs participants about the time and length of the meeting, what topics will be discussed, who is responsible for leading the topic discussions, and the gives the time frame for each topic. Development and distribution of a well-prepared agenda represents applying good leadership behaviors of open communication. The formally designated team leader is responsible for developing the agenda. However, it is also customary for the team leader to solicit suggestions from all team members and then determine final agenda items, taking into consideration the meeting's purpose.

Agenda items should be clear and specific. Decision making and informational meetings should last no longer than one hour; anything exceeding this time limit usually indicates an overloaded or poorly created agenda, insufficient meeting planning, or ineffective meeting management. Meetings lasting over an hour should be reserved for strategic planning, brainstorming new ideas, or identifying problem solutions. In these cases, specific time limits are imposed upon the meeting in advance. Figure 14.1 is an example of a meeting agenda.

Notice the agenda in figure 14.1 specifies the date and place of the meeting and meeting start and end times. Each topic is clearly defined with a specific time period allocated and with an identified facilitator. Also note that each topic is written with a verb and indicates what action or decision is required.

The team leader prepares the agenda and aligns agenda topics with the team's project plan and the needs of the team at the time. The team leader distributes the agenda to all team members before the meeting. The team charter should specify how far in advance agendas should be distributed and depends on the nature of the team's work and expectations for what information, data, or work products will be reviewed or what decisions will be made. For example, if team members are expected to review a complicated work product, such as a data model, before attending a meeting then they should be given sufficient time to accomplish this task.

Figure 14.1. Sample agenda

Agenda Weekly Meeting of Pharmacy Inventory Management System Development Team Date: December 1, 20XX Place: Meeting Room #487 Members: L. Eckert, T. Roberts, P. Collins, M. Rucker		
Time	Topic	Facilitator
7:00 a.m.	Meeting convenes	Eckert
	Approval of minutes of 12/1/XX	
7:02	Approve final project scope statement	Roberts
7:07	Approve draft diagram of current system	Rucker
7:10	Approve current system functions	Eckert
7:15	Determine functions that fit within project scope	Collins
7:40	Make assignments for: Flow diagram, entity relationship, and use case development	Eckert
7:45	Identify and assign action items for next meeting	Eckert
7:55 a.m.	Meeting adjourns	

Advanced distribution of the agenda alerts team members to the meeting topics for discussion and is applies several ethical leadership behaviors. First, it shows respect for team members and gives them the opportunity to schedule their work for the meeting in a productive way. Second, it allows team members to prepare for the discussion of the meeting topics and gives them an opportunity to participate and purposefully share in decision making. Third, it clarifies meeting and member expectations. Finally, it supports honesty, trustworthiness, and accountability through open communication and expectations.

Distribute Resources

Resources required for information or decision making should be distributed prior to the meeting. For example, in the agenda in figure 14.1, the minutes of the previous meeting and the draft diagram of the current system should be circulated prior to the meeting. This gives team members time to review information and come prepared to make decisions; and it shortens meeting times because team members will analyze information in advance. The meeting norms in the team charter should specify how far in advance of the meeting resource materials and agenda are distributed.

Like distribution of an advanced agenda, providing the necessary resources to team members prior to a team meeting demonstrates several leadership behaviors. It respects the time of team members, allows them to come prepared to provide their insights and knowledge and share in decision making, clarifies expectations and accountability, and increases honesty and trust through open communication.

Distribute Materials and Supplies

The team should identify what materials and supplies are needed for each meeting. For example, arrangements should be made for materials such as flip charts, laptop computers, and overhead projectors. When teams do not have the necessary materials and supplies available, their work can be delayed or impeded, which in turn may adversely impact the project timeline or other resources.

Manage the Meeting

In addition to appropriate preparation, a productive meeting must be conducted well. Both the team leader and team members are responsible for ensuring that the meeting is well managed. The roles and associated activities of the team leader, team members, and team secretary discussed in this section demonstrate how good leadership behaviors are applied. For example, when the meeting process is well managed, team members are likely to respect and listen to each other, provide their input, and actively participate in the meeting. It is also more probable that team members will make thoughtful decisions by weighing facts and consequences rather than self-interests. Finally, an efficient meeting process helps team members hold themselves accountable and ensure prosocial behaviors such as trust, inclusiveness, commitment, and motivation.

Role of the Team Leader

The goal of each meeting is to accomplish the agenda objectives, make decisions, and determine action items linked to positive results. As the meeting facilitator, the team leader must exhibit leadership behaviors like having a positive attitude, empowering participants, being honest and trustworthy, and impartial treatment of both issues and meeting participants. As meeting facilitator, the team leader assumes the following responsibilities.

- **Takes charge of the proceedings**. The team leader guides the team through the meeting agenda and makes sure that each agenda item is fully addressed. The team leader makes certain that team meeting norms are observed during the meeting process, and usually appoints a team member to serve as timekeeper. The timekeeper's task is to monitor the time spent on each agenda topic, alert the team two or three minutes before time runs out for each topic, and notify the team when time has expired for a topic.
- **Develops and distributes the agenda.** As noted previously, the team leader develops the agenda and distributes it to all participants before the meeting.
- **Starts and ends the meeting on time.** The team leader ensures the meeting starts and ends on time. If it appears during the meeting that scheduled business will not be accomplished in the allotted time, the team leader can ask members for permission to extend the meeting in increments of five minutes, readjust the agenda items, or carry over business to the next meeting. The final decision for making any of these changes rests on the consensus of the team members.
- **Follows established meeting rules.** Meeting norms should be listed in the team's charter. The team leader is responsible for making sure that all meetings follow these norms. Examples of meeting norms are provided in chapter 12.
- **Keeps the discussion relevant and balanced.** The team leader keeps the discussion relevant, ensuring that the group does not digress from the agenda. The team leader makes certain that everyone participates in the conversation. If there are any silent team members, the team leader can conduct a round robin, asking each member in turn for input on the agenda item under discussion.
- **Summarizes the proceedings after each topic.** At the conclusion of each agenda topic, the team leader summarizes the discussion and the action taken. This process clarifies and openly communicates the important aspects of the discussion or

decisions to ensure everyone understands the implications and consequences of the team's actions.

- **Brings team to consensus, decisions, and action items.** The team leader is responsible for ensuring the group arrives at consensus, makes decisions, and determines follow-up actions. Most agenda items will require some type of decision. Depending on the team norms, decisions can be made by consensus (agreement) or vote. Action items arising from the team meeting are follow-up measures required to implement group decisions. Example action items are found in figure 14.2 in the section on assignments under the column heading "Action."
- **Ensures that meeting records are kept.** Written minutes of every meeting must be recorded. If a secretary has not been identified in the team charter, the chair can appoint a team member to record the minutes. To give everyone experience taking minutes, the team leader can rotate this function among team members. Minutes and other records of team meetings are maintained in the team notebook.

An example of the format and content of meeting minutes appears in figure 14.2. Notice how the minutes follow the agenda topics in figure 14.1. Observe that the minutes are concise but cover the details of the meeting.

Sometimes teams feel that minutes are burdensome to keep. But minutes are important for a successful team for several reasons:

- People's memories are often unreliable. Minutes provide a history of the team's work for future reference and review.
- Minutes not only describe the discussion but the decisions and responsibility for action items.
- Minutes help hold team members accountable for tasks.
- Minutes help avoid conflict among team members.

Role of Meeting Members

The responsibility for a well-run meeting does not just rest with the team leader. Team members are equally accountable for practicing leadership behaviors such as respect for and valuing others' strengths, listening to others and considering their input, making decisions by weighing facts and consequences and not self-interest,

Figure 14.2. Sample meeting minutes

Minutes: Weekly Team Meeting of Pharmacy Inventory Management System Development Team

Date: December 1, 20XX

Place: Meeting Room #487

Members: L. Exhert, T. Roberts, P. Collins, M. Rucker   Absent: All present

Topic	Discussion	Action	Follow-up
Minutes of 11/24/20XX	Meeting started at 7 a.m. Minutes reviewed	Approved	
Appointment of timekeeper and recorder	T. Roberts: secretary M. Rucker: timekeeper		
Approve project scope statement	The goals of the project were reviewed and the client's desired functionalities discussed. Given time and current resources, a limited project scope that delivered the basic functionalities was decided to be most feasible to pursue.	Approved project scope includes development of a relational database for pharmacy inventory management including screens for input, modification, and deletion of inventory items, and generation or reports.	
Approve draft diagram of current system	The draft of the diagram of the client's current system was reviewed. No corrections or additions to the draft.	Draft of current system diagram approved as submitted.	Diagram is to be filed in team notebook by T. Roberts
Approve current system functions	Fifteen functionalities for the new system presented. M. Eckert noted that security functionality was not on the list.	New system functionality was approved with the addition of security protections and passwords for end user.	
Determine functions that fit within project scope	The list of desired functionalities was compared to the project scope. Six of the fifteen functionalities were determined to be within the project scope.	The final list of functionalities to be delivered was approved including input, update, deletion of inventory items, and generation of reports by item number.	

Figure 14.2. Sample meeting minutes (continued)

Assignments	Assignments were made for development of data flow diagrams, entity relationship, and use case development.	Action item: Develop data flow diagram Action item: Develop entity relationship Action item: Develop use cases	T. Roberts is assigned to complete data flow diagram by 12/8. M. Rucker is assigned to complete entity relationship diagram by 12/8. P. Eckert is assigned to complete use cases by 12/15.
Action items next meeting	Action items for next meeting include: review and approval of drafts of DFDs & ERDs.	Next meeting December 20, 20XX, Room 456	
Adjournment	Meeting adjourned at 9 a.m.		

and being trustworthy and accountable. Responsibilities of team members should be defined in the team norms in the team charter. Among them are the following:

- **Attend meetings**. The first responsibility of team members is to attend all team meetings. Meetings are where work and decisions gets done. It is essential that every team member attend all team meetings.
- **Arrive at meetings on time**. Latecomers are disruptive to productive meetings. Arriving late at a meeting is inconsiderate to others and demonstrates a lack of discipline and commitment to the team effort.
- **Come prepared to meetings**. Unprepared team members cannot participate productively in meetings. Team members should have read the agenda for the meeting, the minutes of the previous meeting, and any reports distributed prior to the meeting. Team members should have completed all assignments at an acceptable level.

- **Follow meeting norms**. Every team member is responsible for following the team's meeting norms. When a member does not comply with meeting norms, the other team members should bring this to the attention of that member and bring the meeting back into compliance with team norms.
- **Follow meeting agenda**. Team members should adhere to the agenda topics. If a team member feels that an additional topic should be added for discussion, this issue should be raised with the team leader at the time the agenda is distributed. This gives the team leader time to consider the appropriateness of adding the agenda item before the meeting and allocating sufficient time to it.
- **Participate in the meeting**. Every team member is responsible for active participation in every meeting. Remaining silent on issues, withholding information, and not asking questions or seeking clarification are nonproductive behaviors. Team members are responsible for using leadership behaviors in cultivating a positive meeting climate, listening and respecting other's opinions and input, and working toward achieving team goals.

Role of Timekeeper

The team leader may appoint a meeting timekeeper or a team member may volunteer for this role. The role can rotate among team members, giving everyone an opportunity to gain experience in this role. The timekeeper's job is to ensure that the meeting stays on schedule. Approximately two to three minutes before the end of the time period allotted to an agenda item, the timekeeper makes an announcement that the time for discussion on the topic is almost finished. This allows the team leader time to wrap up discussion and proceed with bringing the group to consensus or making decisions. The timekeeper announces to the group when time has expired for an agenda topic. At that point, the team leader ends the topic discussion.

The timekeeper can also be assigned to help the team leader make sure that discussions are relevant and following the agenda. In this capacity, when digressions occur, the timekeeper can remind the group of the agenda item and help return the conversation to the agenda item at hand.

Role of the Team Secretary

The role of team secretary is usually identified in the team charter. The role can rotate among team members to balance out workload and give everyone the opportunity to gain experience in this role. The meeting secretary is responsible for recording the minutes of the meeting. After the meeting, the secretary types the minutes and forwards them to the team leader for circulation to team members. To guarantee that minutes are accurate, the secretary should type them up no more than a day or two after the meeting. The minutes follow a prescribed format, as shown in figure 14.2.

Assess Team Meeting Process

How well planned, organized, and executed are the team meetings you attend? Use the checklist in table 14.1 to assess how the team meetings you have attended meet the criteria for effective meetings then answer the questions that follow.

Answer the following questions after the assessment.

1. For those criteria that were never or only sometimes met, how did these deficiencies contribute to poor team performance in managing team work and reaching positive outcomes?

2. Could the team have been more productive with the process controls in place?

3. Give specific examples of how the team could have been more productive. Write these observations in the space that follows.

Table 14.1. Checklist for meeting process

Criteria for Managing Meetings Productively			
Use the following criteria to evaluate how the teams have used the appropriate process controls for managing meetings.	**Never**	**Sometimes**	**Always**
1. Has a team leader been identified?			
2. Has the role of the team leader been agreed upon and written in the team charter?			
3. Have the roles of team members been agreed upon and written in the team charter?			
4. Have meeting dates, times, and place been established?			
5. Is there an established format for meeting agendas?			
6. Is there an established format for meeting minutes?			
7. Has the role of timekeeper been designated?			
8. Has the role of secretary been designated?			
9. Have team norms been established in relation to meetings, such as:			
a. Attendance rules			
b. Participation rules			
c. Rules for agendas and minutes			
d. Decision rules (how decisions are made)			
e. Preparation rules			
10. Have all team norms been written in the team charter?			

Defining the Project

After the team has developed its team charter, it then defines the requirements of the project. Similar to the activities described earlier, defining the team project requires the team leader and team members to exercise ethical leadership behaviors such as actively participating in development of the project; respecting and valuing all team members; listening to and considering the ideas and input of others; making decisions based on facts and weighing consequences instead of self-interest or bias; and being honest, trustworthy, and accountable.

Before beginning the project, team members must agree on its scope, objectives, and outcomes that are outlined in a project-definition document. A project definition document describes the common understanding among team members and the project sponsor or manager about the nature of the project (shown in figure 14.3). The project definition is added as an appendix to the team charter and serves as a contract between the team members and the team sponsor, clearly stating expectations for project scope, timeline, resources, and results. Developing a project definition in the beginning saves team time and helps to avoid misunderstandings between the team and team sponsor and among all team members. Teams without a clearly written project definition usually end up making changes throughout the project that waste time, causing frustration and disagreement among team members and ultimately raising project costs.

The team develops the project definition document together. Usually the project sponsor provides the team with an outline, concept, or description of the project. This information is used as a basis for creating the project definition document. Like all other project materials, the project definition document is maintained in the team notebook.

The project definition document consists of several components:

- **Project name**. The team or project name should express what the team is to accomplish and why this is important (chapter 12).
- **Project description**. The description includes two sections:
  - The project's background
  - The project's current status

  In a project assessing the physician practice in figure 14.3, for example, the background could include information about the history of the company or stakeholders, a description of the current environment, a list of the significant stakeholders, a description of the physical facilities, names of employees, and other resources. The current project status is a description of the current operation of the project, perceived deficiencies, and desired improvements.
- **Problem statement**. The problem to be addressed is defined in a few sentences. Using figure 14.3 as an example, notice how

Figure 14.3. Sample project definition

Project Definition Document

Date prepared: September 7, 20XX

Project name: Huntley Physician Group Practice (HPGP) Registration Process Efficiency Assessment

Project members: J. Barnes, K. Davis, O. Holms, M. Prentice, J. O'Rafferty

Project Description:

Background: HPGP has six physicians, two nurse practitioners, and employs a staff of 20 personnel. The practice is located in a rural area and is the only group practice within a 50-mile radius. The group practice sees on average 300 patients a day including physician and nurse practitioner office visits and laboratory visits.

Current status**:** A mixture of manual and automated processing of patient appointments and registration is currently in place. The current mix of manual and automated processing of patient appointments and registration leads to inaccuracies in patient scheduling, results in a backlog for patient registration, and also causes double-booking of providers. The practice wants to capture opportunities for better efficiency by automating all of its appointment and registration processes. Currently there is a backlog at the registration desk and an estimated wait time on the phone of three minutes when patients want to make appointments. The group practice also wants to track appointments and registrations, and produce reports on provider productivity (such as number of patients seen by provider, diagnoses of patients by provider, services provided by patient).

Problem Statement:

Assess the process flows for patient scheduling and pinpoint efficiency gaps, identify opportunities for decreasing inaccuracies in patient scheduling and increasing registration productivity, and determine if there are solutions by use of information technology considering the business goals, budget, and capacity of the group practice for decreasing inaccuracies in patient scheduling and increasing registration productivity.

Project Scope:

The project scope will focus solely on improving the registration process.

1. Map current registration processes
2. Identify efficiency problems in current registration process that impact patient or client throughput
3. Identify areas for process improvement that will decrease patient/client throughput in minutes per patient or client
4. Recommend changes in process flow to improve efficiency as measured in registration time and patient or client throughput
5. Recommend automation solutions that will support new process flows given budgetary and personnel constraints

Functionalities that will not be addressed in this phase of the project include:

- Scheduling inefficiencies
- Automated reporting tracking physician and nurse productivity, patient/client diagnoses

Project Constraints:

The project is to be completed in four weeks. The project recommendations are constrained by the $50,000 budget allocated for automation software and the number of current registration personnel at the group practice.

Figure 14.3. Sample project definition (continued)

Project Objectives:

1. Map current registration processes
2. Identify interrelationships among activities and duplicative, unnecessary, or repetitive processes
3. Identify the current time it takes in minutes per patient or client to complete registration process starting from the time patient or client arrives at the clinic through completion of the entire registration process
4. Identify areas for process improvement eliminating duplicative, unnecessary, or repetitive processes that will decrease registration time and throughput in minutes per patient or client
5. Recommend changes in process flow to improve efficiency as measured in registration time and patient or client throughput
6. Recommend automation solutions that will support new process flows given budgetary and personnel constraints

Project Timeline

Project start date is January 4, 20XX. Project end date is February 4, 20XX.

Project Costs

Project costs include salaries for project personnel, travel expenses, and $10,000 in supplies

Required Resources

Personal computers with Windows Operating System. Systems analysis software.

Team Leader: Janice Barnes. Ph: 815-220-9000.

the problem statement defines the problem to be solved. The problem definition guides the team in its work. In this case, the problem definition identifies several specific things the team has to do. First, the team must evaluate the current patient scheduling and registration process flows of the group practice and identify where inaccuracies and efficiency gaps are occurring. The team then must come up with ideas for decreasing inefficiencies and increasing the productivity of the group practice by changing processes. Finally the team needs to assess information technology solutions and determine if these can increase productivity and decrease inaccuracies. The team must perform all of these tasks while taking into consideration the goals of the group practice, its capacity, and budget. In other words, the final project solutions are constrained by budgetary and other resources.

- **Project scope**. Many projects fail because of something called "scope creep." Scope creep happens when the project continually grows because more and more work is added to it. Sometimes this is referred to as a runaway project. If project boundaries are not set at the start, the team runs the risk of a runaway project. As more work is added to the project, team tensions run high and adds to team frustration and conflict, ultimately resulting in the team not finishing the project on time. Therefore, the team must identify the scope of the project and state what will and will not be included in the final deliverable or product. An example of limiting the project scope appears in figure 14.3, where the team determined that several of the proposed functionalities were outside of the project scope and eliminated these.

- **Project constraints**. Every project has limits to what can reasonably be done. For example, time, money, and people resources are common elements that constrain or restrict a project. Project constraints that the team may consider include the time allotted to complete the project, skills of team members, and resources available to them. Understanding the constraints helps the team establish the boundaries and scope of the project.
- **Project objectives**. Project objectives are the specifics of what the team will achieve and deliver. Examples of project objectives for a registration process evaluation are listed in figure 14.3. Notice these objectives are specific and list the products to be produced.
- **Project timeline**. All projects have a start date and an end date. The estimated timeline includes a task list and identifies responsibilities for completion.
- **Project costs**. All projects involve some type of costs. Costs include such things as office supplies, equipment, software, space, and human resource costs. Since all projects have budgets, the costs of a project may or may not be a limiting factor in what can actually be delivered as the project's final product.
- **Required resources**. Projects usually require a number of resources. For example, resources might include access to computer software, computers, meeting space, reference books and materials, and such. Identifying required resources at the start of the project is important and helps to ensure that the team has the right materials when they need them.
- **Project leader and oversight**: The final component of the project definition is the name and contact information of the team leader, who provides oversight for the entire project.

Notice how the team has limited the project scope. The current status description lists several efficiency issues the clinic needs to address. However, this project is limited to the registration process and excludes scheduling processes. The project objectives are specific statements that elaborate on the project scope. The project definition document concludes with a statement of timeline, project costs, and the required resources to complete the project. Lastly, the document lists the team leader's contact information.

Planning the Project

After the project is defined, the project plan consisting of several steps is developed. This includes identifying tasks to be performed and the timeline for completion of each; assigning responsibility for completion of each task; identifying resources needed for project completion; and defining how communication within and external to the team will be handled. Project planning depends on applying good leadership behaviors by all team members. For example, identifying tasks and necessary resources to complete them involves active participation of team members by listening to and considering others' ideas and opinions, contributing one's own ideas, and making decisions based on facts and weighing consequences. Assigning tasks and assuming responsibility for their completion requires each team member to be accountable and dependable. Finally, the results of the planning process provide clarification of what is to be accomplished, the expectations for each team member's contribution, and clarification of the roles each team member will perform and be accountable for. The next sections describe each of the planning steps.

Develop Project Task List

Developing the task list is the first step in project planning. The task list is the roadmap for the action plan. Once the team prepares the list, each task is analyzed to determine what resources are needed to complete the task, how long it should take to complete each task, and if there are interdependencies among tasks. It is usually easier to develop a task list by first identifying categories of jobs that need to be done. For example, if the team is working on developing a database application the categories of tasks might include the following:

- System analysis tasks
- System design tasks
- System development tasks

Once the main categories are identified, specific tasks within each category are listed. Continuing with the given example, the tasks within the systems analysis category might include:

1. Conduct an initial client meeting.
2. Review the current system.
3. Hold a joint application development meeting.
4. Compile a report of the joint application development meeting.
5. Develop data flow diagrams of the current system.
6. Develop data flow diagrams of the new system.
7. Meet with the client to confirm functionalities of the new system.
8. Determine functions to be incorporated into the first prototype design.

Once all the tasks within each category are identified they are arranged in the order in which they should be performed.

Develop Task Timeline

After the team identifies the tasks and puts them in a logical sequence for completion, start and end dates are assigned to each. A Gantt chart, such as that in figure 14.4, or similar chart is usually used to plot the tasks and their time frames, and to identify who is responsible for completing each task. Tools such as the Gantt chart are essential to organize tasks and identify their sequence, prioritize tasks, indicate potential task interdependences, map out estimates of task completion times, and identify task responsibilities and when specific resources to support tasks (such as materials and equipment) will be needed.

There are several software programs that can be used to create Gantt and similar charts for tracking tasks. The sample Gantt chart in figure 14.4 is developed in Microsoft Word and shows the first four weeks of a database development project. Notice each task is given an identification number. Each task is assigned a start and an end date, and a team member has been assigned responsibility for completion of each task.

Figure 14.4. Sample Gantt chart

ID	Task Name	Feb 24							Mar 3							Mar 10							Mar 17						
		S	M	T	W	T	F	S	S	M	T	W	T	F	S	S	M	T	W	T	F	S	S	M	T	W	T	F	S
1	Team Meetings			T							T							T							T				
2	Develop Team Charter			T	T	T	T	T	T	T	T																		
3	Project Definition											E	E	E															
4	Conduct User Meetings																	J	J	J	J								
5	Develop DFDs																							M	M	M			
6	Develop ERDs																									R	R	R	
Legend: T:team E:Evans J:Johnson M:Moore R:Redding																													

Assign Task Responsibility

Assigning the right person to the right task is one of the standards for a successful team. Here the team matches the tasks to the skills and interests of the team members. The team also ensures that team members are provided time to complete the assigned tasks. Often members work simultaneously on multiple projects and on many different teams. Therefore, it is important that enough time is allocated to individual team members so that assigned components of the project are completed on time. It is the responsibility of all team members to ensure that sufficient resources and time are adequately estimated.

Identify Project Resources and Costs

Besides people and time, projects require other resources that need to be considered for planning purposes. These may include resources such as facilities, meeting rooms, computers, software programs, office supplies, and other materials. Documentation of what resources are required and associated costs and potential vendors should be documented in the team notebook and accounted for in the project budget.

Develop a Communication Plan

Once the team considers project resources, identifies tasks and timelines, and assigns responsibilities, it is ready to develop its communication plan. A communication plan is an integral part of project planning. The plan defines how communication is exchanged within the team and to other stakeholders. A communication plan ensures that all parties who need to be informed about project activities and results get the information they need.

The communication plan identifies stakeholders, their communication needs, and how information will be communicated to them. Stakeholders may include team members, managers, clients, departments, and other teams. The team specifies how it handles internal communication. For instance, the team may use e-mail as a primary medium to transfer information or an Internet project management and tracking application. The team specifies the expectations for checking e-mail and message boards for project information and updates, such as checking e-mail every day, perhaps including weekends. Some of these expectations may already be in the communication norms in the team charter.

However, the communication plan is broader than communication within the team. The communication plan also includes the following:

- **Project stakeholders**. Who are the stakeholders?
- **Stakeholder information needs**. What type of information does each stakeholder need? For example, some stakeholders may need regular status reports; others may require review of project deliverables.
- **Communication methods**. How will information be communicated to each of the stakeholders? Some possibilities are formal written project status reports, oral presentations, e-mail updates, and meetings.

Figure 14.5 is an example of a team's communication plan. Notice the team has identified the project stakeholders, their information needs, and how communication will be handled. The team has also included its communication norms as part of the plan.

Figure 14.5. Team communication plan

Project Name: Delta Database Project			
Stakeholder	**Information Needs**	**Communication Type**	**Frequency**
Team members	Project task status	Team meetings	Weekly
	Agendas, minutes	Web bulletin board	Weekly
	Collaborative work update	Web bulletin board	Daily
Sponsor	Progress report	Internal interim reports – e-mail	Weekly
Client	Progress reports	External interim reports – paper format by mail	Every two weeks

Communication Norms:

- Team meetings are held each Wednesday morning from 8:30 a.m. to 9:30 a.m.
- The team Web bulletin board is used as the primary means of communication among team members.
- Web bulletin board messages are checked by all team members on a daily basis during the workweek.
- All agendas and minutes of team meetings are posted to the team Web bulletin board.
- All interim and other reports are posted to the team Web bulletin board.
- All work materials are posted to the team Web bulletin board.

Assess Project Planning

Use the checklist in table 14.2 to assess how well the last two projects that you participated in as a team member were defined. These projects could have been a student team project, work project, volunteer-group project, or other group project. Then answer the questions that follow.

1. What did you discover about the planning process of the two projects from this exercise?
2. How well-prepared were your projects? Explain the level of preparation and what made them prepared or not prepared.
3. Are there improvements you would recommend in the planning process for these projects? If so, what are they and why are these improvements important?

Table 14.2. Assessment of project planning

Project Definition Steps	Project 1 Name		Project 2 Name	
	Yes	No	Yes	No
Did your team develop a complete task list prior to starting the project?				
Were the project tasks divided by categories?				
Were beginning and end dates assigned for each task?				
Were team members assigned specific responsibilities for task completion at the beginning of the project?				
Were team member skills appropriately aligned with task responsibilities?				
Was a Gantt or similar chart used to identify and track tasks?				
Was a communication plan put in place at the beginning of the project?				
Were project resources identified for each task and the project as a whole at the start of the project?				

Manage the Project

Once the team has planned the project, it is time to take action and move forward. The following are activities that help ensure the team meets the project's goals, schedule, and costs.

Hold Team Meetings

A team assesses whether goals are being met, if tasks are being completed on schedule, and potential resource needs by holding team meetings throughout the project. Team meetings also serve to identify problems in adhering to the project schedule or task completion and to readjust the project plan if needed. Team meetings should be held as often as necessary. For example, some teams conduct a morning huddle every day. A huddle is a brief meeting, perhaps 10 to 15 minutes long where a report is given by each team member on the status of tasks. Some teams meet weekly, bi-weekly, or monthly, depending on the specific project or task. Regardless of length, meetings held throughout the project should focus on

- Reviewing project status
- Communicating each member's progress in meeting assignments
- Determining the percentage of completion of each project task
- Identifying potential problems and how these may affect project schedule, resources, or costs
- Determining solutions to problems affecting the project
- Making changes to the project plan if required
- Sharing information from external stakeholders

Prepare Interim Reports

Interim written reports are regularly compiled throughout the project by the team leader. The timing of these may be determined by the project sponsor or by the team as part of their communication plan to keep the project sponsor and project stakeholders updated on the project. The reports show which team members have been responsible for tasks during a given period and what the workload of team members will be for the upcoming period. In this way, the interim report holds team members accountable for their work.

Reports are compiled in a specific format determined by the project team or by the reporting standards established by the department or organization that employs the team. A copy of all interim reports is maintained in the team notebook. Interim reports do not take the place of meeting minutes. Figure 14.6 shows a sample team interim report.

Notice the first part of the report in figure 14.6 includes a running list of the team's accomplishments to date. The team lists all the tasks completed since its last interim report and lists what tasks were assigned but not completed. (In this example, one team member did not complete an assigned task.) Listing completed and incomplete tasks in this way documents who has performed work

Figure 14.6. Sample interim project report

Project name: Huntley Physician Group Practice (HPGP) Registration Process Efficiency Assessment
Interim report date: Oct 1, 20XX
Prepared by: J. Barnes
Accomplishments to date: • Team charter developed • Project definition document completed • Project tasks identified • Gantt chart completed • Initial client interviews conducted **Project milestones not met:** All milestones have been met. Project is on schedule. **Task assignments completed this week:** • Interim report completed and submitted to client sponsor – J. Barnes • Client interviews completed – K. Davis and O. Holms **Project costs:** Project costs are within allocated budget for this time period. **Task assignments scheduled but not completed this week:** Minutes from last meeting were not complied by K. Davis. K. Davis has been asked to have these prepared as per meeting norms. **Assignments for next period:** • Map current registration processes and document in process flow charts. – M. Prentice and J. O'Rafferty • Identify efficiency issues in current registration process. – M. Prentice and J. O'Rafferty

and who has not. This type of documentation is important for giving credit to appropriate team members when the project is completed.

This example shows how interim reports are essential in documenting how a team has managed a project. The team, the project sponsor, and the manager can review the interim reports and assess the degree to which the team stayed on schedule, whether there was an appropriate task assignment among team members, and how well team members met deadlines. This assessment is important, particularly in evaluating each team participant and individual effort for the project work.

The team should use the interim reports to assess the following:

- Is the team staying on schedule?
- If the team is not on schedule, what is the underlying cause? How will the team make adjustments and correct the problem so that it does not occur again?
- Is each team member completing tasks as assigned and on time?
- Is the task load for each member appropriate?
- Are assigned task loads reasonable?
- If task loads are not reasonable, how does the team plan to make adjustments?

Leadership behaviors are threaded throughout project management activities. Team meetings and interim project reports are demonstrations of open communication within the project team and to the project sponsor and other project stakeholders. They also demonstrate honesty, trustworthiness, and accountability on the part of the team. The interim reports, for example, document what work has been accomplished, what work is yet to be done, and honestly communicates when tasks have not met projected deadlines and holds individual team members accountable. These also demonstrate the dimension of effectiveness in leadership ethics (chapter 8) by communicating how the team is staying focused on the project purpose and the degree to which they are fulfilling the project scope, objectives, timeline, and budget.

Project Closeout

After project completion, the team still has a number of activities to perform. This phase of the project is normally called project closeout. These activities tie up the loose ends in a project and provide final documentation to the project sponsor or manager and the client. Some of the activities associated with project closeout include preparation of final project report, conducting a final meeting with the project sponsor or the project client and stakeholders, performing post-project and team member evaluations, and compilation of the final team notebook. Combined these activities demonstrate several ethical leadership behaviors. Specifically, they support clear communication, trustworthiness, honesty, and accountability.

- The team practices solid communication and transparency behaviors in preparing a detailed written and complete final report and by conducting a final meeting with the meeting sponsor and stakeholders that allows for open dialogue and questions.
- The final report and meeting with stakeholders exhibits the team's trustworthiness in carrying out its responsibilities for the project. The team is honest and accountable in its reporting by matching the results of the project to the project objectives, deliverables, and costs as stated in the project definition document.
- By performing post-project and team evaluations, the team demonstrates its accountability and its readiness to review the results of the evaluations in order to learn from their experience and to continually improve their work.
- By preserving project documentation in a final team notebook, the team leaves a historical record of the project. The historical record is a communication and evaluation document that can be used as a resource by future teams working on a similar project or by the organization for insight about what went right or wrong within the project; and to leverage the project strengths and minimize weaknesses in future projects.

Each of these activities is discussed in the next sections.

Prepare Final Project Report

The team is responsible for preparing a final project report and distributing it to all team members and project sponsor or manager. The final report content depends on the type of project the team completed and the promised deliverables in the project definition document. For example, in the physician practice project in figure 14.3, the final report included the following:

- Cover letter
- Table of contents
- Executive summary
- List of project objectives
- Statement of project scope and constraints
- Process flow diagrams of current registration system with explanations
- Identification of interrelationships among activities and duplicative, unnecessary, or repetitive processes
- Registration process efficiency
- Identification of areas for process improvement
- Recommendations for changes in process flow to improve efficiency as measured in registration time and patient/client throughput
- Recommendations for automation solutions that will support new process flows
- Estimated costs for implementation of recommendations
- Appendices

Hold Final Project Sponsor and Meeting

At the completion of a project, the project team holds a final meeting with the project sponsor and stakeholders. If the project involved working directly with a client, the team holds a final client meeting. The team gives the client a final project report along with the project deliverable. The following is a list of the usual contents of the final project report to the project sponsor or client.

- If applicable, cover letter thanking the sponsor or client for the opportunity to conduct the project and outlining the contents of the report
- Executive summary of the project definition, background, scope, work completed, and description of deliverable(s)
- Details of work completed, schedule, costs, and description of the deliverable(s)
- Appendices, which may include original contract or proposal, diagrams, flow charts, and other supporting documentation
- A sign-off form or checklist to be signed by the sponsor or client; the sign-off form verifies that all work has been completed according to the original proposal or contract with the client

Conduct Post-Project Evaluation

As a final step in finishing the project, the team performs a post-project evaluation, sometimes called a project retrospective or post-mortem review. This review is performed to identify how well the team did in planning and executing the project. A major purpose of the project is to develop both team and technical skills. Evaluations of what did and did not go well, and how project teamwork could be improved are addressed in the post-project evaluation. The team uses this evaluation as an opportunity to fully assess team skills and how these might be improved.

Perform Individual Team Member Evaluations

Each team member should evaluate the contributions of every other team member and also themselves by using an evaluation form such as the example in figure 14.7. Depending on the organizational standards and team norms, copies of a team member's evaluation may be provided to the project sponsor, manager, or team leader and may also be given to the individual evaluated. Ideally, there should be sufficient trust and honesty among team members so that the evaluations are used by each member as a continual improvement tool for future team work activities.

The evaluation has several purposes. First it provides feedback to the individual team member. This feedback is useful for helping team members assess their interpersonal, technical, and team skills. Second the evaluation is useful in helping the manager or project sponsor perform individual evaluations.

In completing the individual evaluation, team members must be certain that assessments are backed by evidence. This is where the team notebook plays an important role. For example, if someone rates a team member low in attending team meetings, the evaluation should be supported by the copies of the minutes in the team notebook. The minutes should show that the team member was frequently absent at team meetings. Or if a team member is rated high in being counted on to finish tasks, then the interim project reports should support the assessment by showing that the team member always completed her or his tasks on time.

Figure 14.7. Sample evaluation of team member

Individual Team Evaluation Form

Team member evaluated:

Evaluated by:

Place an X in the bracket closest to the statement that best describes the team member's contribution, participation, and activities on the team.

1. Could be counted on to be present at all team meetings	( ) ( ) ( ) ( ) ( ) ( )	Was not always on time or present at all team meetings
2. Shares opinions with team freely	( ) ( ) ( ) ( ) ( ) ( )	Usually withholds opinions unless team asks
3. Is likely to be impartial during team conflict	( ) ( ) ( ) ( ) ( ) ( )	Is likely to take one side during team conflict
4. Accepts constructive criticism	( ) ( ) ( ) ( ) ( ) ( )	Resists criticism and team input
5. Generates ideas for the team	( ) ( ) ( ) ( ) ( ) ( )	Relies on others to generate ideas
6. Can be counted on to complete tasks on time	( ) ( ) ( ) ( ) ( ) ( )	Cannot be counted on to have tasks completed on time
7. Can be counted on to complete tasks at a high quality level	( ) ( ) ( ) ( ) ( ) ( )	Cannot be counted on to complete tasks at a high quality level
8. Willing to work through conflict and negotiate solution	( ) ( ) ( ) ( ) ( ) ( )	Seeks to avoid conflict and confrontation
9. Can be relied on to follow team norms	( ) ( ) ( ) ( ) ( ) ( )	Cannot be relied on to follow team norms
10. Made an equitable contribution to project tasks	( ) ( ) ( ) ( ) ( ) ( )	Did not make an equitable contribution to project tasks

Provide an explanation for any item that you rated on the right hand side of the column.

Provide any additional relevant information for this evaluation.

Assemble Final Team Notebook

The last step in closing out the project is assembling the final project notebook. The team should have been compiling the team notebook throughout the project. However, this is the final opportunity to ensure all documentation about how the team carried out the project is included in the notebook.

The notebook is important because it is the repository of all the team's work and a history of how the team conducted its work. As the repository, it provides documentation for the organization, project sponsor, manager, and the team in assessing and evaluating how well the project was organized, planned, and managed. There should be an organization-wide policy that governs how project records are curated including identifying what documents should be gathered and the criteria used for determining temporary or permanent documents, and how the documents are processed, maintained, accessed, and disposed. In some cases, the maintenance of project documents may be subject to accreditation standards, vendor or client contract stipulations, or to state or federal law.

Team Leader in Practice

The team leader sees to it that projects are planned and managed so that they meet their goals and are successful. Planning and management includes establishing an enabling structure and processes that help the team progress from the beginning to the conclusion of a project. Use the checklist in figure 14.8 as a guide to help you in the planning and management of your next project.

Figure 14.8. Project planning and management activity checklist

Activity	Target date	Completed date	Comments on challenges or other observations in carrying out the activity
Define the project			
1. Develop a clear, written problem statement.			
2. Provide a project name that represents the project deliverables.			
3. Develop a project description that includes an explanation and background of the client and context of the project and provides an overview of the current status of the problem.			
4. Clearly identify the project boundaries and scope.			
5. Identify project constraints.			
6. Develop project objectives.			
7. Provide an estimated project timeline with expected start and completion dates.			
8. Provide an estimate of project costs.			
9. Identify resources required to support the project.			
10. Prepare a project definition document that includes documentation on steps one through nine and present to client for sign-off.			
Plan the project			
1. Develop project task list.			

Figure 14.8. Project planning and management activity checklist (continued)

Activity	Target date	Completed date	Comments on challenges or other observations in carrying out the activity
2. Identify major task categories and assign tasks to a category.			
3. Identify task interdependencies. Place tasks in the order in which they need to be completed.			
4. Identify start and end dates for each task.			
5. Assign team member responsibility for each task.			
6. Develop a Gantt chart to plan and track all tasks.			
7. Identify project resources and costs for each task and for the project as a whole.			
8. Secure resources for project.			
9. Develop communication plan.			
Manage the project			
1. Develop meeting norms, documentation policies, and structure for productive team meetings including: a. Establish dates and times for meetings b. Use a meeting agenda for every meeting and distribute prior to meeting c. Develop minutes and distribute after every meeting d. Develop and abide by meeting rules and norms e. Assign secretary f. Assign timekeeper g. Establish techniques for guiding behaviors			

Figure 14.8. Project planning and management activity checklist (continued)

Activity	Target date	Completed date	Comments on challenges or other observations in carrying out the activity
2. Prepare interim reports on a weekly basis.			
3. Hold interim meetings as needed.			
4. Track the status of each task on a daily or weekly basis.			
5. Identify schedule problems and develop solutions to ensure project stays on track.			
6. Readjust schedule as needed.			
7. Hold final client meeting.			
8. Develop project final report including: a. Cover letter b. Table of contents c. Executive summary d. List of project objectives e. Statement of project scope and constraints f. Description of project work g. Deliverable(s)			
9. Conduct post-project evaluation.			

Reference

Johns, M. 2007. Creating, Coaching, and Managing High-Powered Work Teams. Raleigh: Lulu Press.

Part IV
The Visionary Leader

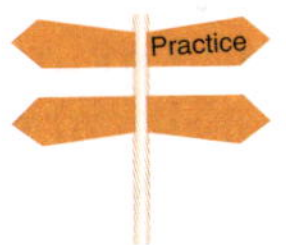

Leadership is fundamentally about looking forward, not backward. Leadership depends on taking that forward-looking perspective, developing a vision of what is possible, and leveraging the leader–follower relationship to turn vision into reality. The visionary leader is proactive, looks for opportunities, and seizes the initiative to challenge the status quo through innovation and change.

Visionary leaders do not monopolize or keep vision for themselves. Instead, they encourage their followers to be fellow participants in the exploration of new ideas, processes, and perspectives. The visionary leader is also a change agent who understands that change can be seen as a threat to followers who may exercise either fight or flight behaviors to allay their fears.

Sympathetic to the concerns and needs of their followers, visionary leaders include their followers in developing a shared vision. They exercise leadership behaviors that build a culture of securing employee emotional commitment by being transparent, communicating, listening, motivating, and encouraging followers to identify problems and create solutions themselves. Part 4 examines the behaviors of the visionary leader and consolidates the concepts provided in parts 1 through 3 in applying leadership behaviors for change advocacy and management.

Why Vision Matters

Leadership cannot exist without vision. Positional leaders—ones who hold a title such as manager, vice president, or chief executive officer—often fail at leadership because they focus on planning and budgeting, organizing and staffing, and solving day-to-day crises rather than setting direction, seizing opportunities for innovation, and leveraging change. Time does not stand still and today, more than ever before, change in healthcare is increasing exponentially. Just a few years ago, for example, health information management (HIM) departments were consolidated into one physical space in a healthcare facility. Today the change has been dramatic as HIM functions are spread throughout a healthcare facility and have been assumed by a variety of departments. For instance, in many healthcare facilities the coding staff reports to revenue cycle management, not an HIM department. Issues involving patient privacy were always under the jurisdiction of the HIM department, but today they likely are the responsibility of a separate privacy or compliance department. In many cases today, HIM departments are virtual with many of the employees working hundreds or even thousands of miles from the physical medical center.

Reacting to change, rather than anticipating and being proactive to it, quickly leaves organizations behind competitors and makes survival more difficult. Healthy organizations do not react to change—they create change and innovation that keeps propelling them forward, not backward. Vision matters because it is the key factor in fostering innovation and directing changes that keep organizations relevant. Without that kind of direction, organizations fail to thrive and ultimately collapse.

Leading with Vision

Visionary leadership is one of the most challenging, yet one of the most important, aspects of leadership. Without forward thinking there is no leadership. This part of the book presents an overview of the characteristics and behaviors of visionary leaders and shows that consolidating the leadership behaviors presented in this book provides the foundation for leading with vision and leveraging change.

Chapter 15: Vision and Transformation

This chapter introduces the concept of transformational leadership, examines the behaviors and characteristics of visionary leaders, and makes the case for why visionary leaders are essential for organizations to flourish.

Chapter 16: Leading Change and Transformation

This chapter provides an overview of how people, teams, and organizations approach, plan, and control change. It also examines why change efforts succeed or fail, and explores how ethical and inclusive leadership behaviors are vital in supporting successful change efforts.

15 Vision and Transformation

"Every organization, every social movement, begins with a dream. The dream or vision is the force that invents the future," (Kouzes and Posner 2007, 17). Inspiring a shared vision is common to personal-best experiences by leaders (Kouzes and Posner 2007, 14). Leading begins with having an eye toward the future with a desire to make positive change and create something new. Leaders look to the future with curiosity and optimism and find opportunities for changing the status quo. To make positive change agents leaders must be visionary and enlist and energize followers who enjoy the same commitment and drive in seeing the leader's vision achieved. They lead change by motivating others to embrace change. They accomplish this by creating positive relationships with their followers and exercising ethical and inclusive leadership behaviors such as social awareness, allowing for and considering the input of others, valuing and respecting others, and being fair and consistent decision makers.

This chapter looks at the rationale for vision as an inseparable element from leadership and examines the behaviors of visionary leaders who make positive change happen. The first section examines the relationship between vision and transformational leadership that attempts to achieve positive change within and beyond the organization that impacts public policy and challenges all stakeholders to higher ethical behaviors. Next, the behaviors of transformational leaders are explored. The chapter concludes with a discussion of how organizations benefit from transformational change.

Transformational Leadership

A person can hold a positional leadership role with an organizational title—such as health information management (HIM) director, chief information officer, or chief medical officer—but not be visionary or create transformational change. Indeed, this situation exists every day in all organizations. In these circumstances it can be argued that holding a positional role as an organization's leader but engaging in only transactional work like day-to-day operations that maintain the status quo is not leadership at all. Rather, this behavior conforms to the definition of management and not leadership (part 3 introduction). Because a person holds the title of leader, does not mean that he or she functions as a leader.

Vision and leadership go hand-in-hand and vision is associated with a category of leadership called transformational. Transformational leadership involves elevating the level of motivation and morality of the leader and follower to create change that achieves outcomes such as liberty, justice, and equality that are beyond the self-interests of an organization or company and may also impact public policy. Leaders who are transformative change the culture of their organizations by articulating a motivating vision that sets challenging goals for achieving a higher good and ultimately transforms their followers' aspirations and expectations (Burns 2012).

The Pursuing Perfection Project is an example of a demonstration project showing how the integration of vision and transformational leadership in healthcare organizations led to positive change and can impact public policy. The project, an international effort between 2001 and 2008, was composed of seven hospitals and healthcare systems in the United States, four communities in England's national health service, a teaching hospital in the Netherlands, and a three-hospital county healthcare system in Sweden (Reinertsen 2004). The demonstration project was funded by the Robert Wood Johnson (RWJ) Foundation and focused on improving the quality of healthcare. The participants set ambitious goals and embraced the vision that a transformed healthcare organization would be one where there were no needless deaths, no needless pain, no needless helplessness, no needless delays, and no needless waste (Reinertsen 2004).

At the end of the project, the conclusion was that raising expectations to "levels that were thought to be unattainable is not only possible but within reach when aims are ambitious, the science is strong, and leaders are willing to deploy resources to get the work done," (Kabcenell et al. 2010, 9). Specifically, they made headway in achieving outcomes for a transformed healthcare organization.

To achieve these results, project participants identified six major leadership challenges that had to be met and established specific, measurable goals that defined more precisely what a transformed organization would look like. In other words, they articulated a clear picture of the outcomes of change.

The following is a summary of the six leadership challenges identified by the Pursuing Perfection Project with an example of some of the measurable goals for each (Reinertsen 2004). Notice how these transformational leadership challenges align with principles of ethical leadership and leadership ethics (chapter 8) and an inclusive organization (chapter 10). Notice how the emphasis is on elevating all staff members' motivation and moral behavior to create change that achieves a higher good beyond oneself or the organization.

- **Leadership Challenge 1: Reframe core cultural values**. This challenge requires changing current cultural values to new ones. Current values hold that the responsibility for patient care rests in the autonomy of the doctor who knows best and the healthcare professionals who are the center of care and control it. Reframing core cultural values involved transformation of the core value of individual autonomy to practicing the science of medicine as a team where doctors, healthcare professionals, and the patient worked together in a transparent environment. The following are examples of goals designed to meet this challenge:
    - In partnership with healthcare professionals, patients are given the opportunity to design the goals for their care, plan of care, and determine their care team
    - There is full transparency concerning care and its quality to patients, staff, and community using industry standards as measurement
- **Leadership Challenge 2: Create improved capability.** Capability in this context means building leadership competency and a team of leaders who promote and ensure transformational change.

Creating improved leadership capability requires creating a plan for staff leadership development supported by the highest level of organizational executives and implementing the plan by means such as leadership training, hiring methods, performance measures and feedback, and compensation programs. The following are examples of goals designed to meet this challenge:

- Transformation is built into succession management where newly hired leaders are committed to transformational change
- Promotion is based on being a star performer in quality improvement and transformational change

- **Leadership Challenge 3: Collaborate across competitive boundaries.** Meeting this challenge requires that healthcare systems depart from old competitive roles and move into new collaborative relationships, operating with the best interests of the patients in mind, not just meeting the organization's financial bottom line. Healthcare systems in the community and beyond must work with each other and share clinical data to avoid fragmentation of patient care. The following is a goal designed to support this challenge:
    - All staff seek innovation and ideas worldwide
- **Leadership Challenge 4: Create a business environment that simultaneously drives business results and community benefit.** To meet this challenge leaders must create new business models that include collaboration with partners such as purchasers of care, payers of care, and regulators of care who support a clear relationship between improvement in quality and producing business results. The following is an example of a goal designed to meet this challenge:
    - Quality improvement is a strategic organizational goal supported by using system-level and project-level measures
- **Leadership Challenge 5: Drive system level rather than project level results.** To meet this challenge, organizations must take a systems perspective to quality improvement rather than viewing it as project-level success. In other words, quality improvement success must be regarded as a systemwide endeavor, not achieving success at just a departmental level. The following are examples of goals designed to meet this challenge:
    - Quality is an operational line management responsibility throughout the organization, rather than delegated to a few quality staff professionals.
    - All staff work is integrated with organizational strategy and is measurable.

- **Leadership Challenge 6: Maintain constancy of purpose over the long-term transformational journey.** Transformation takes time, perhaps many years, during which the organization's leadership team may change. Therefore, transformation must be embedded within the organizational culture, through such things as succession planning and organizational vision and mission to be achieved.

These leadership goals are a snapshot of transformational leadership in action. Notice the energy and urgency the vision conveys and how it is focused on positive change by achieving outcomes of no needless deaths, no needless pain, no needless helplessness, no needless delays, and no needless waste. Also, creating collaborative environments and seeking to drive business as well as community results support liberty, justice, and equality that benefit all stakeholders including patients, caregivers, and the organization.

Transformational leadership is as much about transforming followers as it is in establishing and achieving a vision. The leadership challenges and examples of associated goals listed clearly demonstrate how all stakeholders—healthcare providers, patients, payers, or healthcare systems—are challenged to higher ethical behavior. Transformational leadership happens when one or more persons engage in such a way that leaders raise one another to higher levels of motivation and morality and transformation occurs (Burns 2012). The following are examples of how stakeholders are raised to a higher ethical level.

1. Setting the expectations that quality improvement becomes a concern of every staff member, it is integrated with the organization's strategy, and it can be quantified and measured.
2. Increasing leadership capability to the degree that promotion is based on an individual being a star performer in quality.
3. Requiring collaborative relationships among healthcare systems.

Characteristics and Behaviors of Transformational Leaders

A transformational leader has specific characteristics and behaviors that take him or her beyond performing transactional tasks. A transactional leader is one who typically focuses on short-term goals and maintaining the status quo, solves problems through a step-by-step approach, and minimizes variation in the organization (Spahr 2015).

On the other hand, the transformational leader strives to create the future by seeking opportunities that change the status quo for the better and beyond self or organizational interests.

Having a vision does not make a leader transformative. A transformational vision goes beyond self-interests or the interests of the organization and extends to achieving a higher good specifically in areas of liberty, justice, and equality. For example, a healthcare chief executive officer (CEO) may promote one of the following visions for the organization:

- Our vision is to be a healthcare system that consistently increases market share through advancing healthcare services
- Our vision is to be a healthcare system that is always in compliance with laws and regulations promoting worker safety
- Our vision is to be the healthcare system of choice by providing quality, value-priced, primary healthcare services

None of these visions can be considered transformational. For instance, the first statement primarily focuses on self-interest; the second statement centers on maintaining the status-quo by following existing rules; and the third statement represents a marketing branding slogan more than a vision. One element all three have in common is an appeal for equilibrium in delivering health services, not a call to action for breakthroughs. For example, none of the visions promote innovation, a desire to achieve remarkable results, or aspirations to accomplish positive change resulting in outcomes such as justice, equality, or autonomy. Compare the following transformational vision to the previous visions:

> Our vision is a healthcare system that continually improves the health and well-being of individuals, families, and our community within a culture that encourages innovation and radical improvement redesign to achieve excellence; and is accomplished in a trusting and transparent environment where all are treated equally and where associates flourish in fulfilling their potential.

This vision statement encompasses elements of transformation. It includes a desire to be innovative and continually redesign its processes so that outcomes are frequently improved. The statement pays attention to the well-being of all of its stakeholders with the vision of supporting them in fulfilling their potential.

Besides embracing a transformative vision, the transformational leader must practice specific behaviors that inspire followers to explore better ways of doing things, mobilize people to get things done, and raise the well-being and motivational level of followers and others (Spahr 2015).

Transformational leaders are self-confident, mindful, and determined (chapter 1) and practice ethical leadership (chapter 8) and inclusive leadership (chapter 10) behaviors. They motivate their followers to go beyond self-interests and aim for consequential change that makes a positive difference beyond the interests of the organization (Cossin and Caballero 2013). Transformational leadership has four factors:

- **Idealized influence**. Transformational leaders influence others by acting as role models. They have ethical behavior and values and followers trust and count on them to do the right thing. Followers identify with the leader's values and behavior and consequently want to imitate these. Through idealized influence leaders are able to build commitment from their followers to organizational goals.
- **Inspirational motivation**. Transformational leaders articulate a positive vision to their followers, challenge them with high expectations and standards, and provide them with a strong sense of purpose greater than self-interest. Transformational leaders are effective communicators who make their vision understandable, engaging, and powerful, and instill self-belief in their followers concerning their abilities and the integral part they play in achieving a shared organizational vision.
- **Intellectual stimulation**. Transformational leaders provide autonomy to their followers and encourage them to be creative and innovative in generating ways to solve problems and determining how to do things better.
- **Individualized consideration**. Transformational leaders provide a supportive climate to followers by listening, acknowledging, and providing empathy to their needs and concerns. Transformational leaders maintain open channels of communication with followers. They respect the unique strengths and attributes of each follower and provide an environment where an individual can develop these strengths and attributes and fulfill his or her potential. (Northouse 2016, 167–169)

The elements of transformational leadership rely on the use of leadership behaviors discussed previously in this book. For example, idealized influence depends upon ethical leadership behaviors of a trust relationship between the leader and followers that is developed through mutual respect, making fair decisions, conscientiousness and dependability, and communicating expectations through actions so that followers model and practice these same behaviors. And intellectual stimulation relies on the leader listening to and considering the input of followers and giving them opportunities to make decisions on their own. Figure 15.1 displays a representation of how these behaviors and transformational leadership are related.

Figure 15.1. Relationship between authentic and ethical leadership and transformational leadership factors

Assess Transformational Vision

To what degree do healthcare systems have a transformational vision? Select the vision statements of three healthcare systems (these are normally on the healthcare system's website). Use the following grid to assess the degree of transformational leadership reflected in these statements. Then answer the questions that follow.

Transformational Behaviors	Health system 1 Vision	Health system 2 Vision	Health system 3 Vision
Uses innovation to solve problems			
Concerned with employee development			
Goes beyond usual benchmarks			
Includes outcomes such as justice, equity, and autonomy			
Strives to achieve breakthroughs providing healthcare services			

1. What insights have you gained from reviewing and assessing the vision statements? Write your observations in the following space.

2. Do you believe that healthcare organizations can have transformational visions? Or are they more suited to transactional leadership? Explain your reasoning.

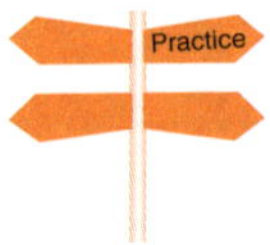

Develop a Transformational Vision

Select one vision statement you analyzed that had more transactional than transformational aspirations. Rewrite the vision statement in the following space to make it more transformational.

Organizational Benefits of Transformational Leadership

Studies support that beyond the positive outcomes transformational leadership gives the greater community, multiple individual and organizational benefits are derived as well. Transformational leaders establish challenging goals and are stimulated by individualized consideration, intellectual stimulation, and inspirational motivation (Northouse 2016). Application of these transformational factors likely accounts for the significant variance found between high and low performing organizations and is cited as a key determinant of successful change and leadership and organizational effectiveness. Transformational behaviors are important in building team cohesion and self-belief in accomplishing goals. In addition, transformational leadership behaviors have been found to be associated with employee commitment, motivation, task performance, and organizational performance (Hargis et al. 2011).

Practicing Transformational Leadership

The following exercises help you put transformational leadership into practice. The first exercise helps you synthesize material about leadership behaviors from other parts of the book and align these with specific transformational leadership factors. The second exercise challenges you to join a student, volunteer, or work team and use transformational leadership behaviors.

Create a Model of Transformational Leadership

Based on the material presented in this chapter, identify the behaviors of a transformational leader for each quadrant in the model in figure 15.2. Copy the model (including the behaviors you have identified) and create a reminder for yourself of transformational leadership that you can use. For example you could

- Create bookmarks with the model on them
- Create a face cover for a tablet that you use
- Create a digital picture and use as a screen saver on your computer
- Create a digital picture and use as the background on your phone or other electronic device

Practice Transformational Behaviors in a Team

For this exercise you can use an existing team of which you are a member or join a student, volunteer, or work team. Prepare a list of the transformational behaviors you have identified in figure 15.2 and put these in table 15.1. For two consecutive weeks, document when you have used each of these, a brief description of the situation in which each was used, and comments about the outcome. Then answer the questions that follow.

Figure 15.2. Transformational leadership model

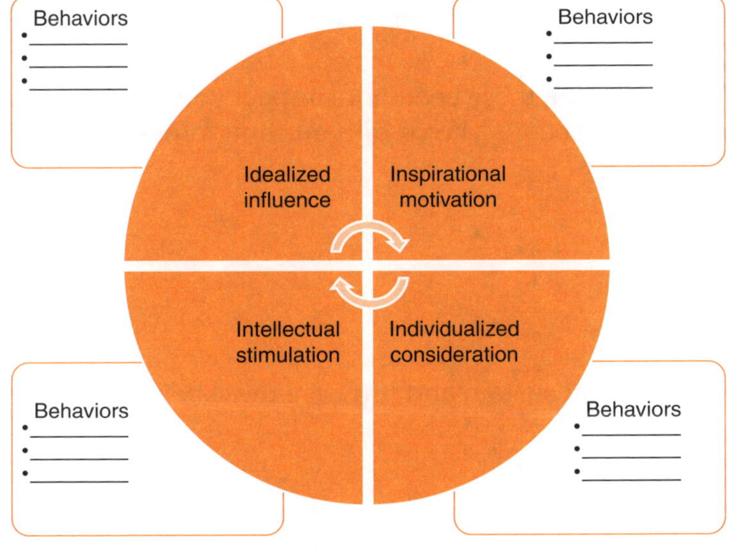

Table 15.1. Practicing transformational leadership behaviors

Behavior	Date used	Situation description	Comments about the outcome

- How did using the transformational leadership behaviors impact your team?

- How did using these behaviors impact you? How did you feel about your actions? What do you think others thought about your actions?

- How can you sustain and improve these behaviors?

References

Burns, J. 2012. *Leadership*. New York: Open Road Media.

Cossin, D. and J. Caballero. 2013. Transformational Leadership Background. IMD. http://www.imd.org/uupload/IMD.WebSite/BoardCenter/Web/213/Literature%20Review_Transformational%20Leadership.pdf

Hargis, M., J. Watt, and C. Piotrowski. 2011. Developing leaders: Examining the role of transactional and transformational leadership across business contexts. *Organization Development Journal* 29(3):51–66.

Kabcenell, A., T. Nolan, L. Martin, and Y. Gill. 2010. *The Pursuing Perfection Initiative: Lessons on Transforming Health Care*. IHI Innovation Series white paper. Cambridge, MA: Institute for Healthcare Improvement.

Kouzes, J.M. and B.Z. Posner. 2007. *The Leadership Challenge*. San Francisco: Wiley.

Northouse, P. 2016. *Leadership Theory and Practice*, 7th ed. Thousand Oaks: Sage Publications.

Reinertsen, J. 2004 (January 13). A Theory of Leadership for the Transformation for Health Care Organizations. http://www.uft-a.com/PDF/Transformation.pdf

Spahr, P. 2015 (October 30). What Is Transformational Leadership? How New Ideas Produce Impressive Results. http://online.stu.edu/transformational-leadership/

16 Leading Change and Transformation

People experience continual change in their lives. When they perceive a change is non-threatening and beneficial and believe they can adapt to it, they generally adjust fairly well. Resistance to change arises for many reasons but, fundamentally, opposition is based on people perceiving a change as a threat, as something either unnecessary or undesirable, and as something they do not have the ability to control. Resistance usually manifests itself in behaviors associated with a fight or flight response to a threat. Flight behaviors may take the form of denial or avoidance, for example, while fight behaviors may include unhealthy behaviors such as sabotage or aggressiveness. The leader's role is to help lessen the stressors that cause unhealthy fight or flight responses by using leadership behaviors that support follower needs (chapter 9). For instance, listening to followers, considering their input, and giving them opportunities for participating in decision making are behaviors that support follower needs for respect, belonging, and autonomy. Consequently, fears of being isolated and not being in control are lessened.

This chapter adopts the perspective that managing change, referred to as change management, is different from leading change, referred to as change leadership. Managing change is composed of a set of tools and processes that are used to maintain control of events during a change initiative. Using some of the tools and processes described in chapter 14 such as the Gantt chart and meeting agendas are ways of maintaining control and implementing a change with as little disruption as possible.

Leading change, however, is about creating a vision for the future that includes change, motivating others to embrace the change vision, gathering the resources needed to make the change, and using leadership behaviors to accomplish change. Promoting change and motivating others to adopt change are discussed in this chapter as the foundations of leadership; these always rest on the leader's ability to understand and influence his or her followers.

The first part of this chapter is an overview of various change models. Change models examine how people, teams, and organizations approach, plan, and control change. The second part looks at the reasons why change efforts succeed or fail. Sometimes change efforts fail due to inadequate planning and management, but often efforts fail because of poor leadership. These two sections are followed by a fictional scenario that illustrates how the concepts of authentic, ethical, team, and transformational leadership learned in this book can be applied in mitigating change stressors and leading successful change initiatives. The chapter concludes with a final reflection that leadership is a journey in creating an environment where people, organizations, and communities flourish.

Change Models

Change means to alter or make something different from its current state. Change may involve substituting one thing for another. Upgrading to a new data input screen for collection of cancer registry information, replacing a brand name drug with a generic drug in the hospital formulary, revamping the process for release of healthcare data, or replacing in-house medical transcription with an outsourced alternative are some examples of substitution.

Change may also involve giving something up. When one health system merges with another one, health information management (HIM) director positions and departments may be consolidated, for example. This may result in the elimination of some HIM director positions, discontinuation of some HIM functions and positions at one of the health systems, and implementation of a new organizational and reporting structure for HIM employees.

Both these forms of change impact individuals and organizations alike. From the standpoint of the individual, changes such as these can affect how people's needs are being met. In the healthcare merger example, when HIM functions are consolidated, employees may be moved to a new department and have a new reporting structure. Consequently, their needs for belonging, certainty, and autonomy may be threatened. Change usually means that people need to learn or adjust to something new. These situations can trigger a loss of self-esteem and belief in oneself.

From an organizational perspective, consider a health system merger that has consequences with regard to efficiency and effectiveness of how work gets done. For instance, how does the merger of two hospitals into one health system change the health information system infrastructure and the types of health information system applications that are used in both hospitals? If information systems change as a result it will likely change work processes and how people do their work. How does the merger impact patients? Will patients have to go to a different facility than the one they are used to because services have been distributed differently among the merged health systems? Many models exist to explain how individuals, teams, and organizations face, accept or resist, and manage change. This section provides an overview of thought on individual and organizational change models. Change relating to teams is covered in part 3.

Change Models Relating to Individual Change

Primarily the acceptance or rejection of change rests on the people who are potentially affected by a change. Change can be viewed as either a threat or an opportunity. When people view change as threatening to one or more of their basic needs, resistance to change is manifested through fight or flight behaviors. The fight or flight response is based on physiological science and involves an area of the brain called the limbic and sympathetic nervous system. When faced with a perceived threat, the brain releases hormones into the blood stream that stimulate the body to produce a physical response such as an increased heart rate or blood pressure. In addition to these physical responses, the hormones also increase the emotional response areas of the brain and reduce the ability of the brain's cognitive functions in decision making. This results in behaviors that demonstrate greater emotional response, such as anxiety, anger, or avoidance, and behaviors that result in impaired decision making, such as making snap judgments.

Behavioral models of change focus on how an individual's behavior can be influenced through rewards and punishments. The underlying principle in behavior models is that incentives, also called extrinsic rewards, will increase an individual's performance and result in higher performance (Gneezy et al. 2011). Although incentive programs have been used for decades in business and healthcare as a way of trying to motivate people, the accumulation of research suggests that rewards and incentives such as increased pay, vacation time, and awards only succeed at securing temporary compliance. Neither rewards nor punishment has a lasting effect on changing people's attitudes and behaviors or their performance (Kohn 1993).

Cognitive models of change focus on aligning an individual's mindset or perspectives about change with their beliefs and values. When personal values and beliefs are aligned with change people are less threatened by the change and feel at ease in pursuing it. However, if personal values and beliefs are not affiliated with the change, people become distressed. For organizations, this means proposed change must align with people's overall beliefs (Lawson and Price 2003). For example, if employees believe in an organization's vision, such as the example in chapter 15 where the healthcare system believes in continual improvement and change to better the lives of individuals, then they are more likely to accept and pursue the change because they know it furthers the organization's mission.

When an employee's needs are being threatened by a proposed change, his or her mindset can be changed through coaching strategies (chapter 13) to help the employee become more self-aware. Coaching can help employees identify self-limiting beliefs and attitudes and how to change these. It can help employees recognize and leverage their strengths to overcome unfounded fears and to set new goals for themselves.

Besides reframing mindsets, employees must be supported in the change by being given the skills to participate in the change. For example, if a new automated coding system is being implemented, employees must have training, adequate time for development of new skills, and other resources that help them make the transition from the old to new system and build confidence in themselves.

Another way of framing an individual's reaction to change is to assess a person's readiness for change. Prochaska's stages of change model describes the phases individuals go through before they are ready to take action to change their behavior. Leaders can determine in which stage of change their followers are and then plan appropriate corresponding interventions and actions. The following is a summary of the five phases in this model and what interventions a leader may use to help his or her followers proceed to the next stage (Prochaska et al. 1995, 38–46).

- **Pre-contemplation phase**: People in the pre-contemplation stage see no need for change. They lack information about the problem or reason for change. They are of the attitude, "If it isn't broken, don't fix it." Leaders can move their followers from pre-contemplation by raising the followers' consciousness of the problem and the solution, listening to and acknowledging their followers' fears about the ability to change, and providing encouragement that they will succeed.
- **Contemplation phase**: In this phase people understand there is a problem, but lack an awareness of how the problem's solution can have a positive impact on themselves and their environment. Leaders can help their followers move from the contemplation stage to the preparation stage by helping them evaluate how the change can be a positive impact for them personally as well as for the organization and greater community.
- **Preparation phase**: In this phase people are ready to begin planning for change and leaders can support their followers by helping them set personal goals. For example, if the change requires learning a new skill, the leader can assist the follower in setting SMART goals (chapter 7) so he or she will be prepared for the change.
- **Action phase**: In this phase people take action to change. Leaders can help their followers in this phase by providing resources and social support to achieve the goals the follower has set, by restructuring the environment to support success, and by providing autonomy.
- **Maintenance phase**: In this phase people continue with new behaviors and positive outlook. Leaders can assist their followers by continuing to provide resources, social support, autonomy, and an environment that sustains the implemented change. (Prochaska et al. 1995, 38–46).

These models of individual change highlight how the use of authentic and ethical leadership behaviors is essential in helping followers accept and pursue change. This includes using authentic leadership behaviors such as social awareness and relationship building, mindfulness leadership behaviors such as listening and compassion, goal-setting behaviors, and ethical leadership behaviors such as acknowledging and supporting follower needs, and providing followers with autonomy.

Models Relating to Organizational Change

Organizations are often described by using different metaphors. For example, some view an organization as a machine that is designed and built in a specific way to accomplish an explicit purpose. This perspective contends that the organization has routine operations and a specific hierarchical managerial and functional structure supported by job roles and descriptions as well as policies and procedures. This way of thinking has its roots in early 20th century management thought and many of its key principles are still operational in most organizations today, for example, an employee should have only one manager; work should be divided into specific roles and departments; management should be in control; and employees should be disciplined. In this view of an organization only those in authority are responsible for change, people are assumed to always resist change and their resistance should be managed through rewards or punishment, and change efforts can only be successful if they are well planned and controlled (Cameron and Green 2009, 100). Looking at the organization as a machine implicitly ignores the humanness within organizations and denies the principles of ethical and inclusive leadership practices.

Another way of viewing an organization is to compare it to a political system. This perspective asserts that power is a key differentiator within an organization. Some organizations, for example, may be more democratic and some more autocratic. Regardless of the type or source of power, the way change is accomplished in the organization is only through politics. For example, to get an initiative approved requires the support of a powerful person in the organization. Or, the allocation of resources depends upon who bargains or negotiates best. From this perspective, change can only happen when it is supported by a powerful person or persons, and strategies for securing change rest in creating coalitions or renegotiating issues. This view of organizations, like the machine metaphor, discourages the use of ethical and inclusive leadership behaviors, pitting people against each other, and turns the organization into groups of winners and losers (Cameron and Green 2009, 102).

The most amenable view to the human element in organizations is one that compares the organization to a living organism. This view considers the organization an open system made up internally of interrelated parts or sub-systems that depend on each other, and the entire system is subject to forces of the external environment. Thus, like a living organism, the organization must be able to adapt to the surrounding environment to survive. Because of the interdependency of parts both internal and external to the organization, this perception recognizes it is essential that the organization be concerned with individual, group, organizational, and community health and happiness. This viewpoint corresponds with ethical and inclusive leadership principles for meeting the needs of individuals and groups in the organization, the community, and constituency beyond. From this perspective, change should be a response to the external environment, individuals and groups should be aware of the need for change, change can be designed, and it can be accomplished through participation and psychological support of individuals and groups affected by the change (Cameron and Green 2009, 103).

How a leader perceives an organization and how it operates also affects the way change is viewed and implemented. The perspectives of the organization as a machine and as a political system, for example, employ techniques that manage change as opposed to lead change. Research studies support that management of change is not sufficient by itself to successfully advance change efforts. The reasons for change failure and success are explored more fully later in this chapter.

Another way of approaching change in organizations is to apply the five phase Prochaska model described earlier. Although the model was originally designed to explain the phases an individual goes through to change personal behaviors, the model can be adapted to assess the readiness of the organization for change and to explain the phases of organizational change. Using the same interventions as those used for supporting individual change that are closely aligned with ethical and inclusive leadership behaviors, the organization can move forward as an entity achieving a successful change effort.

Why Change Efforts Succeed or Fail

The difference between change efforts failing and succeeding rests on good leadership (chapter 8). An organization can have appropriate change management tools and processes in place, but studies show these are inadequate if they are not accompanied by change leadership behaviors. For example, one study of a customer relationship management system implementation found that four out of the six contributors to project failure related to leadership issues such as lack of long-term vision, lack of employee motivation and buy-in, and employee resistance. Just one contributor was related to the state of organizational data and none were associated with the technology itself (Myron 2003). Another review of the success and failure of change initiatives found changing a company's organizational structure or implementing training programs does not change employee behavior in regard to motivation and performance. Rather, employee behavior is better predicted by creating a shared vision and engaging and motivating people through commitment. Furthermore, resistance to change is embedded in people's feeling of loss of identity, control, associations, and structures (Washington and Hacker 2004). Several studies conducted on successful change show that involving and engaging people are key factors for success (Prosci 2014). These include having executive sponsors who provide guidance and direction; frequent and open communication about the change, the need for change, and answering employee key questions; providing detailed definitions of how jobs will be done differently; and leveraging support from those closest to the change. All of these factors for success are based on ethical, inclusive, and transformational leadership behaviors.

The following fictional scenario synthesizes the principles of change and change leadership presented in this chapter in the context of how an HIM director might apply ethical and transformational leadership behaviors.

A Change Chronicle at Lobbard Health System

Lobbard Health System is a new health system that formed as a result of the merger of three smaller health systems. Lobbard is composed of 14 acute-care facilities along with 20 physician care locations, five specialty care service centers, and three wellness centers. Each of the 14 acute-care facilities and their associated care and service centers has its own HIM department with different areas of responsibility and reporting structures. To add to the information management complexity, there are four different electronic health record (EHR) applications in addition to different administrative, human resources, materials management, and other electronic applications among the various entities. The health system faces multiple challenges in reorganizing its organizational and information infrastructures, policies, and procedures. The following describes one health information management challenge and the HIM director's response as the organization attempts to integrate its information systems.

The Enterprise Data Dictionary Program

Denise, the newly appointed corporate director of HIM, is responsible for leading the enterprise data dictionary program. The goal of the program is to catalog and define data objects throughout the new health system as a basis for interoperability of the various and disparate information systems and to support efficient retrieval and analysis of data. The data dictionary program aligns perfectly with a key Lobbard strategic initiative to develop an information infrastructure for interoperable EHRs including privacy, security, and data standards.

Returning from a late afternoon meeting with Fred, the corporate chief information officer (CIO) and Denise's boss, Denise thinks about the preliminary first steps she and Fred discussed to launch the program. The program's charter, developed by Lobbard's executive team, made it clear that the data dictionary program was critical to Lobbard's mission.

Denise settles in at her desk and reviews the mass of electronic documents she has collected on the over 500 electronic databases known to exist in the new health system. She knows that understanding the current problem and why change is so important will be vital in positioning the project's vision and getting buy-in from all stakeholders.

Problems abound within these databases. The meanings and structure of the data elements are not consistent. For example, the values for the data element "gender" are represented differently among the systems. Some systems use "m" to designate male, while others use the number "1" or another variation.

Moreover, data representations and data elements are inconsistently named throughout the systems. Even among database applications internal to an organization, there are variations. For instance, names that are applied for an inpatient admission date, include "Admit Date," "Admission Date," and "Day of Admission." Beyond differing data values and names, there are varying lengths for redundant data elements. For example, in one system "patient last name" may have an allocated length of 50 characters, while in another system the allocated length may be 20 characters. Furthermore, there are significant differences in how like-named data elements are defined. For instance, in one system "pediatric age" is defined as less than or equal to 14 years of age, while in another system it is defined as less than 18 years of age.

After an hour of review, Denise considers the difficulty ahead in getting different departments to change their views about how they define their data and come to agreement on new data definitions and their representation. Denise also muses at the complexity of change required in identifying every database within the system and beginning the tedious work of classifying, comparing, and consistently naming and cataloging each data element from all of the systems.

Even though the health system has a newly formed corporate information technology division, information systems at the different care sites are still operating independently to various degrees. Some of the information technology (IT) divisions have very structured processes and have followed best practices in data administration, while others have not. Two of the acute-care facilities, for example, have developed and maintained robust data models with an associated electronic data dictionary. Others, however, have developed and cataloged their data dictionaries using a spreadsheet; and for others a data dictionary is nonexistent.

The mixed authority and responsibility structure and vast differences in using best practices for data management adds another layer of organizational complexity to the problem. Moreover, the program will affect different stakeholders throughout the organization. Certainly each of the IT divisions will be affected. Beyond the technical aspects, designated owners of various databases—such as cancer registry, research databases, and others—are stakeholders and must be included in the program. Others such as data and business analysts, corporate risk management and compliance, nursing, and other clinical departments have a stake in how data are defined. Given the technological, organizational, and human complexity involved, Denise knows she has her work cut out for her in promoting and advancing change in data administration practices at Lobbard.

As Denise prepares her strategy for initiating change, she believes that guiding and achieving change encompasses putting into practice a group of leadership behaviors reflected in authentic, ethical, and team leadership.

Shaping the Effort

Denise understands the importance of the data dictionary program as it relates to the organization and that its alignment with a key Lobbard strategic initiative is a positive first step for its success. Given the program's high priority and visible support from the executive team, Denise believes the program is on solid footing for the guidance and direction the program needs. Denise draws on her leadership knowledge and experience and develops a bulleted list of top considerations and key success factors for the program. She will use these as the basis for developing her strategy for change.

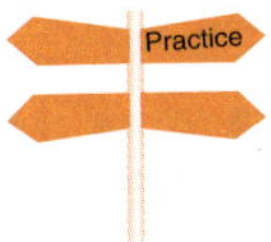

Practicing Leading Change

Use figure 16.1 to identify the ethical leadership behaviors (chapter 8), transformational leadership behaviors (chapter 15), and change leadership behaviors that will be essential for Denise to employ for the program's success. Be specific about how each behavior should be used and what impact or outcome that will contribute to the program's success will be achieved by using it. Then answer the questions that follow.

- Review your responses. For each response identify how the behavior addresses or mitigates one or more major issues associated with change failures identified in this chapter.

- Consider a change initiative you have been part of at your school, work, or in your community that was successful. What behaviors from your list were used that made the change successful? Write these down and explain how each made the change effort successful.

- Reflect on a change initiative you have been part of that was not successful. What behaviors from your list were not applied? Write these down. If applied, would these behaviors have made a difference in the project success? Explain why or why not.

- In the future, what key leadership behaviors will you use to ensure successful change initiatives? Explain why you have chosen these behaviors.

Figure 16.1. Relationship of leadership behaviors and change outcomes

Leadership behavior	How behavior should be used	Impact or outcome
Authentic leadership behaviors		
Ethical leadership behaviors		

Figure 16.1. Relationship of leadership behaviors and change outcomes (continued)

Team leader behaviors		

Creating an Environment Where People, Organizations, and Communities Flourish

This book documents a journey of leadership development based on the premise that leading authentically, leading ethically, and leading others are the foundations for creating a culture of organizational well-being where innovation and transformation flourish. The ultimate goal of leadership is to foster an environment where people are optimistic and engaged, build positive relationships with each other, have a sense of belonging, and are committed to challenging the status quo to accomplish positive things greater than themselves.

There are many leadership theories (appendix A) that attempt to explain what leadership is and how it should be practiced. To date there is not a single theory that totally explains the complicated process of leadership or leader behaviors. That being said, this book brings together elements of several leadership theories with the view that leadership consists of a leader–follower relationship and succeeds in positive transformation of organizations and the greater environment only when authentic and ethical behaviors are applied.

Leadership does not happen as a "big bang." Leadership is an ongoing process in which leaders are all improving their leadership and becoming better leaders. Unlike a race where the winner breaks through the ribbon at the finish line to claim first place, there are no first places in leadership. It is not about being the best, it is about continually striving for being better in developing ourselves and empowering others to fulfill their potential.

Leaders continually seek new learning. They use mindfulness to suspend judgment and discover new things about themselves and others, and they apply their new knowledge and discovery every day to practice better leadership. The book uses this learn–discover–practice paradigm for leadership development and the model should not stop here. Instead, the model should be a key takeaway to use every day as you continue with your journey to be a better leader.

References

Cameron, E. and M. Green. 2009. *Making Sense of Change Management*, 2nd ed. London: Kogan Page Limited.

Gneezy, U., S. Meier, and P. Rey-Beil. 2011. When and why incentives (don't) work to modify behavior. *Journal of Economic Perspectives* 24(4):191–210.

Kohn, A. 1993 (September/October). Why Incentive Plans Cannot Work. *Harvard Business Review*. https://hbr.org/1993/09/why-incentive-plans-cannot-work

Lawson, E. and C. Price. 2003 (June). The Psychology of Change Management. *McKinsey Quarterly*. http://www.mckinsey.com/business-functions/organization/our-insights/the-psychology-of-change-management

Myron, D. 2003 (August). 6 Barriers to CRM Success and How to Overcome Them. *CRM Magazine*. http://www.destinationcrm.com/Articles/Editorial/Magazine-Features/6-Barriers-to-CRM-Success-And-How-to-Overcome-Them-44805.aspx

Prochaska, J., J. Norcross, and C. DiClemente. 1995. *Changing for Good: A Revolutionary Six-Stage Program for Overcoming Bad Habits and Moving Your Life Forward*. New York: HarperCollins.

Prosci. 2014. Prosci's Top Contributors to Success. 2014 Study Results. http://www.change-management.com/Prosci-2014-Report-Contributors-Handout.pdf

Washington, M. and M. Hacker. 2004. Why change fails. *Leadership and Organizational Development Journal* 26(5):400–411.

Appendix
Competing Leadership Theories

A theory is a set of ideas that provides an explanation for a phenomenon. There are many leadership theories that attempt to explain what leadership is and how it should be practiced. However, leadership is a complex process and research shows leadership is dependent upon the confluence of many variables. To date there is not one theory alone that explains leadership or the complicated web of characteristics and behaviors that make exemplary leaders.

A leadership development model is presented in this book, not a theory of leadership. A development model is a framework used as a guide in describing the stages or processes a person or something goes through in changing from one condition to another. In this book, the leadership development model is a framework that helps guide an individual in attaining the behaviors associated with good leadership that incorporates both moral and technical competence (chapter 8). To support people in becoming better leaders, the content of this book combines elements from several contemporary theories of leadership and embraces the following principles in its leadership development model:

- Leadership is a process, not a trait or characteristic
- It consists of a leader–follower relationship that includes self-awareness, self-management, and the awareness of others
- It focuses on bringing about positive transformation extending beyond one's self-interest and the interests of an organization by establishing coalitions through a shared vision and influence
- It includes the practice of authentic and ethical behaviors

Theories about leadership have changed dramatically over the decades. For example, a hundred years ago, leadership was described as the control and centralization of power and was considered more in line with obedience and domination. This concept of leadership is drastically different from theories promoted today such as authentic, servant, or transformational leadership that focus on collaboration, cooperation, and more caring and inclusive ethical principles.

Leadership theories differ from each other because they often represent the perspective of a specific discipline or are built on other theories from that discipline. For example, there are leadership theories based on perspectives from cognitive psychology, behavioral and social sciences, and neuroscience. Additionally, a theory is not valid simply because it exists. Valid theories are grounded in assumptions that fit and are able to explain the facts (Bass 2008). Theories that are ideologically inspired, such as agency theory or transaction cost theory, have been considered unsound theories (Bass 2008). For instance, agency theory assumes that all managers are focused on maximizing their own interests at the expense of anyone else in the organization. The idea that there are no managers who are collaborative and who want to work toward something bigger than themselves is unfounded. Certainly there are many people in leadership roles who are collaborative and want to work toward the common good. Therefore, the leadership theory based on this assumption is lacking because the assumption is unfounded.

To provide a background on the evolution of thought on leadership, some of the more common leadership theories developed between the early 20th century and today are briefly described. The next sections cover representative theories from the following categories: trait, behavioral, situational, and leader–follower. While these theories differ from each other, many have overlapping elements. Generally, however, there has been little attempt to compare and contrast the validity of existing theories or to integrate these in leadership theory research (DeRue et al. 2011). Therefore, the following sections are provided principally for the purpose of understanding the progression and differences in thought on leadership over the past century.

Trait Theories

Trait theories were developed early in the 1900s from research on the characteristics of important leaders throughout history. Among these theories, traits are variously defined demographics and characteristics such as gender, intelligence, personality, dominance, and extroversion. Because of the differences in trait definition among the theories it is difficult to compare one trait theory to another with regard to leadership effectiveness.

Some trait theories, like the Great Man Theory first promoted by Thomas Carlyle in the 1840s, evaluate leadership through the historical assessment of the biographies of great men and propose that certain people have innate traits such as intelligence, personality, education, and class distinction that make them great leaders. In other words, leaders are born, they are not made. Other trait theories maintain that specific leader traits can be learned. Regardless of approach, trait theories hold that people having the "right" traits can be identified, recruited, and hired for leadership positions.

Some trait theories presume that people do not become leaders exclusively because of the traits they possess. Instead, the set of traits people have must fit situations in which they perform for leadership effectiveness. An example of this type of trait theory is Fiedler's contingency theory where a leader's effectiveness is based on a match between leadership style and a specific situation. A leader's style is defined as either task-oriented or relationship-oriented and is assumed to be unchangeable. The leadership situation is based on the level of trust between the leader and his or her followers, whether the tasks are structured or unstructured, and the level of the leader's positional power. For instance, if there is a trust relationship and the tasks are structured and the positional power is strong, then the most effective leadership style is task-oriented and directive rather than a relationship-oriented style.

A key principle of trait theories is that specific traits can be used to differentiate people who are leaders from non-leaders. For example, one study conducted in 1959 identified leaders as having the following traits: intelligence, masculinity, adjustment, dominance, extraversion, and conservatism (Mann 1959). This is a good example where study findings represent the cultural and economic perspectives of the period, rather than providing a universal theory that holds across cultures and time. Today, traits such as masculinity, dominance, and conservatism are routinely rejected by current leadership theories.

A major criticism of trait theories is the lack of consistency in the list of leader characteristics among the theories. In addition, many of the research methods used to identify leader characteristics are dissimilar or lack research rigor, which may suggest one reason why so much variation exists in the characteristics identified among the theories. Variation notwithstanding, some traits appear more frequently than others among the trait theories; these include intelligence, self-confidence, determination, integrity, and sociability (Northouse 2016).

The following section describes personality assessments, which are a specific method for identifying an individual's personality traits, and how these are used within trait theories. Assessments of personality factors are frequently used to identify an individual's collection of traits. The Myers-Briggs type inventory (MBTI) historically is one of the most used personality assessments that measures a continuum of four sets of opposite traits. These traits include extroversion and introversion; sensing and intuiting; thinking and feeling, and judging and perceiving. Although used extensively for career counseling and identification of leader behaviors, the MBTI has been highly criticized since the 1990s as a flawed measure of personality due to its poor reliability and validity statistics (Pittenger 1993).

Another personality model often used for trait identification is referred to as the Big Five Personality Factors. The five traits include neuroticism, extraversion, openness, agreeableness, and conscientiousness and have been studied in relation to leadership. Neuroticism is defined as the tendency to exhibit behaviors related to emotional instability, such as hostility, anxiousness, and depression. Extraversion is a predisposition to exhibit positive effects such as energy and zeal, and to be sociable and assertive. Openness refers to behaviors associated with curiosity, creativity, and autonomy. Agreeableness is the propensity to be trusting, compliant, and conforming. Conscientiousness is measured by indicators such as dependability, organization, and thoroughness. Studies show significant correlations between personality traits and job performance. For example, one study found that high extroversion, conscientiousness, openness, and low neuroticism were related to individuals being perceived as leaders by others and related to a leader's performance in influencing and guiding a group's activities in achieving goals (Judge et al. 2002). The Personality Factors Rating Scale (PFRS) used to assess the Big Five Personality Factors has been shown to have strong reliability and validity statistics.

Behavioral Theories

Behavioral theories attempt to explain what leaders do, how they act, and what relationship they have with followers (Northouse

2016). Different from trait theories, behavioral theories attempt to describe how leader behaviors predict leader effectiveness. Behavioral theories contend that leadership is concerned with two types of task orientations—tasks related to performance and tasks related to people. Three theories that represent the behavioral approach to leadership are prominent—the Ohio State studies conducted at the Ohio State University, the Michigan studies conducted at the University of Michigan, and the Leadership Grid model developed by Blake and Mouton.

Ohio State researchers analyzed leaders' behaviors when they were leading a group or organization using a questionnaire called the Leader Behavior Description Questionnaire (LBDQ) they developed. The researchers found that leaders' behaviors could be grouped into two categories. The first of these were production task behaviors such as organizing work, defining role responsibilities, and scheduling work. The second were people-oriented behaviors associated with developing and maintaining relationships with followers such as building respect and trust. Essentially these categories identified that leaders provide structure for followers and nurture them. Each of these categories is independent of the other. In other words, a specific leader could be more oriented to production behaviors than to people-oriented behaviors or vice versa or could be oriented equally to both.

The researchers at the University of Michigan focused on leader behaviors and their impact on small groups. Similar to the Ohio State studies, the Michigan studies found that leaders engage in two types of behaviors, which they labeled employee orientation and production orientation. Both categories are similar to those codified by the Ohio State studies. Consistent with the Ohio State studies, these orientations are independent of each other. Over the years researchers have attempted to develop a universal theory of leadership to describe how leaders can best leverage the behaviors from task and people orientations in order to maximize employee satisfaction and performance in differing situations. However, studies to date have not been able to identify a model for leadership effectiveness in every situation (Northouse 2016).

Robert Blake and Jane Mouton of the University of Texas developed a two-dimensional model based on the Ohio State and Michigan research. The resulting model called the Leadership Grid views leadership as a blend of production tasks necessary to accomplish organizational goals and people behaviors that are associated with building trust, commitment, and providing good working conditions. The x-axis of the grid represents a concern for production tasks and is measured from 1 to 10, with 1 being a low concern for production and 10 being a high concern for production. The y-axis represents concern for people and is measured from 1 to 10, with 1 being a low concern for people and 10 being high concern for people (Northhouse 2016, 74–78). The model suggests that leaders may exhibit any mixture and degree of these behaviors and can be categorized in one of five resulting leadership styles:

- **Authority-compliance:** Describes a leader high on production concerns and low on people concerns. This leader presents results-driven behaviors with little regard for people and may be viewed as controlling, demanding, and driven.
- **Impoverished management:** Describes a leader low on both production and people concerns. This type of leader goes through the motions of leadership but is uninvolved and withdrawn.
- **Country-club management:** Describes a leader high on people concerns, but low on production concerns. This type of leader is most concerned with interpersonal relationships, but not with accomplishing tasks.
- **Team management:** Describes a leader who is high on production and people concerns. This type of leader promotes participation, teamwork, and accomplishing tasks and can be viewed as behaving open-mindedly, setting and clarifying priorities, and stimulating participation.
- **Middle-of-the-road management:** Describes a leader with intermediate concern for both production and people. This leader is a compromiser who finds a balance between production and people behaviors and may be viewed as nonconfrontational and expedient, and someone who does not adhere to his or her convictions. (Northouse 2016, 74–78)

Situational Theory

The situational leadership theory proposes that the competence and commitment of followers to a goal determines the kind of leadership behavior that should be applied in a given situation. Leadership behaviors are viewed from two dimensions. The first dimension is directive behavior that includes such tasks as setting goals and timelines and developing methods of evaluations. The second dimension is supportive behavior that includes actions such as two-way communications, solicitation of input, and sharing information.

The Situational Leadership II model was developed by Paul Hersey and Ken Blanchard. This model represents directive and supportive behaviors along two axes. The x-axis is directive behavior and the y-axis is supportive behavior with each measured on a scale of low to high. The model has four styles. Examples of directive behaviors include the leader explaining the task or goal, giving directions how to perform or reach it, and monitoring follower performance. Supportive behaviors include two-way communication between the leader and followers that offer social and emotional support. The following is a description of each style and situations in which they should be used.

- **Directing style.** This style includes high directive and low supportive behaviors. It would be used in situations where followers have low competence but a high commitment. Because of follower low competence, the leader would communicate clearly what the goals or tasks are and how they are to be achieved. For instance, a new process for copying patient records is being introduced to the release of information (ROI) team. The ROI team is highly committed to following HIPAA (Health Insurance Portability and Accountability Act) and state regulations for release of patient information. Because the process is new but the commitment of the ROI team is high, the ROI supervisor will clearly define the task and steps to achieve it. She may do this by providing and reviewing a detailed written procedure of the new tasks with the team and monitoring the team's actions as they complete the task.
- **Coaching style.** This style includes high supportive and high directive behaviors. It would be used in situations where followers had low to some confidence and low commitment. Because follower commitment is low, the leader would use coaching behaviors to encourage followers as a means of increasing their commitment; and because followers have low to moderate competence the leader would need to communicate goals and the methods to achieve them clearly. This style may be used by a health information management (HIM) director, for instance, where a process has been introduced to improve coding efficiency,

but the coding staff does not believe it will achieve the desired outcomes. In this case, the HIM director will need to clearly demonstrate how the new process would increase efficiency and provide benefits to the coders in order to increase their commitment. She will also have to increase their confidence by communicating and showing them how to perform the new process.

- **Supporting style.** This style includes high supportive and low directive behaviors. It would be used in situations where followers had medium to high competence and variable commitment. Because the followers have high competence, the leader does not have to micromanage followers, but can give them autonomy. However, because commitment is variable, the leader would provide recognition and social support to followers to increase their motivation. An example of this may be a team with excellent technical skills that is working on a data model for an admission and registration system, but is not motivated to complete the project on time. In this case, the project sponsor would work to increase motivation by making clear how the team's work contributes to the overall mission of the organization and specifically to improving the patient experience.
- **Delegating style.** In this style the leader is less directive and less supportive. This style would be used when followers have high competence and high commitment and do not require intense involvement of the leader. Followers in this situation are able to achieve designated goals with minimal supervision or oversight and are provided with ample autonomy to get the job done. (Blanchard et al. 1993)

Leader–Follower Theories

Leader–follower theories do not focus on leader behaviors, but instead propose leadership is primarily concerned with the relationship leaders have with their followers and the interdependency between the two roles. Some of the more prominent theories are described in this section.

Servant Leadership

The foundation of this theory is that leaders have the duty to be attentive to the needs of their followers. Servant leadership theory originated in an essay published in 1970 by Robert Greenleaf and is defined as a set of leadership practices that creates a more caring world by making the serving of followers' needs the highest priority and ensuring that followers develop their potential (Greenleaf 1970, 6) There are many leadership scholars who support the servant leader theory. Among them are Ken Blanchard, Peter Senge, and Larry Spears. The characteristics of a servant leader include:

- **Listening.** The servant leader listens deeply to others, to both what is said and unsaid. This deep listening is similar to the mindfulness concept of being present in the moment and learning new things.
- **Empathy.** Similar to being nonjudgmental in mindfulness, the servant leader assumes the best in colleagues and co-workers and accepts them for their unique characteristics. The servant leader may reject the unacceptable behaviors of others, but does not reject them as people.
- **Healing.** Healing in this context means reestablishing positive relationships. Servant leaders care about the well-being of their followers.
- **Awareness.** Similar to mindfulness, servant leaders are aware, receptive, and nonjudgmental of their environments, which helps them understand issues involving power, ethics, and values.
- **Persuasion.** Servant leaders help people change in positive ways by consensus building and nonjudgmental argument rather than coercion.
- **Conceptualization.** Servant leaders are visionaries who can set clear goals for their organizations, provide direction, and who can face complex challenges with creative and innovative solutions to problems.
- **Foresight.** Servant leaders are able to conceptualize what the future holds through awareness of the current state of affairs and an understanding of the past. This foresight allows servant leaders to reasonably deduce what may occur and anticipate the consequences of their actions.
- **Stewardship.** Servant leaders readily assume the responsibilities of the roles in which they are entrusted. They carefully manage their organizations and hold them in trust for the greater good of society.
- **Commitment to the growth of people.** Servant leaders respect their followers as unique individuals, having value in themselves

as individuals and beyond their contributions to the organization. Servant leaders are committed to helping each person grow and fulfill her or his potential.

- **Building community.** Servant leaders foster shared interests and pursuits, are inclusive, and bring people together in creating a common identity. (Spears 2010)

Many characteristics of the servant leader theory are embodied in the Developing Leaders for Leadership model presented in this book. These include self-awareness and social awareness (chapter 2), mindfulness (chapter 6), ethical leadership and leadership ethics (chapter 8), inclusive leadership (chapter 9) and visionary and transformational leadership (chapters 15 and 16).

Team Leadership

Interest in the differences between team and traditional leadership has escalated as organizations increasingly rely on both face-to-face and virtual teams in achieving organizational goals and competitive advantage. Teams are a departure from the traditional hierarchical organizational structure that embodies positional leadership where the solo leader has complete power and authority. Teams have a flat structure where members play different roles, have broadly equal status and authority, and have autonomy in making decisions affecting their work. These characteristics make team leadership different from usual organizational leadership (Belbin 2010). Similar to other leadership approaches, team leadership is explained by different theories, two of which are discussed as follows.

Belbin Team Role Theory

The Belbin team role theory suggests that successful teams accomplish their work through nine different roles. A team role is defined as the way a team member behaves, contributes, and relates to others on the team, and is not their functional or technical role (Belbin 2010). Team members may assume one or more roles and all roles must be executed for team success. Each role is categorized into one of three groups—action oriented, socially oriented, or thinking oriented. The following is a description of each category and its associated roles and contribution of each to the team.

- Action-oriented roles include:
  - Completer finisher: Pays attention to details and makes sure that team projects or tasks are thoroughly completed
  - Implementer: Turns ideas into action by organizing work that the team needs to accomplish
  - Shaper: Challenges the status-quo, drives the team to consider different possibilities, and exercises persistence in meeting challenges
- Socially-oriented roles include:
  - Coordinator: Clarifies goals and delegates tasks; usually assumed by the team leader
  - Resource investigator: Explores opportunities, develops necessary contacts outside of the team, and negotiates for resources on behalf of the team
  - Team worker: Conflict manager who ensures that team members get along and work effectively with each other
- Thinking-oriented roles include:
  - Monitor evaluator: Analyzes, evaluates, and weighs the pros and cons of others' ideas
  - Plant: Develops innovative ideas and solutions
  - Specialist: Provides specialized knowledge and skills that are scarce (Belbin 2010)

Each role has a specific strength but is also accompanied by weaknesses or shortcomings. The shortcomings are balanced by other roles. For example, the resource investigator (RI) is an extrovert, highly optimistic, and good at exploring opportunities and gathering ideas from the external environment. However, the RI's shortcomings manifest in being overly optimistic and losing interest after an initial spurt of enthusiasm. These shortcomings can be balanced by the shaper who thrives on pressure and has the drive and courage to overcome obstacles.

Hill Model for Team Leadership

Different from the Belbin model suggesting that successful teams rely on the performance of a variety of roles among team members, the Hill model of team leadership focuses on what roles the team leader must perform to ensure team effectiveness. The premise is that the leader's job is to monitor the team and then take the necessary actions to ensure its effectiveness (Hill 2013). A team leader must have a broad scope of skills and behaviors and be flexible in responding and adapting to challenges and team member needs. Team leaders encourage team-based problem solving and collaboration among team members.

Leadership decisions are focused on monitoring team effectiveness and determining when it is appropriate to intervene in the team's functions and take action. Intervention can take the form of action either internal or external to the team. External actions may include negotiating for additional resources, advocating for the project, or sharing information with others outside the team. Internal actions are focused either on task-related actions or relationship building. These include behaviors such as focusing on goals, structuring the team and developing processes to achieve results, monitoring work to maintain standards, and facilitating problem solving and decision making within the team. Relational actions include coaching team members, managing conflict, building commitment, and ensuring that members' needs (that is, autonomy and identity) are met.

Transactional Leadership Theory

As the name implies, transactional leadership theory is based on a relationship in which an exchange occurs between two people; in this case, the leader approaches the follower to make an exchange. An exchange can be a valued economic, political, or psychological good. The exchange is referred to as a contingent reward. In other words, a reward is given contingent on receiving something else in return. The objective of transactional leadership is to ensure goals are met. Many forms of transactional leadership occur every day in organizations. For example, a healthcare system provides vacation time to employees after they are employed with the organization for a specified amount of time.

Transactional leadership is not concerned with the individual needs of the followers nor with their development. While sometimes rewards are negotiated (for example, salaries in the hiring process), more often the leader offers a reward and it is the follower's responsibility to engage in the activities necessary to achieve it. Besides reward exchanges between leader and follower, transactional leadership involves both active and passive management-by-exception (MBE). Active MBE involves anticipation of follower mistakes through enforcement of rules; and passive MBE involves monitoring followers' behaviors and actions, and providing corrective and negative feedback and reinforcement when mistakes occur. Some studies show that providing contingent rewards can increase follower engagement, particularly when they are combined with transformational leadership behaviors discussed in the next section. Active MBE, however, has been found to reduce followers' autonomy and, as a consequence, their work engagement (Breevaart et al. 2014).

Because transactional leadership is not based on raising human moral conduct and motivating the ethical aspirations of both the leader and follower, many leadership authorities do not consider transactional leadership as leadership at all (Ciulla 2014, 206).

Transformational Leadership Theory

Transformational leadership is defined as leadership where both leaders and followers engage in a way so that they are both raised to higher moral and motivational levels (Burns 2012). The goal of transformational leadership is to convert followers to leaders by influencing them to seek the common good of a group instead of focusing on self-interests, engage in long-term self-development, seek change opportunities, and envision long-term possibilities beyond immediate needs.

Transformational leadership is associated with leaders who develop people, build teams, and influence their followers to aspire to high expectations. The transformational leader is identified as having the following behaviors.

- Charismatic leadership involves behaviors such as making personal connections with followers that build follower respect and trust of the leader
- Inspirational leadership consists of communicating a positive vision for the future and demonstrating optimism of its achievement
- Intellectual stimulation involves helping followers to look at problems and challenges from different perspectives and adjusting ideas accordingly
- Individualized consideration involves the leader acting as a mentor and recognizing that every follower is unique and has specific needs and abilities

Transformational leadership behaviors have been associated with higher follower satisfaction with the leader, higher follower motivation, and higher leader effectiveness than transactional leadership behaviors. However, studies have also found correlations between transformational behaviors and contingent rewards. In other words, when transformational leadership and contingent rewards are provided together, there is higher follower motivation and engagement (Judge and Piccolo 2004).

The characteristics of transformational leadership (chapter 16) are embraced by the Developing Leaders for Leadership model presented in this book.

Authentic Leadership Theory

Authentic leadership is a relatively new theory developed in the early 2000s that has its roots in positive psychology. As this theory continues to evolve, several definitions of authentic leadership emerge. One perspective is that authentic leadership involves intrapersonal introspection that incorporates self-knowledge, self-regulation, and beliefs about oneself. Another view is authentic leadership is a relational process between leaders and their followers. This perspective asserts that leaders affect followers' development and vice versa. A third view is that authentic leadership is a developmental process where leader behavior is continuously developed in areas of positive psychological capital, positive moral perspective, self-awareness, influence on follower development, and relational transparency. The following summarizes the components of the developmental view of authentic leadership.

- Positive psychological capital consists of confidence, optimism, hope, and resiliency as personal resources of the authentic leader.
- Positive moral perspective consists of ethical and transparent decision-making processes by which authentic leaders use strengths of efficacy, courage, and resiliency in addressing ethical issues to achieve sustained moral action.
- Self-awareness is a continuing process where the authentic leader comes to understand his or her unique talents, strengths, sense of purpose, core values, beliefs, and desires.
- Self-regulation is the process of aligning personal values with intentions and actions. The authentic leader uses behaviors such

as maintaining self-control, setting standards, assessing discrepancies between standards and expected outcomes, and identifying actions to reconcile these discrepancies to achieve self-regulation.
- Influencing followers' development is accomplished through leading by modeling authenticity including self-awareness, self-regulatory processes, positive psychological states, and moral perspectives.
- Relational transparency is the open sharing of information, decisions, thoughts, and values. (Avolio and Gardner 2005)

Many characteristics of authentic leadership provide the foundation for the Developing Leaders for Leadership model presented in this book. Among these are self-awareness, social awareness, and self-management (chapter 2); mindfulness (chapter 6) ethical leadership; and leadership ethics (chapter 8); and inclusive leadership (chapter 9).

Adaptive Leadership Theory

Adaptive leadership focuses on supporting people in adapting to changing environments. The role of the leader is not to solve problems, but to mobilize people and exercise leadership behaviors such as organizing, orientating, and providing focus to face tough challenges.

Adaptive leadership takes a systems perspective that change is embedded in complex systems. Complex systems consist of a network of subsystems, with a change in one subsystem potentially affecting one, many, or all subsystems. Thus, the adaptive leader recognizes change is a complex process and pauses to understand its many facets and consider the big picture. Adaptive leaders assess the environment to determine the type of change facing followers. For example, they decide if the change is technological and requires followers to adapt their skills, or if change is behavioral and mandates that followers adjust their attitudes, beliefs, or perspectives. Based on this assessment, leaders are in a better position to mobilize, position, or help organize change solutions. For instance, a behavioral change in HIM may be aligning attitudes, procedures, and processes with new regulations. Historically, for example, HIPAA requirements necessitated a behavioral change in attitudes of HIM department employees in allowing patients more open access to their own health records.

Adaptive leadership is based on the premise that people are able to develop and adapt to change. Therefore, the adaptive leader's responsibility is to support people in making adaptations. This is accomplished by using leadership behaviors such as regulating stress, reducing uncertainty, and providing direction.

References

Avolio, B. and W. Gardner. 2005. Authentic leadership development: Getting to the root of positive forms of leadership. *The Leadership Quarterly* 16(3):315–338.

Bass, B. 2008. *The Bass Handbook of Leadership Theory, Research, and Managerial Applications*, 4th ed. New York: Free Press.

Belbin, M. 2010. *Team Roles at Work*, 2nd ed. London: Taylor and Francis.

Blanchard, K., D. Zigarmi, and R. Nelson. 1993. Situational Leadership After 25 Years: A Retrospective. *Journal of Leadership and Organizational Studies* 1(1):21–37.

Breevaart, K., A. Bakker, J. Hetland, E. Demerouti, O. Olsen, and R. Espevik. 2014. Daily transactional and transformational leadership and daily employee engagement. *Journal of Occupational and Organizational Psychology* 87:138–157.

Burns, J. 2012. *Leadership*. New York: Open Road Media.

Ciulla, J. 2014. *Ethics: The Heart of Leadership*. Santa Barbara: ABC-CLIO, LLC.

DeRue, D., J. Nahrgang, N. Wellman, and S. Humphrey. 2011. Trait and behavioral theories of leadership: An integration and meta-analytic test of their relative validity. *Personnel Psychology* 64:7–52.

Greenleaf, R. 1970. The Servant as Leader. http://www.benning.army.mil/infantry/199th/OCS/content/pdf/The%20Servant%20as%20Leader.pdf

Hill, S. 2013. Team Leadership. Chapter 12 in *Leadership Theory and Practice*, 6th ed. Edited by Northouse, P. Thousand Oaks: Sage Publications.

Judge, T. and R. Piccolo. 2004. Transformational and transactional leadership: A meta-analytic test of their relative validity. *Journal of Applied Psychology* 89(5):755–768.

Judge, T., J. Bono, R. Ilies, and M. Gerhardt. 2002. Personality and leadership: A qualitative and quantitative review. *Journal of Applied Psychology* 87(4):765–80.

Mann, R. 1959. A review of the relationships between personality and performance in small groups. *Psychological Bulletin* 54(4):241–270.

Northouse, P. 2016. *Leadership Theory and Practice*, 7th ed. Thousand Oaks: Sage Publications.

Pittenger, D. 1993. Measuring the MBTI and coming up short. *Journal of Career Planning and Employment* 54(1):48–52.

Spears, L. 2010. Character and servant leadership: The ten characteristics of effective, caring leaders. *The Journal of Virtues & Leadership* 1(1):25–30.

Index

F

G

H

I

K

L

M

N

O

P

T

U

V

W